Learning to write

Gunther Kress

Routledge & Kegan Paul
London, Boston and Henley

First published in 1982
by Routledge & Kegan Paul Ltd
39 Store Street, London WC1E 7DD,
9 Park Street, Boston, Mass. 02108, USA and
Broadway House, Newtown Road,
Henley-on-Thames, Oxon RG9 1EN
Set in IBM Press Roman and Univers by
Hope Services, Abingdon, Oxon.
Printed and bound in Great Britain by
T. J. Press Ltd, Padstow, Cornwall
© Gunther Kress 1982

Library of Congress Cataloging in Publication Data

Kress, Gunther R.
Learning to write.
Bibliography: p.
Includes index.
1. Children — Writing.   I. Title.
LB1139.W7K73   372.6'23   81-21072

ISBN 0-7100-9048-X   AACR2
ISBN 0-7100-9082-X Pbk

To Jonathan and Rachel,
who taught me most

Contents

Preface

Considering how painlessly children learn to talk, the difficulties they face in learning to write are quite pronounced. Indeed, some children never learn to write at all, and many fall far short of full proficiency in the skills of writing. It seems from this that there is more involved in the learning of writing than fairly mechanical translation skills. I became interested in the questions associated with learning to write by seeing my own children grappling with the problems, and then through working in an institution which is primarily concerned with the education of primary-school teachers. To watch children writing is to see focused energy and intelligence at work; anyone who has done so cannot dismiss the products of that work as insignificant, deficient, wrong. However, in teaching linguistics to intending and practising teachers it became quickly apparent to me that teachers found it difficult to see anything of great import in the texts, or to say much about them either to the writers or when discussing such texts in class. More than that, it was obvious that linguistics had very little to say about such materials and therefore had seemingly little relevance to the practical concerns of teachers. I therefore set about demonstrating that this was not the case.

The exculpation of linguistics, however worthy a cause, would not have led me to write the book. Rather it was the realization that the fact that nothing could be seen in or said about the early writings of children had a great potential for harm. It could lead too readily to the assumption that there was, quite simply, nothing in the texts to say anything about, and that that was due to the limited abilities of the children who wrote the texts. To show that such was not the case seemed a sufficiently good cause for writing a book.

There was also a further reason. Because there exists no mode for

looking at the texts produced by very young writers — between six and
twelve — the focus of investigations of writing fell on much later writing,
from eleven or twelve years onwards. There the most readily accessible
methodology to apply to such texts came from literary criticism, and
with it came its criteria for good writing. A quotation from Donald
Ferris's 'Teaching children to write' may show what such criteria are,
and how they are taken into the teaching of writing:

> The product of the writer is a more tangible thing to evaluate; for
> example, if the quality of originality in writing is defined as being
> related to how frequently a particular idea occurs among a number
> of written products, it is possible to rate writing products as being
> more or less original.
>
> Even though the qualities of original writing may be listed, the task
> of evaluating the writing of a particular student is still difficult.
> Through a survey of several professional publications during the
> period from 1929 to 1959 Carlson suggests seventeen possible
> qualities which might be found in original writing and suggests that
> there probably are many more. The qualities which Carlson found
> are listed following and will not be discussed in detail. The reader is
> referred to Carlson's excellent article for a more complete explanation
> of the qualities.
>
> '(1) novelty or freshness, (2) individuality, (3) a personal quality
> revealing the self, (4) emotion or feeling, (5) "becomingness,"
> related to identification, (6) imagination, (7) a recombination or
> restructuring quality, (8) an abstractive element consisting of
> finding the essence, (9) immediacy, (10) dynamic vitality, (11)
> curiosity, (12) reservoir of experimental data, (13) perceptive
> sensitivity, (14) flexibility or versatility, (15) symbolism, (16)
> coherent unity, and (17) an expressive-communicative element.'
>
> An expressive list! some of the qualities probably are not immediately
> meaningful and not directly applicable to elementary school children's
> writing. Carlson simplified her findings on originality for use in a
> study of original stories of fourth, fifth, and sixth grade children.
> She defined an original story as 'a form of narrative or descriptive
> composition which is novel, non-imitative, and one which appears
> with statistical infrequency.' (pp. 174-5)

There are two related problems with this approach. One, it is *not* about
writing, but about the qualities listed here. James Moffett and Betty
Wagner make a related point, about reading:

The misconception of 'reading skills'
There is a widely held misconception about the nature of the reading process. It is that reading comprehension is somewhat distinct from general comprehension and thus can be concentrated on as a 'reading skill'. A long list of mental activities that any psychologist would consider general properties of thinking that occur in many different areas of human experience have somehow or other all been tucked under the skirts of reading. Recalling, comprehending, relating facts, making inferences, drawing conclusions, interpreting, and predicting outcomes are all mental operations that go on in the head of a non-literate aborigine navigating his outrigger according to cues from weather, sea life, currents, and the positions of heavenly bodies. Not only do these kinds of thinking have no necessary connection with reading, but they have no necessary connection with language whatever. (*Student-Centered Language Arts and Reading, K-13* p. 123)

The notorious difficulty of judging any one of the characteristics in Ferris's list is well known; a student failing to meet a teacher's expectations in any one of these becomes a failure *not* in 'perceptive sensitivity' or 'dynamic vitality', but in *writing*. That seems to me most unfortunate. The other problem is the highly implicit nature of such criteria: a writing syllabus based on such criteria is unlikely to be made public by the teacher. Hence students not only fail in writing, but have no means of knowing why they failed or how to remedy such failures. And this leaves aside how 'dynamic vitality' would be taught!

There are several omissions in the book, which I regret. I have not included pictures in my discussion, although nearly every text that I discuss had a picture with it, and it is quite clear to me that the picture forms a part of the whole text for the child; it seemed to show the same conception expressed in non-verbal form. Perhaps a book on writing need not concern itself with pictures, though a more comprehensive notion of 'text' will have to include both the verbal and pictorial elements of the one text. Although I have included a number of spoken texts in the book, I have not provided a framework for representing their phonetic character, stress and intonation in particular. This is a serious shortcoming. However, to establish a full framework for representing the sound-aspect of these texts would go well beyond the scope of this book; even then such representations give only approximations to the actual spoken utterance. I have aimed to write the book at a level which will make it accessible to the greatest number of readers; generally I hope that a reasonable knowledge of traditional grammar will be sufficient to follow the argument. As a result I have steered away from linguistic debate even where I am aware of the controversial nature of my statements. Some kinds of writing are not dealt with here. It has not been my intention to be exhaustive in the treatment of kinds of texts, but to provide a methodology for looking at children's writing which will apply to all types of text written by them. I have left the orthography, punctuation, etc., as it was in the written texts; in some instances I have not shown the child's or the teacher's corrections, depending on my purposes in discussing the text. The spoken texts, of course, had no punctuation or spelling, so that has been imposed by me, and may, in some cases, be a distortion of the utterance. Many of the texts are discussed in several chapters so that I could build up a fuller description and analysis of some texts at least.

The debts I owe are many: to the child writers of the texts; to the many teachers with whom I have discussed children's writing and whose immense concern to do what is right for the children in their classrooms, coupled with their great insight, has caused me to change my ideas so often. My approach to language owes most to the work of Michael Halliday. My interest in the structure of speech derives entirely from his descriptions of the intonational and informational organizations of spoken English. In his theories he has consistently put the language user right in the middle of the picture, as an active participant in linguistic/social processes. These ideas have shaped my thinking about language, about language users, including children. I benefited from discussions with Michael Rowan; I enjoyed writing a chapter jointly with him. Noel King and Stephen Muecke read parts of the manuscript and their comments were most helpful to me. Of course, none of the people from whom I have profited is to blame for my inability to make full use of their ideas, or for my at times wilful ignorance.

Handing over impossible manuscripts and seeing them accurately and beautifully interpreted ensures that thanks to the person who produced the typescript are always genuine. Jill Brewster typed this book under constant pressures of time and of a demanding job, remained cheerful, found time to read what she was typing, and gave me most constructive comments. Without her help in this and other areas the book would not have been written.

Lastly my thanks to Tricia, Jonathan and Rachel, who have put up with far too many 'not now, laters' and still treat me as a full member of the family.

Chapter 1
Learning to write

i Putting language into writing

This book sets out to answer two related questions: 'What is it that a child learns when he or she learns to write?'; and 'What can we learn about children, society, and ourselves, by looking at this process?'

Two answers are usually given to the first question. One concentrates on the problem experienced by children at an early stage in their writing experience, with problems such as the control of the writing implement, concentration and attention-span, spelling, letter-formation, forming the focus of attention. The other looks at children at a much later age. Here the approach is a broadly literary one, with the emphasis firmly on 'creative writing'. The questions asked are about the literary and aesthetic quality of the writing: is it 'good writing', does it show 'quality', judged by criteria which are derived from the study of 'Great Writing'. Other approaches, closely allied in their concerns, are broadly psychological: 'What is this piece of writing telling us about the child author?', 'Is it "sincere" writing?', that is, is the child writer actually revealing something about him or herself rather than merely going through a routine or a performance, insincerely?

Whatever the merits of such approaches, they can hardly be said to deal with the full process (and product) of *writing*, and in particular, they pay the scantest attention to language. One deals with largely mechanical problems, while the other deals with the contents of the final product, the intentions of the writer, or the effects of the written piece. They deal with psychological states of the writer, but not with the linguistic process and substance of writing.

The second question, 'What can we learn about children, society, and ourselves by looking at this process?', has been posed and answered in the terms I have just mentioned. Again, I wish to put the emphasis firmly on language, and explore the connections of language and the processes of writing, thinking, and perceiving. I put it forward as a hypothesis that the forms of written language which children use at different stages point to cognitive models which are distinctive in their character, and have an independence and validity of their own. There are close connections between language, social structures, and writing: the written language is close to the standard language accepted by a community, so that some social dialects may be either closer or more distant from the grammar of the written language. This has important consequences for the learning of writing. Access to writing is not equally available to all members of a society. Furthermore, the kinds of writing which children are taught and learn to produce at school may provide an insight into the value-system of our societies, particularly given the fact that few children grow up to be writers in any significant sense of the word. For many or most of these children once they leave school writing will mean the jotting down of a shopping list, or the filling in of a docket at work. What has been the function of learning to write for them? The process of learning to write represents one instance of social learning, where pre-existent norms are imposed on the individual, so that a knowledge of these norms should give revealing insights about ourselves.

Hence it is my intention to put the starting point of any discussion of the learning of writing where I firmly believe it is: with the learners when they are first learning, and within language. To state such utterly self-evident aims simply exposes the major shortcomings in treatments of the subject. Discussions of writing have focused on two periods: the very earliest stages of writing, and on writers from the ages of eleven to twelve years onwards. That is, problems of handwriting, letter-formation, spelling, punctuation have received attention as matters which need to be taught when children first learn to write. There is then a gap of four to five years, spanning the age-range of seven to twelve, and attention again focuses on the process of writing when children are, or are beginning to be, competent writers, from eleven or twelve years of age onwards. The interest of investigators has then been not so much with writing as with what writers do with their writing. The reasons for this seem to have been twofold. The tools which were available for the analysis of writing — those of literary criticism — were unsuited to the analysis of texts produced by younger writers; that is, it is difficult to apply the criteria used in the discussion of 'Great Writing' to stories written by eight-, nine- or ten-year-olds. In addition, linguistics has not provided the theoretical and methodological tools either for the analysis of writing, as distinct from language in general, or for the analysis and understanding of the developmental processes and stages in the learning of writing. Consequently that is the period particularly focused on in this book. The ages of the writers represented by the texts in the book range from six to fourteen.

ii   Reading and writing

One startling fact, and one which needs explanation, is the massive discrepancy between the amount of work which has been done on reading, compared to the work done on writing. The number of books on the learning of reading is vast; by contrast there are few on the learning of writing. The impact of linguistics on theories of reading has been pronounced, and just about totally absent from writing. The processes involved in learning to read are not well understood; the functions of reading are. In writing, on the other hand, neither the processes nor the functions are well understood. It may well be that the greater emphasis in research on reading is an appropriate reflection of the fact that this less active linguistic skill is more widespread in developed societies, and more needed. More members of a literate society have to be able to read than have to be able to write. Indeed, the number of writers even in highly literate societies is relatively small compared to the number of readers. Proportionately speaking, few people write. And much of the writing done by these few is highly stereotyped writing. The causes of the unequal distribution of active writing are of course social, deriving from the economic, political and ideological structures of any given society. It has economic, political and ideological effects: those able to produce meanings and messages are few by comparison with those who consume meanings and messages. Hence the control of messages and meanings is in the hands of a relatively small number of people.

The emphasis on reading research may also have been an effect of the types of linguistic theories which were current over the last fifty years. Theories which focus on structures below the sentence, on decontextualized sentences, on meaning as inherent in the individual linguistic item, on reading as a decoding skill, are unlikely to treat the learning of writing as problematic, nor indeed are they likely to be able to deal adequately with the textual aspects of writing.

Changes in attitudes are now beginning to be evident in the teaching of reading. That is, it is beginning to be realized that the processes involved in reading engage a much more far-reaching range of abilities than the more simplistic decoding approaches had supposed. It has become recognized that reading is an active process, in which the reader is engaged in the (re)construction of meaning, indeed in the (re)construction of the text which is being read. This is a far remove from the attitude which saw reading as a passive linguistic skill, one merely of decoding a meaning which resides there in the text. One recent book on the early stages of a child's learning of language is entitled *Learning How to Mean*. Terms such as 'meaning-making' are now popular currency in the discussion of the learning of reading. This is not the place to comment on the theories of language or of linguistic and cognitive processes implicit in the different approaches to the learning of reading (flashcards, the phonic method, direct accessing, etc.) except to say that they are clear evidence of a poverty of theory both in linguistic and cognitive terms. Fortunately there are signs of changes in this area.

But while research on reading was marked by an impoverishment of theory, no attention was given to syntactic aspects of learning to write. This is exceedingly puzzling; it seems that no problem was seen in that area. Yet why the decoding skills of reading should receive massive attention, and the encoding skills of writing not, is strange. Perhaps the very metaphor of 'coding' has proved to be the major problem. Undoubtedly the metaphor has been taken seriously, and literally, as an account of the linguistic process. Meaning is seen as having some existence independent of language, which is encoded by the speaker, into linguistic form. The point is well made in Britton et al.'s chapter on 'The process of writing', quoting D. W. Harding:

> The notion that in putting an experience into words we always start
> from a definite something and seek words adequate to convey it
> may be an oversimplification. It seems necessary to add that language
> and experience interpenetrate one another. The language available
> to us influences our experience at intimate levels and if we manage
> to convey experience precisely, that may be due partly to the fact
> that available modes of expression were influencing the experience
> from the start. (Britton et al., *The Development of Writing Abilities*
> *(11–18)*, p. 39)

The hearer receives the encoded form, and from this must decode the intended meaning. From this point of view decoding is the problematic part of the process: the encoder knows both meaning and code, the decoder knows only the code. The message has to be decoded, deciphered, by him in order to recover the meaning encoded by the writer. So this aspect of the metaphor, that is, the recovery of meaning, may have caused the emphasis in research on the decoding end, on reading rather than on writing.

The 'code' metaphor has another effect in that it predisposes the user of the metaphor to regard the code as empty or vacuous, without meaning in itself. That is, the medium of the code itself has no content. It is true that the dots and dashes of morse-code contribute no meaning to a message, and contain no meaning in themselves. The same is not true of language. As the quotation above suggests, linguistic form is not semantically empty or neutral. Hence one cannot speak of a pre-existent meaning being encoded in language. Rather it is a case of a meaning which exists in a vague, non- or pre-linguistic form being expressed through the 'meaning-potential' of a given language, where it is assumed that the linguistic form contributes to and shapes the meaning intended by the speaker/writer. The match between intended meaning and its expressibility in a language is never guaranteed. It is a happy coincidence when it comes about, but frequently it does not. Of course, learning to speak and write a language is learning precisely what is and what is not sayable or writable. And that, eventually, becomes the learning of what is and what is not thinkable.

It is a minor irony that the coding view, depending as it does on a code–meaning conjunction, paid no attention to meaning, concentrating instead on the mechanics of de-*coding*, such as letter-sound, letter–image, picture–image correspondences.

Approaches to reading affect the teaching of writing in several respects. Implicitly they provide models for thinking about the other end of the process. So if reading is seen as primarily a decoding skill, then it is quite likely that writing will be regarded as a process of encoding in a quite analogous manner. And indeed, as the heavy emphasis on matters such as letter–sound correspondences show, that has been the case. From this point of view the learning of writing is often regarded as the learning of the mechanics of translating, either speech into writing, or meaning into visual symbols. Specific theories of reading lead to the production of reading materials which enshrine the theoretical assumptions of the theories on which they are based. These reading materials constitute one form in which children meet written language; for some children these materials will be their first and only experience of the written form of the language. The effect of this can be readily assessed by looking at early (and not so early) Readers, and comparing these (a) with the teacher's assumptions of what written language is and her or his expectations of the language which children should be producing, and (b) with what written language is actually like. The models provided by Readers are positively detrimental to the child learner as models of the written language.

iii   Linguistic theories and writing

Although there is at times a healthy suspicion of theoreticians on the part of practitioners in the field of language learning, it is nevertheless true that practices depend on and derive from theory. This theory may be an unofficial, unarticulated one, held by one or several practitioners, or it may be an official theory, widely held and supported. Hence criticism of practices should always be traced back to the theories which originally gave rise to them. Changes in theory are, conversely, bound to affect practices. In short, practices can only be as good as the theory underlying them. It is the case that linguistic theories have, on the whole, not been conducive to enlightened and effective practice in either reading or writing. This may have been due to the indifference of theoreticians of language to the needs of practitioners, or to inherent limitations in linguistic theories. The history of linguistics may be described as the struggle from smallest to larger linguistic unit: that is, modern linguistics begins with a heavy concentration on the problems of phonetics and phonology, and slowly moves to a consideration of sentence grammar. Moreover, linguistic theory has not made a clear distinction between written and spoken language. That is, linguistics has paid attention to the sound features of language, but has assumed that the grammar of speech and the grammar of writing are in all essentials the same. Writing has been regarded as an alternative medium of language, giving permanence to utterances.

It is small wonder that with such notions (however implicit they may have been) attention focused on the mechanical and largely trivial features of learning to write. Indeed, if one assumes that the syntax of speech and that of writing *are* the same, then the learning of writing cannot be seen as anything other than the learning of the skills of transposing spoken language into the written medium. After all, when children come to school they do speak their language competently;

certain aspects of language use still have to be learned by them — in particular the socially and situationally determined variations — but they certainly have command of the major grammatical forms and processes of their language. If, therefore, it is assumed that the grammar of speech and that of writing are the same, then only such matters as learning the letter-forms, spelling-conventions, punctuation, need to be learned.

However, there is now an increasing amount of evidence which indicates that speech and writing do each have a distinct grammatical and syntactic organization. The changed attitudes derive from work in a number of areas: in sociolinguistics and varieties study; in text-linguistics and the study of genre; and work on the grammatical organization of speech itself.

Work in text-linguistics has been taking place predominantly during the last decade. It has sought to establish whether or not linguistic units and rules exist at a level beyond the sentence. In the process it has become clear that there are linguistic patternings above the sentence level, that texts exhibit structural patternings and semantic relations which, while differing from the grammar within the sentence, are no less part of a speaker's and writer's knowledge of language. These matters include aspects such as the internal cohesion of texts, the topical connectedness of parts of texts, the development of thematic material, paragraphing, paraphrase and restatement. In considerations of the learning of writing the significant point is that speech and writing differ most markedly textually.

From the same point of view it also becomes apparent that the sentence is not a unit of typical spoken language. The sentence belongs to writing, forming there the basic unit of textual structures. The sentence may occur in speech as a borrowing from the syntax of writing, but speech, typically, is organized on the basis of clausal complexes which are not sentences. They may be long chains of clauses linked by co-ordination or simply by being adjoined. While the sentence typically is a structure of main and subordinated and embedded clauses, the clausal complex is typically an aggregate rather than a syntactic structure. The thematic structuring of sentences differs markedly from that of clausal complexes. Typically each sentence is a construct with an internal structure which marks the thematic element of each sentence from the non-thematic. The treatment and development of topical material within the sentence is hierarchical and integrative. Within a clausal complex the thematic structure is replaced by two structuring devices.

On the one hand, there is a sequential development of topics, so that clauses in sequence may take over the function of the theme/rheme structure within the sentence. On the other hand, superimposed on this structure is another structure carried or expressed by intonation, which marks some elements as informationally prominent, thereby leaving the unmarked elements as non-prominent. This structure is interpreted by the hearer as presenting some material as being already known to him, and other material as new to him.

It may be that the differing structures of speech and writing could not readily be seen until structures larger than the sentence were considered within linguistics. However, these discoveries do find support from the study of non-European languages which have only recently been described, and have till now been unwritten. Some of these languages do not have sentences in the traditional sense, and operate instead with two units: clausal complexes and paragraphs.

This book cannot hope to rectify the shortcomings which I have described. However, I hope that it may provide a rudimentary sketch which will be helpful to teachers in looking at the writing produced by the children in their classrooms, to parents interested in the language of their children, and to linguists as a suggestion for areas where research seems to me to be needed. My sketch contains at least the following. It regards speech and writing as two models of language with distinctive grammatical and textual structures and organization. Consequently, learning to write has some of the features of learning a second language, including the initial 'interference' from the first language. The distinctive linguistic unit of writing is the sentence, which is not a unit of informal spoken language. Writing and speaking occur in distinct social settings, which have their own different demands, and have significant effects on the syntactic and textual structures of speech and writing. Social dialects differ in their proximity to the standard defined and encoded in the written language. Hence children come to the learning of writing from different starting points, some much closer than others to the syntax of writing, some much further away. Language and cognition are intimately connected; hence the two modes, writing and speaking, will make differing cognitive models available to their users. Writing and speech have their own textual and generic forms, which differ in their structures and in their characteristic functions. These must be learned by the child, as a part of learning to write. These textual forms and genres embody specific ideological contents, which should become the subject of overt discussion and teaching as a part of the learning of writing.

iv Writing and society

Western technological societies are generally assumed to be wholly literate. Over recent years this assumption has taken some knocks as it has been discovered that from 10 to 15 per cent of adults are either completely or functionally illiterate. Clearly, schools do not manage to teach all children to read or write. Among those who are literate, reading is much more widespread than writing, though even reading abilities and reading habits are probably unevenly distributed. It is likely that the larger proportion of a population both reads a more restricted range of materials and reads far less in volume than the smaller proportion. Indeed, newspapers which address the larger group of the population — mass-circulation tabloids — seemingly have a quite specific view of their readers' reading (and general cognitive) abilities, which is reflected in the textual structures of materials in those papers. Texts tend to be brief, and presented in sentence-paragraphs; though contrary to the assumption of many critics of such publications — and perhaps the writers and publishers themselves — the syntactic structure of the language of these papers is no less complex than that of 'quality' newspapers.

While the use of reading is unevenly distributed, the use of writing is much more so. Even in highly literate societies and among highly literate groups writing is proportionately far outstripped by reading in quantitative terms. No one writes more than he or she reads. At the other end of this scale there are a large number of people, the majority in any society, who never or hardly ever write. If one takes into consideration the *type* of writing, then this discrepancy becomes even greater. If by writing one means something other than such minimal activities as making shopping lists and filling out forms, and leaves aside writing which is the reproduction of writing (typing, transcribing, etc.), and considers only writing which involves the production of *new* texts, then it is clear that only a very small percentage of the population is engaged in writing. Even among these, most writing is still highly routinized: the production of fairly standardized letters, memos, notices. The kind of writing most widely taught and most highly prized in schools — such as essays, narratives, poetry — is engaged in by very few members indeed of any society.

It is quite clear, and reasonably obvious, that exclusion from the consumption of messages — being unable to read — carries with it heavy penalties in terms of exclusion from a wide range of knowledge, activities and hence power, in a society. Conversely, the ability to produce written messages is equally necessary for sharing in and contributing to knowledge and to ideological activity, and for gaining a measure of power. Hence the unequal distribution of the uses of and participation in reading and writing have fundamental social, economic, and political consequences. Inability to use and control the forms brings with it exclusion from the benefits associated with their exercise.

It is perhaps less obvious that the forms of the written language — due to their high social and political status, their wide dissemination, and their permanence, have a constant effect on the forms of the spoken language. That is, the syntax of the spoken language is constantly being invaded by forms from the syntax of writing. This is particularly so for those speakers who wish to gain social, economic and political power. For them the syntax of spontaneous speech is replaced by the syntax of the written language. To be able to speak as one writes is a highly valued ability, and carries with it favourable judgments about the speaker's level of intellectual ability and control.

In part such judgments no doubt also derive from the connection between cognition and language. If language and cognition are closely interrelated, then different forms of language will be a sign of different modes of cognition. In so far as written language differs from spoken language it may be accompanied by, and be a sign of, different modes of cognition. This is not implausible. The co-ordinating, 'chaining' syntax of speech presents conceptual materials in a distinctly different form from the subordinating, embedding syntax of writing. The one points towards the order of sequence, the other points towards the order of hierarchy. The habitual and unreflecting use of either may lead to differing modes of cognition. It is quite likely that a society will attach greater value to one than to the other, not because of any inherent superiority or inferiority in the one or the other, but because of judgments extraneous to the potentials and meanings of that form itself. Western technological societies have clearly declared their preference for the subordinating syntax, for the order of hierarchy rather than that of sequence. This may be related to the structure of knowledge and power in those societies, or it may not. It is a point which I shall discuss in detail later in the book.

Within our own society the various forms of writing — exposition, argument, analysis, report, narrative — are used in different contexts and for different purposes. In their most general form they are enshrined and codified in the genres which exist within the repertoire of textual forms of any language. Genres are, consequently, not neutral in their cognitive, social and ideological effects. Learning to write becomes the learning of the forms, demands, and potentialities of different genres. This occurs through the increasing specialization of the tasks of writing, beginning in the second or third year of formal schooling, from subjective accounts of the child's activities to 'projects' in which special kinds of genre are developed: objective historical writing, factual scientific and technological writing, to 'creative' writing of different kinds. In secondary school the process of specialization continues apace, so that eventual mastery of and initiation into the disciplines is constituted by the mastery of the genres in which they are reported and written about, in which they exist. The genres are fixed, formalized and codified. Hence the learning of the genres involves an increasing loss of creativity on the child's part, and a subordination of the child's creative abilities to the demands of the norms of genre. The child learns to control the genre, but in the process the genre comes to control the child. Given the cognitive and social implications of these generic forms, the consequences for the child are immense.

v   Teaching practical writing

Given the preceding arguments, it is clear that writing is not an ideologically neutral activity. Certain genres are linked inextricably with certain social practices, and indeed the social practices to a large extent find their articulation in the appropriate linguistic practice. It follows from this that the teaching of writing is more than the mere transmission of a necessary though neutral skill. Failure and success both have negative and positive effects for the taught.

As I pointed out above, few of those who leave school, particularly those who leave early, will have occasion and opportunity to write to any significant extent. Few of those who leave university will have occasion to write productively, let alone 'creatively'. This should have immense implications for the teaching of writing. It is a fact that the most highly valued writing in schools is 'creative' writing. Textbooks in the 'Language Arts' generally quickly dispense with the 'mechanics' of learning to write in order to deal with the real business of writing, creative writing. To demonstrate what I mean, here are two quotations from John Stewig's *Exploring Language with Children* (1974). Both come from a chapter entitled 'Writing with children', the first under the heading 'Editing and correcting', the second under the heading 'Evaluating creative writing'.

1 Which of my sentences say what I want to say the 'best' way they can? Are there some which don't really say anything at all? Are there places where I've expected a reader to jump wider gaps in action than anyone can safely jump? Is there a way I can rearrange my sentence to make it more interesting (funny, engaging, descriptive, unexpected, shorter, longer, tantalizing)?

2 Are there words in my story which need to be made stronger? For example, *nice*, that pale modern-day ancestor of the vigorous Middle English adjective meaning wanton, is now so anemic it can seldom hold its own in a sentence. Children can be helped to see that many words need to be weeded out of their writing vocabulary because they are today too feeble to be effective.

3 Is there anything in my story as a whole which: a) needs to be somewhere else or b) doesn't need to be in the story at all? In this, of course, one is trying to get children to do basic plot revision, to think about what happened to whom, when, and why. (p. 204)

Questions related to the plot

1 Are the ideas in my stories becoming more interesting? Am I learning to make things happen sequentially so the reader can follow easily?

2 Am I learning how to make plots go in more than one direction? Can I sometimes start at the end of my story to work backwards, or in the middle and go in both directions, instead of always having to start at the beginning and work toward the end?

3 Am I learning how to write different kinds of plots including both realistic and fantasy ones? Am I learning how to write plots which both boys and girls find interesting?

Questions related to setting

1 Am I improving in my ability to look at some object and write a clear, concise description of it which will share my impressions with a reader?

2 Am I becoming able to combine descriptions of several objects into a unified paragraph which helps my story?

3 If I write made-up descriptions, are they getting better at making a reader 'see' the objects or situation I am describing?

4 Am I developing the ability to reread what I have written and to eliminate detail which I may like but which doesn't help my story? (pp. 206-7)

I wish to ask two questions in relation to these quotations. To what extent could one achieve the same aims and ask the same questions by getting a child to model something (whatever the topic happened to be) in plasticine or to paint a picture of it? Which of these skills will be useful to the child in his or her later life?

Clearly my first question attempts to see what aspects essential to *writing* — rather than imagination, creativity, wit, (self-)analytic and critical ability, awareness of audience, etc. — are examined. My answer is: few. What focus is there on the contribution of language as such? Very little. In other words, we are dealing here with the development of quite general abilities and skills, which can, among other media, be developed, expressed, and tested, in writing. But the choice of medium is, I suggest, largely incidental. Of course there is the pay-off that writing is a more highly valued skill than modelling in plasticine, and that skill is being developed incidentally. I do not wish to argue against the development of these skills, all of which should be the right and prerogative of all humans. I am arguing against the error of talking about one thing inappropriately in terms of another.

My answer to the second question is perhaps predictable. I believe that all these abilities and skills are valuable - essential even - if a human being is to lead a full life. The fact that few people's lives are so constructed as to permit them to exercise creativity, imagination, criticism, is a fault not of the teaching of writing but of society. Given the lives that most school-leavers will lead, I believe that there are, in addition to these, other skills with which the teaching of writing should provide them. They should have exposure to and practice in the genres which will impinge most on their lives. The ideological contents of the various forms, genres, of writing should become the subject of overt discussion and direct teaching. In this way it could be that all school-leavers would gain some insight into the meanings of their own and others' writing, to understand the content of the messages to which they are subjected, and to provide them with the essential skills necessary to manipulate, control, and organize language for their *own* purposes. This might ensure them some rudimentary freedoms, and the possibility of becoming creative in their own sphere.

vi   Sources and context

In teacher education institutions the discussion of writing is usually dealt with under the 'Language Arts'. These discussions tend to draw on linguistics at a great remove and quite indirectly, due no doubt to the fact that linguistics as such is not a part of the core teacher training course. In this book I have used a sampling of textbooks: Pose Lamb's *Guiding Children's Language Learning*, Stewig's *Exploring Language with Children*, Mitchell's *Speech Communication in the Classroom*, Pflaum-Connor's *The Development of Language and Reading in Young Children*. I do not think that they provide a sufficient insight into the nature of language for intending teachers; indeed, language as such is hardly discussed. A brilliant exception to these is James Moffett and Betty Wagner's *Student-Centred Language Arts and Reading, K–13*. The work of the London Institute group (Britton, Burgess, Martin, McLeod, Rosen) has a more linguistic orientation, in that it looks at the functions of student writing — the expressive, transactional, and poetic functions — and the roles and interrelations of relevant categories, such as writer and audience. Their work does not consider the grammatical organization of language, including written language. There are signs of changes in approach: two papers, by Jim Martin and Joan Rothery, in *No. 1 Writing Project Report 1980*, provide linguistic descriptions of student writing. The project's first phase 'is examining samples of student writing from later primary through secondary school'.

The question of the relation between the grammatical organization of spoken and written English, and its effects on children's writing, is explored in Chapters 2 and 3. However, there is no single uniform 'spoken English', rather there are a large number of dialects, both social and geographical, which may co-exist in one geographical region. Some of these dialects may be closer to the standard form of English than others, and therefore there may be children in the same classroom for whom the grammar of the written language is less familiar than for others. Some of these issues are discussed in Peter Trudgill's *Accent, Dialect and the School*.

Developments in research on writing are influenced by available theories. The dearth of research focusing on language is related to the aims of the dominant linguistic theories. Between 1960 and 1970 the most prominent theory — the one which defined the orthodoxy in linguistic research — was transformational generative grammar. Its emphasis was exclusively on discovering the (deep) abstract set of rules which could account for (surface) linguistic form. Hence the actual behaviour of speakers or writers received no attention within this theory. The two major works are Noam Chomsky's *Syntactic Structures* and *Aspects of the Theory of Syntax*. Of course other linguistic theories existed, and work based on these continued. In Britain the work of Michael Halliday continued to be prominent, and this had most significant effects on language in education. His *Explorations in the Functions of Language, Language as Social Semiotic*, and *Learning How to Mean: Explorations in the Development of Language* provide a good sampling of his ideas. The more theoretical aspect of his work is represented by *Halliday: System and Function in Language* (ed. Kress). Halliday's work on the grammatical organization of speech is reported in chapter 12 of the last-mentioned book, as well as in his *Course in Spoken English*.

A number of developments caused the weakening of the Chomskyan orthodoxy. Work in sociolinguistics led to the realization that social factors influence and are intimately related to the use of linguistic rules, and are reflected in linguistic form. N. Dittmar's *Sociolinguistics* is an excellent critical survey. Some exemplifications of these connections can be found in Fowler et al., *Language and Control*, where the interrelations of social and linguistic structures are explored through the close analysis of interviews, newspaper language, rules and regulations. The analyses demonstrate that specific modes of writing, genres, encode ideological positions, quite irrespective of the 'content' of an individual instance of the genre. Work in discourse studies and in text-linguistics demonstrated that the sentence cannot be regarded as the focal linguistic unit, as it was within transformational generative grammar. Malcolm Coulthard's *Introduction to Discourse Analysis* provides a summary of work done in that area. Teun van Dijk's *Text and Context* illustrates the concerns of text-linguistics.

Chapter 2
Speech and writing

i   The recent history of the study of speech and writing

Recent work in sociolinguistics has clearly established the responsiveness of language to situational and contextual variation. This can be put more strongly by saying that the very structure of language reflects the significant features of the situation in which it is produced, and whose meanings it encodes. If this is so for language in general, it would be most surprising if it were not the case for the two distinctly different modes in which language occurs: speech on the one hand, and writing on the other.

Linguists have long recognized that speech is the prior form. Historically it occurs well before writing emerges. Even now there are probably still more languages which exist only in a spoken form than exist in spoken and written form, though massive investment by missionary groups, linguistic researchers, and governmental agencies is changing this picture rapidly. Children learn to speak long before they learn to read and write. There is no question that spoken language constitutes by far the greater bulk and volume of language use, far outstripping the bulk of written language. This remains true even today, with mass-circulation newspapers, teleprinters, word-processors, and all the technological modes of reproduction of writing. For every word written there are a hundred thousand words spoken.

From the point of view of linguistic theory, speech has also been given primacy. Linguists aver that they study the spoken form of the language, not the written. In reality this means that linguists are prepared to accept the linguistic ability of the individual language user as constituting perfectly good evidence for the study of linguistic forms, rules and processes. It does not mean, in most cases, that linguists study speech. Linguists study language. Until recently when and if speech has been studied it has been studied only from its sound-aspect. As far as the grammatical structure of the language is concerned (in all this I am talking about English), linguists have looked either at abstractions or at written language; or, more often, at abstractions based on the written language. In the process the grammatical structure of speech has been ignored in the main (I will come to exceptions in a moment). Theoretical discussions of language have dealt with language 'as such', and this notion of language was based on the written form. This point is made in a slightly different way from an anthropologist's viewpoint:

> In the 1930s and 40s . . . writing systems figured prominently in discussions of stimulus diffusion, independent invention, internal patterning, and the acceptance, rejection, and modification of cultural traits . . . . During the same period, however, the study of writing began to suffer at the hands of linguists. Depicted by members of the emergent structural school as a pale and impoverished reflection of language, writing was consigned to a position of minor importance. Textbooks continued to include brief chapters on the subject, but usually this was to emphasize that writing and language were entirely distinct and that the former had no place in the domain of modern linguistics (e.g. Hockett 1958; Gleason 1961; Bolinger 1968; Langacker 1968). As a consequence of these views, and the uncompromising way in which they were expressed research on forms of written communication declined abruptly. It continued at a low ebb throughout the 1950s and for a while, in the mid-60s, seemed destined to stop completely. (Basso, 1980)

While I regard the tendency of this criticism as correct, in its specific detail it is wide of the mark. It is the case that writing as such has not received serious attention from recent linguistic research. However, this was not because of a concentration on the study of speech, which has been similarly neglected. Rather this has been the case because of the focus in linguistics on the language system abstractly considered. Paradoxically, in so far as examples have been used in the study of syntax, they have tended to be based on the linguists' intuitions about written language; though this fact has not been acknowledged. In short, the assumption in modern linguistic studies has been that there is a single language system, and its rules have been drawn out by an unacknowledged use of the forms of the written language. No doubt this sleight of hand (unrecognized by linguists themselves) was facilitated by the socially higher valuations of writing, which placed the normal forms of speech in the categories of substandard, incorrect, lower-class language.

The effect, in the event, can be seen in another passage, taken this time from a textbook in which the insights — and prejudices — of modern linguistics are mediated to teacher training students as the results of scientific research and therefore as unchallengeable wisdom. The author of the book was at the time of the first publication of the book a senior lecturer at a Teachers' Training College (a College of Education) in Great Britain.

> Speech is an activity, whilst language is the structural pattern or system we use to convey our message in speech. The pattern of language consists of words and of the structural relationship between words and phrases, which is known as grammar. (A. Mitchell, *Speech Communication in the Classroom*, p. 1)

That is the sum total of statements on speech in the first chapter, 'Effective speech for the teacher', under a subheading, 'Speech and language'. The rest of this chapter, and of the book, contains nothing further on the structure of *speech*. (The other subheadings are 'Speech communication', 'Communication in the classroom', 'The acquisition of language'.) Chapter 2, 'Linguistic studies and speech', has the sub-headings 'Descriptive linguistics', 'Phonology', 'Grammar', 'Lexis', 'Institutional linguistics', 'Variety according to use register', 'Addressor-addressee registers', 'Style', 'Sociolinguistics'. The remaining chapters are 'Voice improvement', 'Articulation', 'Speech communication for the teacher in the classroom', 'Organization of material', 'Storytelling and reading aloud', 'Discussion in the classroom', 'Mixed-media projects'. In other words, there is nothing on the structure and the characteristics of speech in a book entitled *Speech Communication in the Classroom*. No doubt it contains much of general value to intending teachers, though as far as speech is concerned students will finish reading the book believing that they have authoritative knowledge about speech when in fact they have been given a most impoverished view of the structure, character and function of spoken language, and of children's uses of it. The book is characteristic of countless others, and it may stand for the level at which knowledge of speech is mediated to intending teachers.

ii   The contexts of speech and writing, and their effects

Under the pressure of more recent work in sociolinguistics, particularly in register studies and in discourse-analysis, the varying contexts and situations in which language occurs have been studied and their effect on language noted. It is clear that the contexts and situations in which either speech or writing typically occurs differ significantly, and one could not but expect similarly significant effects on these two modes of language.

The major variable is no doubt the immediate presence of an audience (a single hearer or a larger audience) in speech, and the lack of such an audience (in a single or a multiple addressee) in writing. This single variable has a large number of consequences, which ultimately affect the structure of speech and of writing. Typically speech happens in interaction with another speaker. The language is generated mutually in the interaction, with both participants contributing to the text, which is consequently not a single-speaker text. The linguistic forms of interaction are typical of speech: questions and responses, and forms which solicit agreement from the other participant. These can occur in writing, but when they do, they do so as echoes of the forms of the spoken language.

The nature of the interaction depends on at least two connected variables: the status and power relation of the two speakers, and the type of interaction in which the participants are engaged. The more powerful speaker tends to have speaking-rights, which he may accord to the less powerful, though he need not do so fully. The type of interaction also distributes speaking-rights unevenly. For instance, in interviews the interviewer has control, and interviewees do not ask questions; if they do, the interaction-type changes. In lectures only the lecturer speaks. These two variables have their effect on the form of language: a speaker with power, speaking to a large number of addressees (a lecture, typically) will tend to use language which has fewer interactive forms, becomes more planned, and therefore begins to have some of the features of the written language.

Writing, by contrast, is characterized by the physical absence of the addressee. Consequently the language is not generated in interaction, and the resulting text is produced by a single writer. Interactive forms do not occur other than as echoes of spoken interactions. The differences in status and power which exist between writer and intended reader will affect and find their expression in the language being used.

The question of speaking rights, or rather writing rights, arises in a different form here, for even in highly literate societies access to writing is not evenly distributed among all members of a society. It is true that some societies prevent some groups from speaking — temporarily, normally: children, servants, members of committees, generally those of low status and little power in the presence of those with high status and great power. However, in writing, such unequal access is the rule rather than the exception. Productive writing rather than reproductive writing, such as that of scribes, secretaries, school-children (though even much of this writing is highly restricted), is open to few members even of highly developed literate societies. It is nearly always associated with a high educational level and high economic and political power.

What linguistic effects arise from this variable of absence or presence of the addressee? As I have mentioned, spoken interactions give rise to texts which are the product of at least two speakers, who together form a unified text. It is not possible to regard the individual contribution of each speaker separately as constituting a text. This has important consequences for the development of a topic, for instance, and for the manner in which the topic is developed linguistically. It can be seen in the following brief extract. The setting is year one of secondary school, the student is twelve years old; the conversation is taking place outside the classroom.

> *Teacher*: You've got the two German-shepherd dogs? What are they
>   called?
> *Student*: King the big one, and Thunder the small one.
> *Teacher*: Is King the father or mother . . . or . . .?
> *Student*: No (*pause*) we got them separate, see, the big one . . .

The teacher asks the questions even though this is outside of a lesson in a relatively informal situation. The child's response is shaped by the teacher's question, and by his perception of how the information may best be presented to the questioner. In *King the big one, and Thunder the small one*, the most important element of information has been brought to the front of each clause (compared with a more 'normal' syntax, 'The big one is called King, and the small one (is called) Thunder'). In the child's next response, the *see* is there as an acknowledgment of the questioner, checking on whether she is keeping up with the information being provided. Apart from these direct linguistic effects it is clear that the text is generated as a result of the interaction of the two participants. In fact, though the child actually speaks more than the teacher, he is in one sense perhaps the less active participant; the motive force for the generation of the discourse comes in this instance from the teacher.

The child's *see* points to another aspect of speaking as compared to writing. The speaker knows the addressee and is directly aware of her or him, and can and must structure his language to take account of the addressee, of his or her knowledge of the topic at issue, his or her apparent receptiveness and responsiveness in the interaction. In other words, the language of a spoken text can be, and to be effective must be, precisely addressed to one specific audience. In writing, the audience may be known, though (more) frequently it is not. Or, at any rate, I as the writer have no control over who may see my written text, just as I have no control over the circumstances in which my written text is received. I have no real possibility of assessing whether my text was explicit enough for the reader at the time when he or she received it. Anyone who writes memos to a large group of people will know the dangers of assuming that his readers have a specific kind of knowledge.

A phrase is not normally plurisemantic for the hearer, but for him the phrase is not isolated: he hears it in a precise setting made up of all he knows about the person who pronounces it, about his past experiences, his plans, about what the author of the phrase knows and thinks about those for whom the phrase is intended, and so forth. (A. Cicourel, *Cognitive Sociology*, p. 78)

In speaking I get an immediate response and can therefore amend my message, rephrase it, tone it down, make it more explicit. Another brief extract from the same text will illustrate my point.

... we got him from my ... eh ... we got him from my brother's friend ... my oldest brother ...

Here the speaker has had three attempts at formulating one expression, *my oldest brother's friend*. At first he hesitates after *my*, wondering what will be the best way of putting this, continues with *my brother's friend*, and then adds the last piece of information, *my oldest brother*. This last addition may have been triggered by a quizzical look on the teacher's face, if for instance she knew that the child had a number of male siblings. Such elaboration is not possible in writing. A written text either contains all the information necessary for its adequate interpretation and is received without problems, or it does not and problems ensue. Consequently it is necessary to make written texts much fuller of information, to make them more explicit than spoken texts, for there is no chance of adding information. Spoken texts may leave information implicit because the speaker knows what the hearer knows and because he can assess as he speaks whether he has been correct in his assessment. Hence writing tends to be marked by greater explicitness and elaboration than speaking, which can be relatively more implicit and consequently less elaborated.

iii   The structures of speech and writing

The immediate presence of the audience in the case of spoken language is reflected in one of its most significant structural characteristics. Superimposed on the clausal structure of speech (which will be discussed below) is a structure determined by the speaker's wish to present information in the form most accessible to the hearer. Consequently the speaker parcels up by intonational means the information which he or she wishes to present to the hearer in what the speaker regards as the relevant chunks or units of information. This structure of *information units* derives from the interactional nature of speech, and encodes some of its major features, namely the exchange of information from one participant to the other, the mutual construction of meaning, and the mutual development of a topic. It also takes account of the transient nature of speech. A hearer cannot usually pause or check back over the message to make sure that he or she has understood it. The structure of speech makes major allowances for this factor by structuring information, providing sound cues which highlight the relevant informational structuring.

This structure is expressed through intonation. The speaker uses intonation to bracket together segments of his utterance which he regards as constituting one relevant parcel or unit of information. The function of intonation in providing clearly marked structures in speech has been the subject of research by a number of linguists, foremost among them Michael Halliday, whose innovative work has in turn been taken up and furthered in important directions by David Brazil. Halliday calls the basic unit of the spoken language the *information unit*. It is expressed intonationally in the *tone group*, a phonological entity. It encodes what the speaker wishes to present as one segment or unit of information. It is marked off in speech by a single unified intonation contour, and above all, by containing one major pitch-movement. The unit has no previously determined length. It may correspond to a clause but need not do so at all. For instance, in the following text, clausal structure and information structure coincide only partially. (The speaker is a six-year-old child.)

// let's have a look in your mouth to make sure //
no // like that // no // none // . . . put the bottom
lip down // . . . no // it's not your teeth //

(The double oblique strokes are used to mark the boundaries of information units.) The clauses in this brief text are *let's have a look in your mouth*, *to make sure*, *like that*, *put the bottom lip down*, *it's not your teeth*. That is, there are five clauses, but eight information units. A clausal analysis inevitably strikes problems with items like *no none*, which either have to be treated as clauses by some theoretical contortion, or else fall uncomfortably outside the description. In terms of informational structure there is no problem of description. It is clear from this example that the information units need not coincide with the clauses or the clause-boundaries; for instance, the first information unit contains two clauses.

The information units are motivated directly by the interaction between the speaker and the other participant. Some response on the addressee's part causes both the specific content and the structure in which it is presented. The speaker can monitor the hearer's reaction from moment to moment, and adjust the informational structure accordingly.

The information units are, as mentioned, segments of speech which have (are spoken with) one unified intonational 'tune'. Each unit has an internal two-term structure, of 'known' and 'unknown' information. That is, within each unit the speaker represents some part of the information contained in the unit as being unknown to the hearer, the other part by implication as being already known to the hearer. The unknown part is marked by intonational prominence, in that the greatest and most pronounced pitch-movement occurs at the beginning of the unknown segment. So in the example just given

// let's have a look in your mouth to make *sure* //

sure receives intonational prominence with a noticeable fall in pitch, thus marking it as informationally unknown. The whole of this text has a known/unknown structure as shown here (with the unknown segment underlined).

// let's have a look in your mouth to make <u>sure</u> // <u>no</u> //
like <u>that</u> // <u>no</u> // <u>none</u> // . . . put the bottom lip <u>down</u> //
. . . <u>no</u> // it's not <u>your</u> teeth //

It can be seen from this that the unknown segment tends to occur at the end of the information unit. An exception is the last information unit, where the second from last segment is prominent. Where the intonation prominence falls other than on the last word, the prominence is noted by the hearer as unusual or marked, and is interpreted as being special in some sense. In this example a contrast is established between *your* teeth and *other* teeth (in this case, the speaker's teeth). From this text it is also clear that information units need not include anything other than unknown information. The known, by definition, can be left unsaid.

The two-part structure implies that there is always some common ground, some known information, between speaker and hearer. The unknown must be said, the known may be said or it may be left unsaid and implicit. It is, of course, the speaker's judgment which determines that something is shared knowledge, and what that shared knowledge is. It is also not clear from the speaker's decision to treat some information as known just how well known this may be to the hearer. David Brazil makes a similar point in *Discourse Intonation*:

> Another way of expressing the same distinction is to say that some
> parts of what a speaker says merely *make reference* to features
> which he takes to be already present in the interpenetrating worlds
> of speaker and hearer. Others have the status of *information* in that
> they are presented as if likely to change the world of the hearer. (p. 6)

Brazil is here introducing a twofold distinction into the element which Halliday regards as unknown. In doing so he draws attention to the fact that it is the speaker's decision to present content either as though it belonged to the shared knowledge of speaker and hearer, or was drawn from outside that area.

In this example the *known* is (among other, much more taken for granted information) that the previous conversation has been about losing teeth, and about whose teeth may have been replaced with a coin by the fairies. *Mouth, looking in one's mouth*, *your*, etc., are all assumed to be known to the hearer as they have been the topic of the preceding conversation and the shared experience of speaker and hearer. What is new, and hence 'unknown' to the hearer, is the suggestion to make *sure*. Of course, the speaker may be wrong in his assumptions about what is and what is not known to the hearer. In that case there will be some perplexity on the hearer's part, a momentary check in the flow of the interaction. Also, the speaker may be deliberately misconstruing and misrepresenting the hearer's knowledge, and by presenting information as known may attempt to coerce the hearer into accepting this insinuated assumption.

In this extract there are a number of information units which consist only of unknown information. That is not unusual. An information unit must consist of an unknown item of information, and it normally includes a known segment of information as well. To some extent the known segment is redundant, by definition. However, in interactional terms the *known* is not redundant, it serves as a link between the two participants: it provides them with common ground and shared knowledge, which serves as a starting point, a bridge almost, for each speaker in turn. (That is, making reference to 'the interpenetrating worlds of speaker and hearer'.) Thus while the known segment is informationally redundant, it is most important from an interactional point of view. Features of this structure of speech have been regarded as faults in speaking. Some parents and teachers have a habit of correcting children who give 'monosyllabic' answers, insisting that children should always speak, and in particular answer, in full sentences. This clearly rests on a misunderstanding of interactive language, as well as on the assumption that sentences are the basic units of spoken language so that any utterance which is not a sentence is defective. That assumption is incorrect, and the view could only persist because of the absence of research and hence understanding of the structure of spoken language.

Many of the interactional aspects reflected in the structure of spoken language are clearly absent from the context in which written language occurs, so that there is no need for linguistic forms to express them. However, written language does have a need for emphasizing particular items; equally, it must have the means for indicating the writer's topical and thematic organization of his material. The written language does not, of course, have intonation available for these purposes (other than parasitically by getting the reader to superimpose intonation – on italicized, underlined items, or words and phrases in inverted commas, or by the use of exclamation marks, etc.). Instead, written syntax uses sequential ordering of items or more thoroughgoing restructurings to express these meanings. Emphasis may be expressed by placing an item out of the normal syntactic order: *John she couldn't stand*, or *couldn't stand John, could Mary* (from *Mary couldn't stand John*). The writer may restructure the sentence more thoroughly: *It was John whom Mary couldn't stand*. These reorderings and restructurings still employ intonation indirectly, in the sense that these forms invite or even determine a particular reading which involves a more or less silent intonational implementation and actualization of the reading. However, even less drastically reordered or restructured sentences allow the writer to organize his material in a manner which presents his content in a particular fashion. All sentences display a two-part structure. One part, the theme, announces what the writer has chosen to make the topic of the sentence; the other part, the rheme, consists of material pertaining to that theme, furthering and developing it in some sense. In the sentence above, *All sentences display a two-part structure, all sentences* is the theme and *display a two-part structure* is the rheme. That is, the first syntactic constituent of a sentence is always theme, the rest rheme. Consequently theme is not another label for subject; frequently the two will coincide, but often they will not. In the preceding sentence *consequently* is the theme, and *theme is not another label for subject* is rheme.

Hence the textual structuring of speech and that of writing proceed from two distinctly different starting points. The structure of speech starts from the question: 'What can I assume as common and shared knowledge for my addressee and myself?' This question, and its answer, are at the basis of the structure of speech. Writing starts with the question: 'What is most important, topically, to me, in this sentence which I am about to write?' This question, and its answer, are at the basis of the structure of writing. The cohesive and continuous development of a topic is thus paramount in writing, while the construction of a world of shared meaning is paramount in speaking.

The immediacy of the interaction and the speaker's awareness of the hearer lead to another major structural difference between speech and writing, a clausal structure which is both evidence of immediate thinking, in that the speaker does not have time to assemble complex structures, and evidence of the needs of the hearer as the recipient of information. Speech is structured by sequences or 'chains' of clauses, which are, generally speaking, co-ordinated, or else adjoined without any co-ordinating particles (rather than subordinated or embedded). An example of a co-ordinated structure is *let's have a look in your mouth and make sure*, where the two clauses have equal status, and are joined by a conjunction. An example of an adjoined structure is *let's have a look in your mouth(,) make sure*, where the two clauses have equal status, and are adjacent but without a conjunction. A subordinating construction would be *when we look in your mouth we'll make sure*, where there is a main clause, *we'll make sure*, and a subordinate when-clause. In the text from which the example is taken the structure is an embedding one, *let's have a look in your mouth to make sure*, where *to make sure* is syntactically integrated into the main clause *let's have a look in your mouth* and forms a syntactic constituent of it. 'Adjoined' is, however, open to a misinterpretation, namely that it means 'simply adjoined, adjoined without indication of the structural and semantic relationship of the clauses'. Such an interpretation is incorrect. The absence of a co-ordinating particle is possible because of the use of intonation to provide the structural connections. The pitch movement and the pitch height at the information unit/clause boundaries give a precise indication of how the following clause connects both structurally and semantically with the preceding clause. The direction of the intonation contour in the new clause makes this structural connection, and further develops it. The pitch movements involved in this are minute but absolutely clear indications of the structure. Taking a further extract from the text already discussed as an example (numbering the information units)

// No // we got them separate // see // the big one //
we got him from my // ... uh ... // we got him from my
brother's friend // my oldest brother //

1 would have a falling intonation to a medium low position with a slight rising 'hook'; 2 would begin at that level, rise slightly, fall on *separate* to a medium low position; 3 would be level, at that height; 4 would start at a medium high position, fall on *big*, continue to fall on the first part of *one*, with a slight rising hook at the end; 5 would start at that level, continue to rise slightly to medium level on *my*; *uh* would be on that level; 6 would continue at that level, rise steadily to the end of *brother's*, at a medium level, and fall on *friend*, to a medium low level; 7 would start at the same height as *friend* and fall on *oldest*, to a full low position (without final rising hook) on *brother*. This over-arching link is not broken until an information unit ends in a high rise without any down-turn, or in a full fall without any upturning hook, and where the following information unit is not an exact intonational copy of its preceding unit. For instance, the fact that 7 starts at the same height as the highest point of 6 is interpreted by the hearer as indicating that

7 is a gloss on the item which had the same height in 6, that is, that it is offering further information and elaboration on aspects of one element of 6, namely that with the intonation (and information) focus. Consequently, far from the linking structure being missing or weakly articulated, the structure and the meaning of clausal connections in speech are highly articulated and capable of the finest nuance. In writing, this structure is mirrored to some extent in the system of punctuation, which is not, however, capable of expressing the same detail and precision. In *Discourse Intonation*, Brazil discusses a related feature, namely the semantic connectedness of tone-groups (that is, information units) in discourse. He points out that tone-groups are spoken in one of three *keys*, that is, relative pitch-levels: mid, high, or low.

> Any occurrence of a high-key tone group can be thought of as being
> phonetically bound to a succeeding tone-group; any low-key tone
> group as bound to the preceding one. The former carries the
> implication, 'There is more to follow'; the latter 'This is said in a
> situation created by something that went immediately before'.
> In discourse we can say that one sets up expectations, the other
> has prerequisites. (p. 10)

This suggests that in addition to the linking discussed above, there exists another, superimposed level of intonationally expressed linking, relating the content of tone-groups in the way indicated by Brazil.

Topic development in speech, within this clausal structure, is by sequence, restatement, elaboration, and intonational articulation. The evidence of 'thinking on your feet' is everywhere evident in speech. This is in contrast to writing, where there are, typically, no traces of immediate thinking. Writing is the domain of circumspection, of (self-)censorship, reworking, editing. The development of the topic in writing is by another order: not by sequence but by hierarchy. That which is more important is given structural prominence, the less important is structurally subordinated. Consequently writing is the domain of a more complex syntax, typified by the sentence, by subordination and embedding of various types, by syntactic and conceptual integration. Speech is typified by the syntax of sequence, of the clausal chain, of addition and accretion. To the extent that there is circumspection and self-censorship in speech, it emerges in the form of hesitation phenomena. The greater the need for circumspection, the more prominent hesitation phenomena are likely to be; the less need for care, the less likely hesitation phenomena are to occur. Bernstein and others have noted that hesitation phenomena are more common with middle-class than with working-class speakers.

Perhaps the most obvious and most characteristic unit of the written language is the sentence. It features prominently in linguistic theory (it also features quite prominently in folk linguistics), and we tend to assume that we know what a sentence is. In fact, and this is also well known, there is no agreement in linguistic theory on the definition of sentence. I wish to say that the sentence (whatever its definition) is not a unit of informal spoken language, but that it is the basic textual unit of the written language. Because of the influence of writing on speaking and because of its higher status, the assumption is that speech is also organized by the sentence as its basic linguistic unit. I think that is not correct. There is much evidence, for instance from the description of Australian Aboriginal languages, which seems to suggest that, in some of these languages at least, there are chains of clauses and paragraphs but there are no sentences. One of the problems in attempting to write these languages down, to make them literate languages and to give them a 'literature', is precisely this absence of the sentence, so that in transcribing narratives and myths the transcriber wants to impose a sentence structure on the narrative; this falsifies the narrative, because in its spoken form it is not structured in sentences. The interesting point is that after a while the original tellers of the myth also want to organize the written versions of the narratives in sentence form. There seems to be something about writing which demands a different syntactic and textual organization from that of speech.

To show the difference between these two forms of the language, here is an example of the same adult (myself) speaking and writing. The spoken text is from the transcript of a lecture given without notes; the written text was prepared from the transcript, for publication. I deliberately kept reasonably close to the spoken style of the lecture; a fully fledged translation into writing would have been very different.

Text 1

Spoken text

Now of course an exhortation to be open in the way we
look at things is easier said than done *because* we have
all finished I suppose much of our learning *with* most, I

think all of us have finished probably all of our signi-
5   ficant learning *and* learning has of course positive
aspects it has the positive aspect of enabling us to
live in the culture that we are born into *but* learning
also has um I feel quite negative aspects um the positive
ones as I say are clear enough they enable us to function
10   In our world the negative ones have also been pointed to
um frequently enough, I'll just er perhaps talk about them
very briefly in relation to language um the negative aspects
of learning I think are concerned with a kind of reduction
that goes on with a kind limiting that goes on when we
15   learn cultural things. We come to learn things *and* once
we have learned them they seem to be the only way to do things
um the way we say things seems to be the natural way to say
things *and* so forth.

Text 2

Written text

Now of course, an exhortation to be open in the way we look
at things is easier said than done *because* we have all
finished most of our significant learning. Learning has
positive aspects, enabling us to live in the culture that
5   we are born into; *but* learning also has quite negative aspects.
These are concerned with a kind of reduction, a kind of limiting that goes on when we learn cultural things. We come to
learn things *and* once we have learned them they seem to be
the only way to do a thing; the way we say things seems to
10   be the natural way to say things *and* so forth.

I had asked a typist to transcribe the tape, which she kindly did. The 'punctuation' of the spoken text is therefore as the typist heard it. Clearly, the main organizing unit of the spoken text is not the sentence. Though it may be unusual to find the structure of speech in the formal register of 'lecture', the structure itself is not at all untypical of speech. It consists of clauses of equal or near equal syntactic status 'chained' together in sequence. This chaining may take the form of co-ordinated clauses, or of main and subordinated clauses, linked by conjunctions such as *and*, *but*, *or*, *if*, *so*, *because*, *though*. That is, the structure of speech is characterized by 'chains' of syntactically relatively complete and independent clauses. For instance, Text 1, lines 3–6: *I think all of us have finished probably all of our significant learning and learning has of course positive aspects it has the positive aspect . . .* – here three syntactically complete clauses are in the chain. Where a clause is significantly changed syntactically in order to make it part of another clause we have examples of either subordinating or embedding constructions; these are less typical of speech. For instance, in Text 1, lines 6–7; *it has the positive aspect of enabling us to live in the culture, enabling us* is a clause which is heavily modified to fit syntactically into its syntactic unit: *to live in the culture* is, similarly, a clause which has been significantly modified to fit into its matrix clause. In Text 1 the chaining syntax predominates, though it is clearly a mixture of chaining and embedding syntax. Examples of the latter are *an exhortation to be open, the way we look at things, enabling us to live, the culture that we are born into.* Informal speech tends to have even fewer instances of embedding than this text.

The written text by contrast is not only much shorter (ten lines compared to eight), it has more sentence (four compared to two) and the number of co-ordinated and adjoined clauses is significantly lower. Proportionately, full subordination and embedding is more prominent in the written text (twenty-one clauses, five-co-ordinated or adjoined clauses, a ratio of 3.2:1) than in the spoken (thirty-four clauses, thirteen co-ordinated or adjoined clauses, a ratio of 1.6:1). It is worth bearing in mind that this spoken text .was a relatively formal one, so that it contains a higher proportion of subordinated and embedded clauses than informal speech. Also, as the written text derives from the spoken one, it preserves some of the latter's informality. A formal written text would show a higher degree of subordination and embedding.

To summarize: speech, typically, consists of chains of co-ordinated, weakly subordinated and adjoined clauses; writing by contrast is marked by full subordination and embedding. There are other characteristics too. The spoken text is longer, to make allowances for the different mode of reception, it shows repetition, allowing the hearer time to assimilate information. It also contains many features of an interpersonal kind, referring to the interrelation of speaker and audience.

The discussion so far suggests that for our society linguistic competence includes a number of things over and above those which are normally assumed to be included in competence. The traditional Chomskyan version of competence assumes that a speaker of a language has internalized the rules of sentence formation and transformation of that language and uses them as a basis for the production of an infinite set of sentences. There is also a sociolinguist's definition of competence, for instance that of Dell Hymes (1972), who talks about the rules we use in correctly applying these sentences in given situations. I would like to extend this notion of competence, and speak about differentiated competences for speaking and writing. These would include at least two additional types of rule. One would indicate how the structure-forming rules are to be applied in either speaking or writing. Further, if *sentence* is not a linguistic category of speech, then the competence for writing would include rules of sentence-formation, and the competence for speaking would not. In either case the competencies for speech and writing would include knowledge about strategies of conjunction — predominantly chaining for speech and embedding for writing. However, beyond these, the competence for writing would need to include a second type of rule, which indicates the knowledge of those syntactic structures which occur only in the written mode of language; and similarly for speaking. For instance, if a speaker said *Mary was supposed to do the trifle* with intonational prominence on *Mary*, then the most likely form of this in writing is *It was Mary who was supposed to do the trifle*. This structure belongs to writing; when it occurs in speech it is there as an importation, much like a loan-word from another language. Lastly, there would need to be a differentiated textual competence, as textual structures and processes differ significantly from one mode to the other, in areas such as cohesion, topic development, staging. In speaking, the text is usually constructed in interaction with another participant, whereas typically in writing that is not the case.

In the discussion so far I have proceeded as though all speakers and writers were identical. That is not the case. I mentioned above that access to writing is unevenly distributed in Western technological societies. Some members of these societies have no competence at all in writing (or reading) — the figure for countries such as Britain or Australia is between 10 and 15 per cent. Full competence in writing may be restricted to as few as 10 per cent of the population. Obviously there are strong links between the structures of those societies and this uneven distribution of written competence. Speakers too are differentiated according to regional and social dialects. For certain social groups – the professional classes, for instance – the structure of the spoken form of their dialects is very strongly influenced by the structures of writing. As a result, the difference between the syntax of speech and that of writing is far less for such groups than it is for groups whose dialects are little if at all influenced by the structure of writing. This factor has important implications for children learning to write. For some children the syntax of writing will be more familiar than for others, to whom it may be totally unfamiliar. Hence in a group of children some may start with knowledge which others have yet to acquire. This difference in knowledge is unacknowledged, because the fundamental differences between the two forms of language is not a well-understood and widely known fact. Teachers are likely to attribute this difference in the performance of children to differences in intelligence. There exists therefore an initial unnoticed hurdle in the learning of writing on which many children stumble and never recover. They will not be fully competent writers and will be regarded as failures in the eyes of our literate society and in terms of our educational system.

iv Children's speech and children's writing

What are the implications of the structure of speech for children's writing? It may be well to summarize the main points made so far, and then attempt to suggest some of the main effects which these may be expected to have in the learning of writing by children. In Chapter 3 these matters will be explored in detail through the use of examples of children's spoken and written language.

Speech is learned before writing. Hence the grammatical and textual (and of course the phonological) rules of speech are learned first and form the basis of the child's knowledge and use of language. Speech is characterized by the immediate presence of an addressee (a single or multiple-person addressee). The audience tends to be known to the speaker, and the speaker is able to gauge the effectiveness of his or her message by verbal and non-verbal responses of the addressee. Spoken texts are typically created in interaction and a single speaker's contribution to the text is not a complete text in itself. Frequently the text is generated more by one speaker than the other, usually by the more powerful participant in the interaction. This does not necessarily mean that the powerful speaker speaks more, but that he or she causes (in some sense) and directs the speech of both participants. Children are frequently the less powerful participants in spoken interactions – in situations where they speak to parents, teachers, relatives, neighbours.

Topics are developed jointly in spoken interactions. The fact that the immediate addressee or the audience generally is known to the speaker means that the speaker is aware of much of the knowledge which is shared by speaker and hearer. Hence much knowledge may be left implicit, much information may be left unsaid. Indeed, in many situations, particularly those characterized by (displays of) solidarity of the participants, a rule seems to be operating which demands that the known be left implicit. Not to do so, to question or to bring into open discussion such implicit knowledge, tends to have implications of formality, even hostility. In the peer-groups of children this rule is unlikely to be broken. Compared to writing, speech is relatively more implicit.

These aspects of the typical contexts and situations of speech have their effect on the structure of speech. The dominant and characteristic unit of speech is the information unit. It is superimposed on a clausal structure marked by co-ordination and adjunction. The known–unknown structure of the succession of information units is closely related to the implicitness of speech. The speaker decides what is to be said at all, and then decides what is to be offered to the addressee as known and unknown information. Implicitness may work in two steps, first by leaving the 'obvious' unsaid, and at the second step by leaving some of the talked about information always at the level of the known – and thus not accessible for serious examination. Nevertheless, the shared knowledge provides a bridge between speaker and hearer.

Sentences are not characteristic of 'natural' and informal speech. Sentences may occur in spoken language as importations from the written form. Sentences are the basic textual unit of writing. When sentences occur in speech they import formality to speech.

Topic development and structuring in speech is handled characteristically and predominantly by intonation. It structures the topic/non-topic distinction within the single information unit, and it also structures larger textual units. Topic development and structuring is also handled through the sequential ordering of clauses, through repetition, elaboration, restatement, all taking place in a sequential clausal structure.

What are the effects and implications of these features for children's writing? The fact that the child learns the grammatical and textual rules of spoken language first, means that these are the rules of language that the child can draw on when he or she first learns to write. We ought therefore to expect that children's early writing shows many of the features of the grammar of speech, or features which derive from the child's knowledge of speaking. While an addressee is in most cases immediately present in situations where language is spoken, this is not so for writing. We might expect this to cause major problems. The child does not know the absent addressee and has to imagine him in some form; or perhaps the child has no addressee in mind in many cases when he or she is called on to write? The child cannot gauge the effect of the language he or she is producing; and this is a major change for the child. (Most of us have had the experience of either speaking to a child on the phone or, more revealingly, seeing a child being spoken to on the phone. In either case the lack of direct, visible signals of interaction is a problem for the child.) Perhaps more significantly still, the stimulation of the interlocutor is missing. And whereas in speech the child creates a text in interaction, now he or she is, for the first time, forced to construct a text without the guide, the prodding, the stimulus of the interaction. Producing speech under such circumstances is very much an abstract exercise. Now the child must produce a self-sufficient text by himself. Given that children are frequently the less powerful participants in speech-interactions, their speech roles (especially in the face of some 'authority') tend to be passive. School presents the paradoxical situation for children that they are in the presence of an authority, who demands that they be active and construct individual texts.

Where the child writer imagines some addressee, the child may well leave as much information implicit as he or she would have done in the presence of this imagined addressee. Hence children's early writing is frequently extraordinarily implicit, to the point of seeming disjointed. Writing demands the development of the habit of explicitness. In situations where there is a conjunction of a home-background of relatively implicit speech, and of the child's own attitude to implicitness in speech, serious problems of learning and adjustment are ahead for the child in school, where the emphasis is on explicit discourse, in both speech and writing.

The structure of writing is fundamentally distinct from that of speech. To start with, the child is faced with the problem of learning a quite new syntactic, semantic, and textual unit, the sentence. In speaking, one clause follows another in a chain which has no predictable and necessary endpoint. In such a sequence of clauses each clause in turn contributes in an additive manner to the topic and to the development of the text generally. The sentence, and in particular the adult notion of sentence, makes quite different assumptions and demands. Normally it includes some reference to a 'complete thought'. This is not an unproblematic notion in itself, but it is particularly so for the child, used to the expression of one thought over a series of syntactically loosely connected clauses. Sentences typically consist of a number of clauses which stand in a hierarchical relation to each other, with one main clause to which others are subordinated in various syntactic ways. The development of the adult concept of sentence therefore demands the development of planning, deciding which is to be the main clause (the main idea?) and how subsidiary clauses (and ideas) are to be integrated with the main clause. Conceptual and syntactic complexity here go hand in hand. The child's gradual development of the adult conception of sentence will be discussed in detail in Chapter 4; here it suffices to say that it constitutes a major problem for a child who is learning to write. Too many textbooks in the 'Language Arts' have treated the sentence as a basically unproblematic notion, a question of teaching children to use capital letters and full stops. A quotation may make my point:

> In teaching children to write it is essential that the teacher remember the relationship between spoken and written language. Spoken language precedes writing and establishes a pattern for it. *A child who can create a clear spoken sentence* has a skill that is necessary in learning how to write. It might be said that *all that remains to be learned are the mechanics and conventions of the language*: handwriting, spelling, punctuation, capitalization and conventional forms. This is in no way to minimize the number or difficulty of the skills which remain to be learned. The point is that *the child already knows the structure of the language well enough to be able to formulate sentences* that are recognizable and understandable to another native speaker. (D. R. Ferris, 'Teaching children to write' in P. Lamb (ed.), *Guiding Children's Language Learning*, p. 172; my italics)

The mixture of helpful insight and perpetuation of fundamental misconceptions usefully sums up the state of current thinking. (The book continues to be heavily used in Language Arts courses. The most recent borrowing was on 18 August 1981.) But basically it conflates speech and writing: writing is speech plus the 'mechanics and conventions'.

The smaller and larger textual structures are developed in speech predominantly through intonational means. Some of these are echoed in writing. For instance, punctuation to some extent (and more for some writers than others) reflects the intonational and informational structures of speech. Commas normally occur where, if the passage were spoken, a significant intonation movement finishes, that is, at the end of an information unit. However, this is by no means an invariable rule. Written language has developed its own structures and conventions, and punctuation can be related to those, deriving from the syntax of writing rather than from that of speech. While all punctuation marks can be translations of intonational features, they need not be. Furthermore the choice of a semicolon rather than a comma is more frequently a grammatical and textual choice deriving from the contingencies of writing than the reflection of an intonational feature. Consequently, in the learning of punctuation much more is involved than mere translation skills. In addition, the larger textual structures, such as paragraphs and episodes, do not exist in speech, and their essential characteristics have to be learned from the start.

v   Sources and context

It may seem somewhat odd to maintain that linguistics has not been concerned with the study of speech, given that the beginnings of modern linguistics are so heavily preoccupied with the study of speech sound, both in its physical form, phonetics, and in the systematic organization of that physical form, phonology. The work of Henry Sweet, *A Primer of Phonetics* (1892), and of Daniel Jones, as in *An Outline of English Phonology* (1918), stand foremost in this tradition in Britain. A more modern work in this tradition is A. C. Gimson's *Introduction to the Pronunciation of English* (1962). Immensely important work was carried on elsewhere, and though this is not the place to provide even a sketchy history of the study of sound, the names of K. L. Pike and N. S. Trubetzkoy should be mentioned as representatives of American and European work. (See the Bibliography.) This work confined itself to the sound-aspects of speech, and did not look at the grammatical organization of speech as a mode of language. Linguists insist that the study of the spoken language should have priority: for instance, Leonard Bloomfield, in his *Language* (1935), says, 'Writing is not language, but merely a way of recording language by means of visible marks' (p. 21); though he was fully aware of the power of the written form, and its effects on speech (pp. 486-7). This has remained a common-place in linguistics. A more recent representative of this view is H. A. Gleason in his book *An Introduction to Descriptive Linguistics* (1961); chapters

25 and 26, 'Writing systems', and 'Written languages', contain many important insights. Hence Keith Basso is only partially correct in his review of Jack Goody's *The Domestication of the Savage Mind*, in which he asserts that the study of writing has been neglected due to linguists' concentration on the study of speech.

The major advance in the study of the grammatical organization of the spoken language has come in the work of Michael Halliday. This lay in two areas: in his integration of the phonological/intonational aspects of English into the grammatical system of the language overall, and in the study of cohesion, which he and Ruqaiya Hasan have made. His findings are reported in a number of places, for instance in 'Notes on transitivity and theme in English (Parts 1-3)', 1967-8; in *A Course in Spoken English: Intonation* (1970); in chapter 12, 'Theme and information in the English clause' in *Halliday: System and Function in Language* (ed. Kress, 1976); and in a very abbreviated form in 'Language structure and language function' in *New Horizons in Linguistics* (ed. Lyons, 1970). The work on cohesion is most accessible in *Cohesion in English* (1976). Halliday's work on intonation and grammar has been extended, and modified, in important ways by David Brazil of the English Language Research Unit at the University of Birmingham. Three monographs published by the group contain his findings: *Discourse Intonation* (1975), *Discourse Intonation II* (1978), and, with Malcolm Coulthard, *Exchange Structure* (1979). An important article which concerns itself with neurological aspects of the structure of speech is John Laver's 'The production of speech' (1970).

The situation concerning the description of the written mode of language is somewhat analogous to that of speech. There has been much work on the relation between sound and spelling, and on orthography of itself, but no serious attention has been given to the study of the grammar of the written form of language. A look at books or articles on linguistics will quickly demonstrate that linguists do not focus on spoken utterances. For instance, example sentences or texts are in ninety-nine cases out of a hundred given without any indication of the phonological/intonational realization of the utterance. Indeed, many texts in this book are no exception. The difficulty lies partly in the lack of an adequate and simple system for indicating and transcribing phonological features. More recently some attention has begun to be paid to the contexts of writing, and to their effects. Such work has come predominantly from outside of linguistics proper, from people working in educational fields, and in sociolinguistics. The work of

James Britton and of Harold Rosen is a good example. This is reported, including contributions by Tony Burgess, Nancy Martin, Alex McLeod, in *The Development of Writing Abilities (11-18)* (1975). The work of the adult literacy campaign has brought into focus the large number of adults who cannot read or write; in addition it has revived discussion of differing levels of literacy. My own distinction between productive and reproductive writing is meant to highlight the fact that on the one hand an exceedingly small proportion of the adult population writes at all — other than the most rudimentary writing such as shopping lists and filling in dockets and forms — and on the other, of the reminder most of their writing is either reproductive or highly routinized or both. Here I would include the writing of stereotyped letters, memos, official notes, all of them forms of writing where convention dictates the content and the syntax. A small proportion of writers are engaged in fully productive writing, that is, writing in a large variety of forms, and with significantly less constraint on content and syntax. A fully competent writer would thus be one who has the ability to perform efficiently in this group.

Some exceedingly penetrating and suggestive remarks on the relation of speech and writing are made by L. S. Vygotsky in *Thought and Language* (1962) (see particularly pp. 98-101). At the April 1979 meeting of the Australian Linguistic Society a joint paper was delivered by Pawley and Syder entitled 'Why have linguists missed the obvious over these last 50 years?' Two quotations from the paper provide strong support for some of the major suggestions in this chapter: 'The position of the sentence as the basic unit of syntax is weakened by the study of spontaneous speech, as opposed to written discourse. In any case, sentence boundaries are often hard to locate in spontaneous connected discourse . . . the sentence is not a very well-defined unit' (pp. 19-20); 'Modern linguistics is to a remarkable degree based on the study of written texts and artificial speech which approximates written speech' (p. 20). Recent work in the description of Australian Aboriginal languages also lends support to the idea that the sentence is not a unit of the spoken language. I have attempted to draw a distinction between the grammatical systems of speech and writing in chapter 3, 'The social values of speech and writing', in *Language and Control* (1979), and in 'Towards an analysis of the language of European intellectuals' (1978). A major force in theorizing about writing, or rather, literacy, has been the article by Jack Goody and Ian Watt, 'The consequences of literacy' (1972). Descriptive work along these lines is reported in Jack Goody (ed.), *Literacy in Traditional Societies* (1968).

This chapter also draws strongly, if perhaps indirectly, on the theoretical work of Basil Bernstein, in particular on his suggestions concerning the nature and contents of distinctive codes used by socially differentiated groups of speakers in English, as well as on more specific matters in his work, such as his findings on hesitation phenomena. His *Class, Codes and Control*, volume 1 (1971) contains most of the important papers.

A brief word on orthography. If one accepts the argument that the relation between speech sounds and their written representation is rule-governed and hence systematic, one needs to explain why the learning of the system causes so much difficulty to children who have at that stage largely mastered the more complex rule-system of syntax. One answer might be that the learning of syntax is continuous, over a very long period, from birth to nine or ten, and takes place without overt teaching. The learning of spelling is highly intermittent, over a relatively short period (considering that children are expected to become reasonably proficient by the age of ten or eleven), and is the subject of overt teaching. K. H. Albrow's *The English Writing System: Notes Towards a Description* (1972) is an excellent introduction.

Chapter 3
Children's speech and children's writing

i Children's speech: the starting point

If it is the case that speech and writing are two modes of language with distinct forms of syntactic and textual organization, then it becomes not only an interesting but necessary task to provide adequate descriptions of the syntax of both forms, and to investigate the influence of the syntax of speech on early stages of writing and on the gradual development of the latter in its own right. In this chapter I wish to make a beginning on both of these tasks. I cannot hope to provide the 'adequate description' which I am demanding. That will be the task of many people over many years. I hope to be able to provide some fundamental suggestions concerning the kinds of approach, methodology, theories, which may prove illuminating. In the process I hope to give some beginnings of descriptions of children's speech and particularly of children's writing. I attempt to do this by commenting on examples of children's spoken and written texts of various ages from the point of view of the features of both forms of language discussed in the previous chapter.

The first five texts are all examples of the spoken texts of children from the age of three to seven. They exemplify language used in different situations. My intention is to give substance to the points made in Chapter 2 and to establish the range of linguistic forms and abilities which are typical of children's speech when they learn to write. These forms represent the grammar which children draw on in making their first writing attempts.

The first text involves a $3\frac{1}{2}$-year-old boy. He is at home with his mother and her friend, and they are engaged in cooking scones. They are following a recipe book in which the major steps in the preparation of the scones are represented by a picture.

Text 3

Cooking Lesson

Friend: Has mummy just done that, do you think?
Mother: No, darling, you don't spit on the spoon. (*Pause. Child trying to crack egg, for some while, unsuccessfully*)
Mother: Shall I do a bit now? Oh dear if only I had a . . .
5   *Child*: Can I read the instructions?
Mother: Emmm, just a minute, love
(*Activity and inaudible speech*)
Child: . . . butter, honey, . . . where have we got up to . . . now what do we do, are we doing it . . .
10 *Mother*: That bit have we done, pet, look those are the instructions, that was the first instruction, and what did that tell us to do?
Child: Crack the eggs
Mother, Friend: (*Approving yeses in chorus*)
15 *Friend*: We have cracked the eggs, and what's that one?
Child: Mix it
Friend: Whisking it all up, yes
Child: That's where we got up to
Friend: Good, yes
20 *Child*: Number three
Friend: What's that one, you think, number four?
Child: (*Inaudible*)
Friend: And mummys just done that, hasn't she?

The typical contextual features of spoken language are present here: addressees are physically present, they are well known to each other, the situation is highly interactive, the text is created in interaction, the speakers can gauge the effectiveness of their utterances from many cues — in this case by, among other things, the appropriateness of the ensuing action. There is also an unequal distribution of power, with mother and friend relatively more powerful than the child. This latter fact is clearly demonstrated by a number of features. The mother and the friend ask the questions, which are covert commands, and therefore act as instructions. Line 1 *Friend: Has mummy just done that, do you think?* translates to the statement *Mummy has just done that,* from which the child has to infer *Therefore don't you continue doing that.*

Line 4 *Mother: Shall I do a bit now?* translates to the statement *I shall do a bit now*, from which the child has to infer *Therefore you stop doing this, and let me.*

This is a general strategy on the part of the adults in this text; it demonstrates the inequality of the participants in this interaction and in general beyond that. The child asks one question, in line 5, but although the mother responds to the question, she ignores the request contained in it or at least defers it. Where the child's speech is a response to a question or a direction it tends to be brief compared to his speech where it is not a response but is self-initiated.

Responses: line 13 *Crack the eggs*; 16 *Mix it*; 20 *Number three.* Self-initiated: line 5 *Can I read the instructions?*; 8-9 *. . . butter honey . . . where have we got up to . . . now what do we do, are we doing it . . .*; 18 *That's where we got up to.*

Directed response and directed speech of this kind are typical of one mode of instruction and become a characteristic feature of language in the school. Text 4 is a typical illustration of it.

Text 4

Lovely Things

    Teacher: Well we're going to have another look at some of the
        things we did first um when we first started we found
        out that we're going to learn our humanities mostly
        through our senses. How many senses do we have?
5   *Child*: Five
    Teacher: Danny
    Child: Five
    Teacher: Right we have five. Who's going to tell me what they
        are yes
10 *Child*: Seeing
    Teacher: Seeing
    Child: Smelling
    Teacher: Yes
    Child: Tasting
15 *Teacher*: Yes
    Child: Hearing
    Teacher: Yes

Child: Feeling

Teacher: Good boy five senses and we're going to do some work
20   looking at all of those senses aren't we? We've looked
at seeing and now we're looking at hearing. Tell me
some of the lovely things we saw with our sense of sight.
Yes. Oh come on what lovely things can you see yes.

Child: Flowers

25 *Teacher*: Flowers

Child: Birds

Teacher: Right

Child: Paintings

Teacher: Right

30 *Child*: Kittens

Teacher: Right

Child: Um flowers

Teacher: Oh we've had those
Yes

35 *Child*: (*Inaudible*)

Teacher: Yes

Teacher: What's the loveliest thing you can see at home?
Yes

Child: My cake

40 *Teacher*: Yes

Child: My baby

Teacher: Yes I think you like your baby very much don't you.

Child: A rabbit

Teacher: Pardon I can't hear speak up very loudly and clearly
45   children yes

Child: My do

Teacher: Pardon

Child: My dog

Teacher: Yes oh the loveliest thing you have at home Oh I can
50   think of somebody lovelier than that no one's told me yet.

Child: Our cat

Teacher: Yes yes

Child: Our kitten

Teacher: Yes

55 *Child*: Um my baby

Teacher: Your baby you love best

Teacher: Who else do you love best at home?

      Child: Your mum
      Teacher: Hum
60   *Child*: Your mummy
      Teacher: Your bubby
      Child: Mummy
      Teacher: Mummy I thought you'd say that first. Isn't mummy
      doesn't she get a vote —
65   All right then some other lovely things we saw. Do you
      remember when we talked about the lovely silent place.
      Yes
      Teacher: Where was it tell me what the lovely silent place was
      like yes.
70   *Child*: Under the trees
      Teacher: Under the trees yes
      Child: Up in the hills
      Teacher: Hills might be yes
      Child: The pond
75   *Teacher*: Yes the pond we didn't know exactly where it was but
      we know we liked it.

In both texts the adjoining and co-ordination of simple clauses is the dominant structural form. The fact that Text 3 contains many questions makes the clausal chains shorter, seemingly like sentences. The 'chains' tend to consist of at least two clauses: line 1 *Has mummy just done that, do you think?*; 4 *Shall I do a bit now? oh dear if only I had a* . . . In the longer sequences the clauses are also in chained constructions. Line 10: *that bit have we done, pet, look those are the instructions,/ that was the first instruction, and what did that tell us to do.* From the syntactic point of view there is very little difference between the speech of the adults and that of the child. The child's clauses are well formed syntactically, and where he utters a longer sequence it has the same chaining clausal structure as that of the adults: *butter, honey* . . . *where have we got up to* . . . *now what do we do, are we doing it* . . .

    In Text 4 there is a clear contrast between the teacher's language and that of the children. It is instructive to bear in mind that the children in this class are six-year-olds, so that their linguistic abilities are no doubt greater than that of the three-year-old in Text 3. Judging from the text one would not think so; the difference is clearly due to the context. Although there is an element of instruction in the first text, in the second one this is much more pronounced and much more formalized. Despite the formal context the teacher's speech shows no signs of formality. The syntax of her language is that of the chaining clausal structure of informal spoken language. In other words the fact that her attention is focused on the immediate problems of the lesson, of keeping control, means that she does not devote time to the formal planning of her language, and so the informal syntax of speech asserts itself. The teacher's language therefore does not differ substantially from that which the children are capable of, even in a context where formal speech and hence the influence of the written form might be expected. The longest utterances (these are not included in the text as quoted) by any child are *Cos it um was splashing and then silent again*, two co-ordinated clauses, and *Um up in the hills um near a waterfall* which may be regarded as two reduced adjoined clauses. However, the most important feature of this text is the effect of this type of situation on the children's language. On the face of it the teacher may be wishing to elicit descriptive statements from the children. *Oh come on what lovely things can you see* seems to call for a more elaborate response. The lesson instead elicits what seems at that stage to be the equivalent of 'facts'. Of course, this is a comment both on this particular lesson and on the genre into which it will develop, the scientific and factually based lesson. It is a serious comment on the conception of knowledge as it exists in schools even at that early stage.

There is an ironic contrast between this reduction or suppression of language and teachers' expectations for children to write 'stories' in which the same material is expected to be treated in an imaginative discursive manner.

The view is put forward at times (deriving from the writings of Piaget) that children are incapable of real interaction at that stage, that is, that at the age of six they are still in the egocentric stage where they do not or cannot pay attention to others, or to the cognitive states of others, but rather talk only to themselves. If this view were correct then the six-year-olds in this lesson might not be capable of more interactive language anyway. The next two texts show that this is not the case. Text 5 comes from a kindergarten group in which the children are all three years old. They have been looking at posters showing jungle animals. The teacher has then given them a box of small wooden animals to look at.

Text 5

Zebras

Teacher: Here, have a look at these. See what . . .
   see what you can find. If you're very careful
   you can have a look at these.
Annabel: Ohh! Ohh! Look.
5   *Sophie*: Look at them
   Annabel: Whoo! Whoo! Did you hear me whistle?
   Sophie: No
   Christina: I want a whistle, let's set them all out
   Sophie: Shall we
10   *Christina*: No, I'm gonna set them all out.
   Sophie: I am . . . Now I'll get . . . now I'll get these . . .
      these whistles, now I'll get these whistles,
      (*in sing-song voice*) I've got all the whistles
   Christina: (*in sing-song voice*) I've got all the whistles
15   *Toby*: So have I
   Sophie: So have I
   Christina: Anyway, I've got a frog.
   Sophie: Shall we go outside?
   Annabel: No, I'm not your friend, I want my Grandma.
20   *Sophie*: She's not here
   Annabel: I know she isn't
   Sophie: You're a pig
   Annabel: Don't. (*Cries*)
   Toby: This is horrible.
25   *Annabel*: A horse?
   Toby: They're like horses?
   Annabel: No, no, that a strebra
   Sophie: Not a strebra
   Annabel: It is
30   *Toby*: Yes it is
   Sophie: Not a strebra
   Annabel: It is
   Sophie: A zebra
   Christina: A debra
35   *Annabel*: It is not
   Annabel: It's a strebra, isn't it?

    Sophie: No it isn't, it isn't, is it, Christina? Have
    a look — a zebra, a zebra.
    Toby: Bra, bra, bra — zebra zebra
40   *Sophie*: Zebra, that's right, it's not a big one though
    is it, Christina? You've got too many, Christina.
    Christina: You've got too many too.
    Sophie: Give me some
    Christina: No I don't want to, (*cries*) naughty girl.

The teacher withdraws and leaves the children to interact. Though there
is some competition for leadership among the children, so that not all
four participate equally in the interaction, their contributions are
startlingly different from those of the six-year-olds in the formal lesson.
Nearly all their utterances consist of full clauses, many of more than
one clause. *Christina: I want a whistle, let's see them all*; *Sophie: No it
isn't, is it, Christina? Have a look — a zebra, a zebra*; *Sophie: Zebra,
that's right, it's not a big one though, is it, Christina? You've got too
many, Christina*. In passing, it is instructive to consider the syntax
which these three-year-olds command. Interrogatives, declaratives,
imperatives are mastered, as are echo-questions, negatives, a variety of
tenses, modal forms, comparatives. It compares favourably with the
syntax of the early written texts of six- and seven-year-olds, and thus
demonstrates that the problems which children face in their early
writing efforts are not due to insufficiently developed grammar.

    Text 6 is a conversation between a four-year-old and a seven-year-old;
Ruth is four, and James is seven.

Text 6

Tooth-Fairies

    James: Is that one of my big teeth there, is it?
    Ruth: Can't see
    James, why don't you get them out
    James: Yes, it looks like two ten p's from here, cause they're
5   bigger, but its really a . . . two fives
    Ruth: Feel the water
    James: Let's have a look in your mouth to make sure, no, like that
    . . . no none, . . . put the bottom lip down . . . no it's not your
    teeth

10   *James*: What's this!!
      Ruth: What?
      James: This isn't English money! One of them isn't English
         money, mummy.
      Ruth: What?

Again clearly there is no question that this speech is (or that the children
are) egocentric. Both texts show the typical structure of speech, with
just one instance of an embedded clause: line 7 *let's have a look in your
mouth to make sure*.

All the texts considered so far have shown language arising in
interaction: addressees are directly present, texts are constructed
mutually, the audience is known to the speaker; consequently there can
be and is much implicitness. For instance in 'Lovely Things' the teacher's
yes picks out a particular child, nominating him or her to answer. The
meaning is left implicit from the point of view of the verbal message
alone, though it is explicit in the context as the teacher will be looking
at a particular child. In lines 17-18 there is an example of implicitness
at a verbal as well as at an immediate contextual level. In *Tell me some
of the lovely things we saw*, *the lovely things we saw* refers to an
experience shared by the whole group: perhaps the class had been on a
nature walk, or had looked at a poster or a book. That knowledge is not
recoverable from the immediate context, it lies further back. Implicitness
may, of course, go back further still; *our humanities* would be such an
example. Here the teacher refers to knowledge which was probably
established in the first few weeks of the children's formal schooling,
when the teacher discussed with them what the curriculum was, and
what its appropriate categories and labels were. Similarly in *when we
first started we found out*, *first started* refers to an experience which
has become common, shared knowledge, and can now be left implicit.
(Rather than 'you remember the second week of your first term at
school, on the Thursday morning . . .'.) Implicitness works equally in
all the other texts. To give one more example, in Text 6 there is
reference to *the water, them, there, out, here*, the specific referents of
which are all implicit if one regards the verbal text alone. The overall
meaning of the text is implicit, and it needs wider and wider contextual
settings to make it explicit: children losing teeth, leaving these in a glass
of water, for fairies to collect (this needs cultural contextualizing),
waking up in the morning to see the result, etc., etc.

Before leaving the discussion of speech, here is an example of speech which is not the result of interaction. The child here is the teller of a story. The activity has a number of interesting affinities with writing, in Western societies. Since these are literate societies, most 'official' stories are written, and children meet them in that form, as examples of written language read to them. This text was created by a single speaker, though within the constraints of fairly strict generic rules, and with the examples of specific stories to provide models. Telling a story (or writing it) is therefore an exercise in learning and mastering the rules of a particular genre, and once these are mastered, to implement them with a (limited) range of contents. The child story-teller is seven years old, and therefore already has some knowledge and experience of writing.

Text 7

Adventure under the Sea

The story of this is called Adventure under the Sea. Once
upon a time there was a boy who lived in in Australia.
He went to, one day he went to India to, and one day he was
in the sea. Um, he got lost, he swam and he swam. He lost
5   his way for three days, and he could swim a hundred miles a
hour. One day, on the second day, some sharks chased him, and
he looked desperately for somewhere to hide. He, he was in,
the English Channel now in this tunnel thing. So on, he
found a hole. He went down it, and at the bottom he found
10   it was oil. He took a deep breath, the sharks couldn't find
him there. He was safe. But, how would he get back to
Australia? He was not, nowhere near his home. He went along
this tunnel, along long long long this tunnel until he found another,
climbed right up and he found that he was at Dungeness. Sandy
15   Dungeness to the lighthouses. He saw a, some little railway
huts on the shingle. He went and looked in. No one there. He
went to the next one. No one there. He went to the next one.
There was some one there, and he went and knocked at the
door. He went to ask the person for some money so that he
20   could, enough so that he could go to Australia. The person
said 'I'll tell you where to go. Here is the money. You
go, you go over to the little railway over there and you
pay some money for that. You go along to Hythe and then
you get out. You go on a bus, and here is some money for that,

25   and then you go to, on a bus, into Ashford. Then, you get off
the bus and ask somebody to tell you where the stations is, they
will tell you. You get on the, you ask someone to, the
porter to ask you when which train is going to London and
when. He will tell you. When that train comes in, you get

30   on it. I'll give you some money for the train. You go along
London and then you go to London airport. And some one will
tell you where that is. And there is some money for you to go
to London airport, on to the aerodrome. Right off you go.' So
off he went under the plank little train, went right the way

35   to Hythe, he ran off and found the bus. Got on, paid his fares
and went upstairs, and went all the way to Ashford. Then, he
got off, and asked some one to show him where the station was.
They showed him. Got on the train and went all the way to
London, where some on showed him where London airport was.

40   They showed him, he paid the money to get on the aeroplane,
he went in the aeroplane and went off in the air, and landed
at Newcastle where he lived. Someone met him there and they
they brought him back to his mummy and daddy.

A number of points may be worth making as a conclusion to this section of the chapter. It is clear that this child, a seven-year-old boy, has a highly developed syntactic competence. On the level of sentence syntax there are very few rules, judging from this text, which he has still to learn. He uses several kinds of embedding constructions, different modes of subordinating clauses, logical constructions ... *so that* ..., he is highly competent in tense use: *(he) asked* someone *to show* him where the station *was*. Overall the text shows the chaining clausal structure of speech. The child is obviously able to construct long and quite elaborate texts; that is, he has sufficient imagination and concentration to sustain this effort. He is able to use cohesive devices in order to integrate the component elements of the text. He knows the generic structure of this kind of narrative tale well enough to keep to the major structure. It is necessary to make these points, for it is sometimes stated that the problems which children have in their first writing efforts are problems of syntax, imagination, concentration, genre, etc. Quite clearly that is not the case. Children are highly proficient in all aspects of the syntax of speech at this stage. That proficiency provides the linguistic foundation on which they build when they first learn to write.

ii   Children's writing: learning a new language

Having discussed the basic knowledge on which children draw when they learn to write, I now wish to show how the structure of speech and the different contexts of writing influence the early writing of children. Text 8 was written by a six-year-old girl.

Text 8

Going to the Shops

When I went to the
Shops I saw a train
and walk on I saw a
King and Queen. I said
5   how do you do they
said very well thank you
then I lost my money
I had to go home agen
I got some nwe money and
10   baute a lolly pop

The child's development of the concept of sentence is the subject of Chapter 4 and therefore I will not comment on it and related matters (punctuation, capitalization) here. The characteristic structure of the spoken language provides the syntax for this child's written story. All the clauses are either co-ordinated or simply adjoined. A noticeable point is the stark simplicity of this language, both syntactically and textually in comparison to 'Adventure under the Sea', for instance, or indeed any of the texts considered so far. This point is obvious but immensely important because children's language ability *as such* is frequently — perhaps more often than not — judged on their capabilities in writing. From the evidence presented so far it is clear that this grossly misrepresents what children are capable of linguistically and, as I hope to show in Chapter 6, conceptually.

Text 9

The Mouse

The mices enemy are cats

and owls. the mices eat
all kinds of thingk. Mices
are little animals. people
5　set traps to catch mouse.
mouses liv in holes in the
skirting board. Baby mouse
dons have their eis opne.
baby mouses can't see and
10　they do not have fer.
Some people are scered
of mouses.

Again, the most immediately noticeable feature of this story is its simplicity, more perhaps in a textual than in a syntactic sense. That is, the sentences consist of single clauses, with two exceptions, and these are simply adjoined, though marked off by full stops. There are no obvious devices to make the clauses cohere and thereby to give the text itself greater cohesion and unity. For instance, there is no pronominal substitution from sentence to sentence. Sentence 2 could have had as its subject the pronoun *they*, as could sentence 3. This would have linked the three sentences, and drawn them together more as constituents of the same text. This is not due to the child's ignorance of the process of pronominal substitution (which might be a too ready inference from the text): in the penultimate sentence the child has substituted *they* for *mouses* in the second, conjoined clause within the same sentence. Also, the same child uses pronominal substitution in speech, as in Text 6, line 4: *It looks like two ten p's from here cause they're bigger, but its really a ... two fives.* Indeed, this substitution extends over a long stretch of speech, so that *them* in line 12 *One of them isn't English money* refers back to *two ten p's*, eight lines back.

The textual simplicity may be due to a number of factors: for instance, the child's conception of what the set task is about (telling a series of 'facts'); related to this, his sense of the wishes and expectations of the addressee, in this case the teacher; perhaps also the sheer difficulty of the task of writing, which makes demands of a kind which preclude the child's attending to more than a certain number of features; and a simple lack of knowledge of the textual conventions of writing. The text is not a story in the conventional sense, so that the child cannot use the familiar genre of narrative. The topic is not developed in the more mature sense; that is, there is no clear indication of a particular ordering of a conceptual kind, neither sequence nor any other internal logic. (This is not to say that the child did not have some scheme, but simply that the scheme is not readily apparent, it is not a conventional and therefore readily recognizable one.)

Syntactically the text shows some variety of clausal structure: single, simple clauses, *Mices are little animals*; two adjoined clauses, *baby mouses can't see and they do not have fer*; and one embedded clause, *people set traps to catch mouse*. Several clause-types are used: noun-phrase (NP) + verb to be + NP complement, *the mices enemy are cats and owls*; transitive clauses, *the mices eat all kinds of thingk*; intransitive clauses here with two prepositional complements, *mouses liv in holes in the skirting board*.

The predominant structure is the adjoined, chained clausal structure, taken over from speech. In this respect it is quite like Text 8. The textual structure of Text 8 differs from that of Text 9 in a number of ways. It uses more conjunctions and a greater range of conjunctions, *when*, *then*, *and*, as well as simple adjunctions. This may be due predominantly to the different genre to which the story belongs: it is clearly the narrative of some imagined or real event. The inherent order of this story is that of sequence, with the linear sequence of clauses mirroring the temporal sequence of the real or imagined events. The text includes sentences in which the child imports the speech of others, *they said very well thank you*, and quotes her own speech: *I said how do you do*. Such quotations, of course, frequently happen in speech too, and children are competent at this. Syntactically the text contains both co-ordinated clauses, *I got some more money and baute a lolly pop*, and subordinated clauses, *I said how do you do*. The when-clause, *when I went to the shops*, may not at this stage be used by the child as a subordinate clause but rather as a normal main clause, which sets the stage for the story. The writer uses intransitive clauses, with a pre-positional complement, *I went to the shops*; transitive clauses, *I saw a train*; a complex verbal group with *had to*, *I had to go home agen*.

Two more texts will serve to demonstrate that these textual and syntactic structures are general and typical of children's writing at this stage, about six to seven years.

Text 10

Scruffy

On Saturday My Dog got run over and the driver did not
stop. The dog's name was scruffy and he died and then
we buried him.

Text 11
(partial text)

The Racehorse

One day the horse
got lost and the
oner was sad
and then the oner
found the horse
and the horse was glad
and then the horse
was ridn in a rase.

Both stories show instances of implicitness; for example, in Text 10,
the use of the definite article in *the driver* assumes that we as readers
know who the driver was. We can and do of course infer that it is the
driver who was involved in the running over of the dog. The implicitness
does not prevent us from deducing the meaning of the phrase; rather
the point is that the use of the definite article with the noun is normal in
situations where speaker and hearer both share some knowledge. The
child's usage therefore suggests that we as readers, or the teacher who
read the story, know that the child writer knows. We may speculate
about the type of reader which the child writer has in mind as the likely
reader of the story. Is the child in fact writing *for* anyone? In so far as
the story is addressed at all it seems to be addressed to someone with
the same knowledge as the child, perhaps a member of the family. What
is most likely is that the child does not envisage any particular reader,
but writes without any reader in mind, perhaps has a generalized conception of 'what the teacher wants' in mind, and perhaps just assumes
that everyone knows what she knows. Of course, that would be a sign
of an egocentric mode of thinking and writing. I have attempted to

show above that three-year-olds do not behave egocentrically in their spoken interactions. It may be that learning to write has the effect of putting the child back into that mode of thinking. That is both surprising and to be expected. Learning to write is generally regarded as a cognitively enhancing activity and process. Here it seems to work in the opposite direction. However, one has to bear in mind that the child is performing a difficult task, which demands much of her attention. Hence the very effort involved may have some retarding effect in some areas; that is, an activity which was previously undertaken unselfconsciously is now undertaken deliberately. To see young children writing is to see studies in single-minded concentration. It is possible that the child's powers of concentration are completely absorbed in the basic aspects of writing — forming the letters, keeping the lines straight and the letters even, spelling words correctly, getting the syntax right and the cohesion between clauses and sentences established. There is thus no room for thoughts of the needs of the potential reader. Perhaps writing is essentially an egocentric activity; certainly it is a lonely activity, in which the writer, no matter how hard he strives to picture the potential reader, is really his own and only immediately effective reader.

At this stage both topical and textual development are closely related to the development and structure of the sentence. That is, there is some textual structuring within the sentence, and not much outside it. At this stage the sentence has a function similar to that of the paragraph in adult writing. (This is described in more detail in Chapter 4.) In texts which are not the narratives of events the sequence of sentences is therefore akin to the sequence of paragraphs in adult texts, and such topical development or textual structuring as there is has to be sought, in the main, within sentences. For instance, in Text 9, the order of sentences themselves seems not to be motivated by 'topic development'; the operative principle seems rather to be 'enumeration'. Consequently the sentences could be rearranged in a different order without destroying the 'text'. For instance, the order might be:

(3) Mices are little animals. (1) The mices enemy
are cats and owls. (4) People set traps to catch mouse.
(2) The mices eat all kinds of thingk, etc.

The grammatical devices which accompany and code topic development are also absent: two reasons why it is perfectly possible to rearrange the sentences are (i) that the sentences themselves show none of the structures which operate in adult language to fit them into a specific place in a text, and (ii), related to this, there is no cohesion between the sentences. It might be thought that this is due to the fact that the text is not a narrative but that is not the case. To exemplify this point here is a non-narrative written text by a twelve-year-old boy:

Text 12

Beaked Whales

(1) The Beaked Whales live out in mid-ocean, where the tasty squid are found. (2) Squid, it seems, provide most of their meals. (3) Men do not know much about their family because even the scientists who study whales have seen very few Beaked Whales. (4) Generally members of this family have long, narrow snouts, or 'beaks'.

(This is about a quarter of the total text, which is reproduced in full below, p. 92.) The sentences in this text cannot be taken out of their existing order. For instance, reordering 2 and 4:

(1) The Beaked Whales live out in mid-ocean, where the tasty squid are found. (4) Generally members of this family have long, narrow snouts or 'beaks'. (2) Squid, it seems, provide most of their meals. (3) Men do not know much about this family because even the scientists who study whales have seen very few Beaked Whales.

This is, perhaps, just about a possible text, though there is a jarring sense about it, especially the transition from 4 to 2. The two factors which I have mentioned are responsible: the sentences are structured to fit them for the specific place they have in the text, and the cohesive devices are strong, so that their disruption is registered by the reader as a sense of a broken flow. To exemplify the first point: in sentence 2 the child has put the noun *squid* in first and therefore thematic position in the sentence. There it immediately signals that an element which was introduced as information about the theme of the first sentence is now the theme of the second sentence, and will be further developed. Even a minor change, to 'It seems that squid . . .', would be textually less satisfactory: '(1) The Beaked Whales live out in mid-ocean, where the tasty squid are found. (2) It seems that squid provide most of their meals.' The structure of sentence 2 here implies that *squid* had been the theme of sentence 1. A major change such as 'Most of their meals are, it seems, provided by squid' would cause a complete interruption of the textual structure, because it definitely suggests that the theme of sentence 1 had been 'meals of the Beaked Whales'. Such textual structuring is absent from Text 9. Also, the opening sentence in Text 12 is unmistakably the opening sentence. The same is by no means true of the first sentence of Text 9. Clearly, then, in Text 12 the sentences have a specific structure due to their place in the text.

As far as cohesive devices are concerned, several examples will make the point. In sentence 2 the noun *squid* is repeated, which establishes the link with the same topic/noun in the previous sentence. However, by repeating *squid* the child writer can use a pronoun for the repeated topic/noun *whale*, namely *their*. If the child had used a pronominal substitute for *squid*, he would have needed to repeat the noun *whale*. The result would have been:

> (1) The Beaked Whales live out in mid-ocean, where the tasty squid are found. (2) They, it seems, provide most of the whale's meals.

This is clearly less satisfactory, and awkward. Using two pronouns in sentence 2 would have led to an awkwardness of a different kind:

> (1) The Beaked Whales live out in mid-ocean, where the tasty squid are found. (2) They, it seems, provide most of their meals.

In the first four sentences of this text the child has chosen to pronominalize the dominant topic-noun of the text, and this provides a cohesive device in that all pronouns refer to the dominant topic. By this means the child also established what the dominant topic is, namely it is that to which the pronouns refer. The dominance of the topic relates also to implicitness: what is fully known does not need to be fully named each time, but can be referred to by the pronoun. Clearly it is an aid to a potential reader. Other topic-nouns are either repeated directly, or else repeated by the use of a substitute noun: 3 *Men do not know much about their family because even <u>the scientists</u> who study whales have seen very few Beaked Whales.* Cohesion is also provided by the set of nouns which represent directly or in an extended manner the major topic: *Beaked Whales, their meals, their family, whales, Beaked Whales.*

It would be possible to use the two factors of textual structuring of sentences, and of cohesion, as a measure of the extent to which a child has become aware of and competent in the handling of the textual structure of language. As I have mentioned, textual structure is the device whereby the conceptual and cognitive process of topic structure and development is expressed in linguistic form. Conversely, therefore, the type of textual and topical structuring can provide insight into the child's conceptual and cognitive processes and ability. This point is developed in some detail in Chapter 6.

Topic development and the textual structures appropriate to it are more or less absent in the very early stages in the learning of writing. Some exceptions are provided by narrative writing, where the sequence of the events suggests its own sequential, linear structure to the child. This is the case with Texts 8, 10 and 11. In each of these the order of clauses or sentences is given by the order of events in the real or imagined world. There are some cohesive features, too. In Text 8, sentence 2 does not mention who the child addressed: *I said (to them) how do you do*; this 'understood' pronoun substitutes for *King and Queen* in sentence 1, and thereby establishes cohesion between the two sentences. Within sentence 2 *they* also refers to *King and Queen* in the first sentence. There is cohesion within the same sentence between *my money* and *nwe money*. Similar points can be made about Texts 10 and 11.

Narrative writing may thus have a specially important place in the learning of writing, in that it permits the child to develop textual structures and devices in writing by drawing on the child's already established abilities in spoken language. Text 7 shows that this is the case: the factors to which I have drawn attention are well in evidence and established in that text. To emphasize the differences between the structures of narrative and non-narrative texts here is another example of a non-narrative text. The writer is an eight-year-old girl.

Text 13

Birds

(1) I have not got a bird but I know some things about them.

(2) The have tow nostrils and They clean Ther feather and They
eat seeds, worms, bread, cuddle fish, and lots of other things.
(3) and they drink water. (4) When he drinks he Puts
his head up and it gose down. (5) A budgie cage gets very dirty
and peopel clean it.

Unlike the (seven-year-old) writer of Text 9, this writer does produce
what is clearly an opening sentence; indeed, all but one of the five
sentences of this text need to be in the order in which they occur, the
exception being sentence 5, which could possibly occur as the second
sentence; though *budgie* may be related cohesively to the prior *cuddle
fish*. However, within sentence 2 the order of clauses could be changed
without serious effect. Sentence 3 was initially part of sentence 2, and
it could have been interchanged both with sentence 2 and with clauses
in it. There is still no necessary order about the arrangement of these
facts. However, the arrangement on which the writer has settled is more
firmly fixed into this particular order by means of textual and cohesive
devices than is that of the seven-year-old writer of Text 9. There is
some development from this point of view between the two texts.

The syntactic and textual structures of speech are clearly present in
the early written texts of children between the ages of six and eight.
Without doubt, learning to write involves much more than learning the
mechanics of writing. A view such as the following is not just misguided
but incorrect: 'Before a child can write independently he must learn to
write the symbols which, when arranged and spaced correctly, create
the written equivalent of his spoken language. To put it more conven-
tionally, he must learn handwriting, spelling, punctuation and capitalization' (D. R. Ferris, 'Teaching children to write', pp. 175-6 of Lamb
(ed.), *Guiding Children's Language Learning*). The assumption that by
learning 'to write the symbols arranged and spaced correctly' the child
is learning to write, or that creating 'the written equivalent of his
spoken language' is what is involved in the learning of writing is a
grotesque misconception. Of course the child 'must learn handwriting,
spelling, punctuation and capitalization'. But beyond these, the child
must learn the syntax of written language, the textual structure of
writing, the conventional forms – the genres – of writing, and with
these the new cognitive modes of organizing the world. In doing this,
children draw on the structures which they know, the structures of the
spoken language. Learning to write involves the learning of new forms
of syntactic and textual structure, new genres, new ways of relating to

unknown addressees. In the last section of this chapter I wish to trace some aspects of this development.

iii   The ascendancy of the written language

Much of the success in achieving full command of the written language rests on the child's mastery of the concept of sentence on the one hand and of the genres in which written language occurs on the other. These will be the subject of more detailed treatment in Chapters 4 and 5 respectively. Here I wish to trace briefly the development of the syntax of writing up to the age of twelve, at which age it tends to be established in all essential characteristics. At the same time I wish to chart and document the effect which the written language is beginning to have on the spoken language in children up to the same age.

Text 14

Our Trip to Ayers House

(1) On Friday 1st July we all got in the bus and waved to Miss Martyn. (2) We're off I thought, there was lots of merry talk in the bus. (3) Tracey was telling some people that the bus would pass her house 'there it is' said Tracey but it soon went by. (4) We soon were there. (5) When we had got out of the bus Mrs. Gilbert said to sketch the front of Ayers House. (6) When I had finished my sketch I looked at some of the other sketches. (7) I thought Prue's was the best.

This text represents about half of the story written by the child, an eight-year-old girl. The contrast with Text 13 is noticeable. Among other things it consists in the greater variety of syntactic forms. There is still some evidence here of the chaining syntax of speech, but there is also quite a considerable degree of subordination and embedding. For instance, in 2 *We're off I thought*, *We're off* is embedded within the main clause *I thought*; the order of the two is inverted for thematic reasons. That is, in terms of topic development the sequence 'into the bus', 'waving good-bye' and 'leaving' is one unbroken whole; whereas if the order had not been inverted, if the child had written *I thought we're off*, then the sequence would have been broken: 'into the bus', 'waving good-bye' 'I thought', 'leaving'. Similarly in sentence 3 *'there it is' said Tracey*. The point is not so much that this ordering is unspeech-like, which it is not, but rather that the child has now begun to gain a sufficient confidence of expression in the new medium to be able to attempt, and achieve, stylistic effects.

The next story, Text 15, also shows a child writer beginning to experience some freedom in expression; the mere mastery of the mechanics of writing is not a real problem at this stage, and further-more, the child has begun to master some of the conventions of syntax and text of the written language.

Text 15

The Pioneer Boy

(1) The boy I am writing about is called Sam he lived in the gold fields of Biggs Flat. (2) Well things weren't going to well for the Lam family they were very poor. (3) The night before Sam heard them talking of leaving and Sam didn't like that and went to bed crying. (4) He had lots of friends in the gold fields his father had a mine shaft but got no gold. (5) The next day it was Sam's turn to go down the mine shaft. (6) He was told to dig to same place he didn't. (7) Sam soon found his father was sick he had to go down the mine shaft. (8) So Sam did he dug in his place he soon saw a glitter. (9) He saw it was fools gold but that ment gold near. (10) The next day Sam went down he dug he found a pile of gold dust and put it in a bucket he pulled himself up and found he did not only have gold dust but a lump of gold from that day on the Lams were neaver poor again. (11) The piece of gold was called the Sitting Lady.

The writer, a nine-year-old girl, feels confident enough to attempt to copy the mode of spoken narrative in her story. (The contrast with Text 23, discussed in Chapter 5, and written as part of the same school-project, shows that this is indeed an experiment in style, rather than being the only mode of writing available to this child.) The text still shows the influence of speech in the many conjoined and adjoined clauses. The latter are particularly prominent: 1 ... *is called Sam/he lived in the* ...; 2 ... *for the Lam family/they were very poor*; 4 ... *in the gold fields/his father had* ...; 8 *So Sam did/he dug in his place/*

he soon saw ... This may well be a result of the child's attempt to achieve the style of spoken narrative, where intonation would provide the structural linking. The text also has many examples of subordinated and embedded clauses: 1 *The boy I am writing about* (relative clause); 3 *The night before Sam heard them talking* (clausal complement); 5 *The next day it was Sam's turn to go down the mine* (embedded clause); 6 *He was told to dig* (embedded clause); etc. The quantitative prevalence and range of types of subordination distinguishes this text from 'Birds', for instance, marking a qualitative distinction between the two texts. From a textual point of view 'The Pioneer Boy' also marks a noticeable advance. The sentences are structurally appropriate to their specific place in the text, and cohesively it is closely linked.

I mentioned in Chapter 2 that speech is affected by the syntax of writing. One might therefore expect that at a stage when children are on the verge of becoming competent writers their speech would begin to show traces of the syntax of writing. Text 16 is a narrative told by the writer of Text 15, about eight weeks after she had written that story.

Text 16

The Wolfling

Father: Okay, now tell me about the most recent book you
have been reading.
Child: The most recent book I have been reading is called
The Wolfling and in it is all about a little boy who
5   finds out there is a wolf, a she-wolf, and she mated
with one of the dogs in their little village that they
live in and who's called, and they call her Old
Three Toes.
Father: They what, sorry
10   *Child*: Old Three Toes
Father: They call what
Child: The wolf Old Three Toes cause she's only got three toes
Father: Oh it's a she, right, carry on
Child: And um they find the wolf's den and because the, they
15   can't they start digging down into it but they strike
limestone and they can't dig any further and there is
this one, there is one of the hunters there, his father
when he was a boy had gone down into the wolf's den
with a rope tied to his leg, ankle, so he could be

20   easily pulled up if he needed to be. So Robby the boy
found out about the wolf. He went down the den, he
started climbing down there and they had seen the wolf
so they knew she was in there and he started going
down there and the rope didn't stretch far enough so
25   he told them that he was untying it.
Father: He what, sorry
Child: The boy told them that he was untying the rope so he
could go down
Father: Mm
30   *Child*: And he only went down so he could get the pick of the
litter so, some pups there, because he wanted one
Father: Mm
Child: And they had all agreed to that
Father: Who are they?
35   *Child*: The hunters and his father. And he went down and he
saw the she-wolf in there but she didn't harm him,
she just took one of the, she took the only, she took
the, what do you call it? Well, they were twins so she
took one of them and Robby took the other and he brought
40   it back and showed it to them.
Father: Mm
Child: And one of the hunters said, Aren't you going to club
him?, and the boy said, No, I'm going to have him round
for a pet and his father said, Oh no, because he had
45   forgotten that that was the bet they'd made. Then his
father said um, if you, if he kills one farm animal
that he's not meant to, or isn't allowed to if it's a pet
he has to be shot, and Robby kept on saying No, he's not
going to, no he's not going to. And the little wolf
50   would sleep in the barn and for company Robby's mother
would take let her in the house and he would follow
everywhere and it was around that time I think it was
at the back of the house and they hired this man called
Dan who had lost his, who had fought in the civil war
55   and he had lost his wife and child in the Chicago
fire, and they hired him for the, for helping them
with the harvest and he stayed with them for a long
time and he helped Robby get days off so he could
go on his daily round for his traps cause Robby had

60   to buy his day for 50 cents. He wanted a free day
        from ploughing. And, er . . .

Syntactically this text is surprisingly like that of the lecture, Text 1, in Chapter 2. Co-ordination, and subordination and embedding both occur. The first seven lines of the narrative contain four relative clauses: *(which) I have been reading*; *who finds out there is a wolf*; *that they live in*; *who's called*. The story contains some embeddings similar to those of Text 14: lines 42–6 *And one of the hunters said, Aren't you going to club him?, and the boy said, No, I'm going to have him round for a pet* . . . *his father said* . . . *if you, if he kills one farm animal*; etc. These forms are typical of speech. They are significant syntactically and cognitively. Syntactically they provide a model for the embedding of clauses; cognitively they provide a model for including concepts within concepts and a model for the hierarchical organization of ideas.

The text contains a number of passives (e.g. lines 7, 20, 47, 48) as does Text 15. These are additional evidence of the influence of more formal language. There is an instance where the syntax of writing intrudes markedly and, at this stage, unsuccessfully, into the syntax of speech. In lines 56 the child says *and they hired him for the* and no doubt wished to complete this clause with a noun. However, the idea which she needs to express is too complex for a simple noun; she has to start again and this time constructs the concept which she needs in the manner typical of speech, by using a fuller clausal form. At a later stage she might have used a nominalizing form such as *the harvesting of* . . . There are a number of places where the child stops in order to recast and rephrase what she intends to say. In each case the rephrasing is in the direction of the syntax of speech. For instance, lines 7–8 . . . *and who's called, and they call her Old Three Toes*, where the embedded relative clause is rephrased as a co-ordinated full main clause; and lines 53–5 . . . *this man called Dan who had lost his, who had fought in the civil war and he had lost his wife and child* . . . where the child rephrases in exactly the same way. It may be that where problems of some kind arise the child uses the syntax which is more familiar, the syntax of speech. The cognitive implications are significant, as the chaining and embedding syntax represent quite distinct cognitive modes. One is the mode of sequence, the other that of hierarchy. It seems that the former is still the preferred form for this child.

Text 17, 'The Cockpit', written by a boy of twelve, shows full mastery of writing and its syntax:

Text 17

The Cockpit

(1) The crew of a modern jet airliner must have all the information they need at their finger tips, so a great amount of work goes into designing the best possible flight deck control panels. (2) The captain and the first officer each must have controls for flying the plane, and there is an automatic pilot for routine flying.

(3) Basic flight instruments are on the panel in front of each pilot. (4) On the panel between them are the engine throttles and gauges, radio and navigation equipment and things like the parking brake.

(5) The flight engineer has his own instrument panel behind the pilots.

It is not particularly complex syntax; it is remarkable rather for its distance from speech. There is, moreover, no evidence of striving for a style; the mastery of the syntax and textual structure here seems effortless. The effective distance from speech can be felt by saying aloud sentences such as *Basic flight instruments are on the panel in front of each pilot*. This does not have the rhythm of speech; it is language for seeing, not for speaking. Textually it shows the full development of the sentence in its adult form, and topic development is now handled through the adult paragraph.

The spoken language of this child shows marked influences of the syntax of writing:

Text 18

The Empire Strikes Back

Father: Now just tell me about the most recent book you have read.

Child: Well it's called, The Empire Strikes Back, and
its the book that carries on after Star Wars, and
5   what happens in it is the rebels find a planet,
Hoth, and they build a base on it and they're
just getting, just about ready to defend it, just

about finished when an Imperial Droid finds them.
Father: What's a Droid?

10 *Child*: It's a sort of robot, and it sends a message back
        to ah, the Imperial Leaders and they are going to
        attack the base and when, when this is happening, the
        all the supplies and everything they have to get them
        off the planet in freighters while defending it and

15   they get them all off and there's one that can't
        get back to, or can't get back into the other spaceships,
        and its the spaceship that the Empire particularly
        wants called The Millennium Falcon.
Father: Millennium or melenium? What's it called?

20 *Child*: Millennium Falcon.
Father: Millennium. Is it a kind of metal or something?
Child: Just the name of it.
Father: Mm
Child: And they are chasing that and it's got important

25   people on board, someone called Princess Leia
Father: Oh, she was on there
Child: Yes, and they also want it because of its speed. It
        can go, it's the fastest ship in the universe and the
        story is just about um, them escaping and also a

30   person called Luke Skywalker he gets trained by the
        Jedi Master, by a teacher called Yoda and he leaves
        and he goes and meets up with Darth Vader and they
        have a fight and Darth Vader wins but he doesn't
        get killed in the fight he survives.

35 *Father*: Luke?
Child: Yes, he survives and then they go off and meet the
        other spaceships and that's the end of the story.
        And then there's another book that comes after that
        that I haven't read yet.

40 *Father*: Mm

The first three lines of narrative show structures which are characteristic of the syntax of writing; if the contractions *it's* are expanded this becomes more obvious:

> *It is called The Empire Strikes Back, and it is the*
> *book that carries on after Star Wars, and what happens*
> *in it is the rebels find a planet . . .*

It is the book that . . . and *what happens in it is* . . . are forms imported from writing. They are cleft and pseudo-cleft sentences respectively. These stand in a determinate relation to non-cleft constructions: *it is the book that carries on* . . . is related to *the book carries on* . . . In the cleft form the subject and predicate of the uncleft form are 'clefted' *the book* // *carries on* . . . and have each become the kernels of separate clauses: *it is* the book where the verb *to be* is introduced and *that carries on.* In the case of the pseudo-cleft form, the uncleft form is *That the rebels find a planet happens in the book.* To rearrange this sentence no existing clause is altered, hence the rearranged form is not in fact clefted. *(X) happens in the book* becomes *what happens in it*; *the rebels find a planet* stays as it is; and the two separate clauses are linked by the newly introduced verb *to be.* This somewhat complex process is used in writing to achieve the writer's desired placement of emphasis, which in speech is achieved by intonation. So a spoken version of *the book carries on after Star Wars* might be presented as two information units, // the book // carries on after Star Wars //, where *book* and *Star Wars* are intonationally focal and therefore marked as unknown information. To be sure that his desired placement of emphasis is recorded by the reader, the writer needs to use the cleft and pseudo-cleft constructions. These constructions are motivated by the specific contexts of writing, and hence they belong to the syntax of writing. Here they are placed within the structures of speech, both the chaining clausal structure, and the overall intonational framework. The basic features of spoken language provide the overall framework, but within this framework the syntax of writing is beginning to assert itself strongly. The text concludes with a clausal structure which contains two relative clauses: *and then there's another book that comes after that that I haven't read yet* A more typical spoken form would have been *and then there's another book it comes after that and/but I haven't read it yet.* It seems that the child is now quite confident with the embedding syntax, and with the cognitive model which that implies.

The final text, 'Kingies', shows a child aiming for and achieving stylistic effects within the syntax of writing. The child is now master of this syntax, of the textual demands of writing, and near-master of a specific written genre. The text is discussed in detail in Chapter 5.

Text 19

Kingies!
of the rocks

(1) John cast out his killer lure, Brian and Clive followed.
(2) John's President reel, Brian's Daiwo reel and Clive's Abu
reel, hummed as their gears meshed and ratchets clicked,
their lures swimming across the white foamy water.

(3) They swam powerfully towards the small bait-fish, gradually
comming closer to the rock wall; the Kingfish were hungry.
(4) Casting out and cranking their reels, and men's arms grew
tired. (5) The fish rose. (6) They took off with the lures,
jumping, weaving, ducking, diving all in vein to get rid of the
lure they had taken so much trouble to catch. (7) They stopped at
about 200yds from the rock-wall. (8) The men engaged the reels,
gaining line and tiring the fish, the fish being dragged and then in
a desperate bid to free the hook, shaking their heads and making
pitiful runs. (9) They were exhausted and could fight no more.

(10) All ƀf the fish felt the gaff where it had stabbed them
and the sugar bag that was coiled around them hurt even
more. ~~but~~ (11) Relief was few and far between when the bag
was opened up and another fish piled on top.

(12) Brian claimed the world record and Clive and John
world records in line to fish ratio weights. (13) A
good ~~sun~~ Sunday's fishing.

Chapter 4
The development of the concept of 'sentence' in children's writing

i   The significance of early sentences

In the previous two chapters I attempted to establish that the sentence
is not a unit of the spoken language although it does intrude into speech
from the syntax of writing at a later stage in the language development
of children. As a consequence, the early writing of children is characterized by the absence of the sentence. Perhaps the major part of learning
to write consists in the mastery of the linguistic unit of sentence,
with all the manifold ramifications entailed in that. When children
first learn to write they have to establish for themselves, gradually,
what a sentence is about. This is an unrecognized factor in discussion of
children's writing, and that teachers, and others, are not aware of this
factor means that they have no way of understanding what is perhaps
the most fundamental aspect of the early writing of children. Hence
many of the corrections of and interventions in children's writing by
the teacher are misconceived and ill-motivated. Placing full-stops,
replacing small letters with capitals, crossing out conjunctions are all
to some measure beside the point. My discussion, in the previous
chapter, of a quotation from *Guiding Children's Language Learning*
(see p. 60) shows that teachers are not to blame for that. They are
acting on what is received opinion within the 'Language Arts', as
taught in teacher training institutions. I hope that this chapter will
provide a better understanding of the long process of experimentation
which leads a child, eventually, to an understanding and mastery of the
adult concept of sentence.

There are two major factors that I will focus on: the development of
the internal structure of the sentence on the one hand, and the development of the structure of the sentence which is due to its function as a

constituent unit of a text on the other. These two are related. The sentence has to meet two kinds of demands: those of its internal integration, coherence, and consistency, and those which arise as the consequence of its specific place in a larger text, expressing cohesion with other elements of the text and integration into that text. Both aspects have to be expressed by the structure of the individual sentence. However, the motivation for each is distinctly different.

The first text discussed here is not one of the very earliest types. It was written by a seven-year-old boy; in fact it was typed by the child. A sheet of paper had been left in a typewriter, the child happened to come along, and he typed out the story in one go. All the child's typographical conventions and spelling-typing errors have been reproduced here, though the corrections which the child made are not indicated. The line-numbering was added by myself.

Text 20

The Two Poor People

1   Once upon a time there lived two poor people.
2   They longed to be rich.
3   One day when they were in the woods looking for fire wood.
4   when they met a prince riding through the woods.
5   The prince stopped and looked at them and said Are you poor.
6   At firt they were to scared to answer.
7   But in the end they answer yes we are poor.
8   The prince said would you like to come to the palace.
9   Oh yes well come on he said.
10   So of they went.
11   They arrived at the palace they were greted.
12   That night they had a feast they were shown to their beds.
13   They had had a wonder time that day.
14   As the dasys went by they by they bgan to like it more and more.
15   So the more they bgan to mis their frineds.
16   Just befor they went to bed king said your frneds are coming tomorrow.
17   They were so excited that they could hardly get to sleep that night.
18   In the morning they said to the king when are they coming.
19   They will be coming at lunchtime he said

20   At lunchtime when their frined came they were verey surprised to see them there.
21   One day when they were walking in the woods they met an old woman.
22   That old woman happened to be a witch.
23   She was begging to be helpt home.
24   So they helped her home.
25   When they got her home the witch gave the king and queen a red apple.
26   The king and queen took the apples and went back home and eat the appler.
27   Nects day the prince found the king and queen dead.
28   The prince knozu a wizard.
29   That day the prince went to tel the wizard.
30   The wizard came and made the king and queen aliv agen and ciled the witch and they live happyly evry erfeder.
    The End.

The manner in which this text was produced falls into the category of lucky accident. Although children at times give some prominence to the 'line' in their early writing, it tends not to be as consistent and thoroughgoing as it is here. Hence the possibility that a difference might exist for the child between line and sentence does not normally emerge clearly enough. Putting it differently, it is quite possible that 'sentence' has no real meaning for the child, and that 'line' may have as great a significance or greater for the child as sentence. The child may be searching for a unit which can express some unified coherent concept which the child needs to express. Hence although there are a number of aspects which deserve linguistic comment, here I will focus on discovering and describing what the child seems to be wishing to express in this unit of line/sentence. The layout of the story seems to indicate that the *line* has real significance for the child. Only one 'sentence' extends beyond a single line in the child's typed text, namely line/sentence 30. This is all the more noteworthy as producing a new line on a typewriter needs a special effort, particularly so for a child, unfamiliar with a typewriter. Each line begins with a capital letter (except line 4) and ends with a full stop, so that the concept of sentence is co-present with that of the line. The variety of syntactic units which the child puts in the line and between capital letters and full stops is striking. At times in the discussion of the early writing efforts of children it tends to be assumed that some of the problems stem from the fact that the child does not have command of a sufficiently complex syntax. However, in this text, complexity of syntax is clearly not the problem. A look at the first six or seven lines reveals an astonishing complexity and richness of syntactic forms. The first line/sentence consists of an adverbial phrase and a clause; the second consists of a matrix and an embedded clause; the third line/sentence consists of an adverbial phrase plus an adverbial phrase which itself consists of a matrix clause plus an embedded clause; line 4 is (in terms of adult grammar) an adverbial phrase which consists of a clause with an embedded clause; line 5 consists of three co-ordinated clauses, with the last conjoined clause containing an embedded clause of direct speech. There are different types of embedding: *They longed to be rich*; *they were in the woods looking for fire wood*; conjunctions with repeated material deleted: *The prince stopped and (he) looked at them and (he) said*; a comparative construction: *they were to scared to answer*; etc.

This is by no means simple syntax; syntax is not the problem. What characterizes this text is that the child is experimenting with the notion of the line/sentence. These line/sentences contain segments of the clausal chains of speech; though, as just pointed out, there are some embedded constructions. Generally speaking, the line/sentence functions to mark off segments of clausal chains. The unifying factor underlying the segmentation which the writer imposes on the narrative seems to depend on and derive from a notion of topical connectedness. The variability in the length of the lines/sentences might lead one to think that the child has made the segmentations arbitrarily. They vary from line 10 *So of they went*, consisting of one clause, to line 26 *The king and queen took the apples and went back home and eat the appler*, consisting of three clauses. However, on closer analysis it seems quite clear that the line/sentences are well motivated on topical grounds. The experiment therefore is not a syntactic but a textual experiment. Textually, there is a wide variety. In line 5 *The prince stopped and looked at them and said Are you poor* there is a chain of three clauses, *The prince stopped and (he) looked at them and (he) said Are you poor* (where the last clause contains within it a clause of direct speech). A number of events are reported in that line, and these are connected topically. The topic would be something like 'The opening encounter with the prince'. In fact all the lines report little episodes within the larger series of events; for instance the seventh line *But in the end they answer yes we are poor*, or line 8 *The prince said would you like to come to the palace.* This applies to all thirty lines. Line 9 makes this point in a particularly interesting way: *Oh yes well come on he said.* It consists of the poor people's response to the previous question by the prince and the prince's consequent response embedded in the main clause *he said.* In this instance the episode is a 'discourse episode', something like 'affirmative response' followed by its consequent reaction response. In lines 11 and 12 *They arrived at the palace they were greted* and *That night they had a feast they were shown to their beds,* the two clauses which are adjoined in each case again clearly demonstrate the nature of the unifying feature. Each describes a specific and precise episode, especially within this genre: arrival at the palace, and the first evening at the palace. The 'motivation' for the line/sentence can be seen to derive from the structure of the story or narrative, rather than from syntax. The episodic nature of the line/sentence means that these early sentences are quite unlike adult sentences. In fact they have more affinity with adult paragraphs. They are in themselves nearly like mini-texts, mini-narratives, with coherence handled within the line. To that extent the line may be a more appropriate unit for the child at this stage: it suggests itself as a unit within which topically connected elements can be handled; visually it suggests the kind of integration, self-containment and completeness which the child wants. The sentence is merely a superimposition, without any clear motivation of its own.

To summarize, the following seems to emerge. The line seems to be more significant, better motivated than the sentence. In this text line and sentence are co-extensive, so that to some extent the child's notion of what a sentence is has also to be taken into consideration. The unifying feature or characteristic for line/sentence arises from narrative and textual considerations rather than from syntactic ones.

However, while the motivation for the line/sentence seems not to be syntactic — lines such as 4, 9, 11, 12 and 15 would be distinctly odd syntactically or even ungrammatical if syntax was the major criterion — the textual characteristic of the line or sentence does have clear syntactic effects. That is, the very co-presence of clausal units within the same larger unit demands some kind of syntactic accommodation. Hence the textual basis of the line here and of the sentence in most other stories written by children of this age has syntactic effects for the sentence. That is, there is some pressure for the co-present clausal units to be syntactically as well as textually integrated. There is some evidence for that within this text. In line 5 *The prince stopped and looked at them and said Are you poor* the identical subject nouns of the second and third clauses are deleted. This leads to some integration of these clauses. In line 17 *They were so excited that they could hardly* . . ., the *so* . . . *that* construction is evidence of linguistic and conceptual integration. Of course, these forms also occur in speech, though perhaps less typically so. The notion of coherence within the line imposes constraints on what the sentence can be, and hence affects what kind of sentence-syntax will emerge. The sentence's internal syntax is therefore motivated and determined to a large extent by textual and narrative constraints and considerations. The movement is interesting: segments of clausal chains are 'taken into' the sentence (or perhaps better, a sentence is superimposed on them). Once within the sentence there is a need to integrate the components more closely, and this leads to greater unification and integration within the sentence by means of more complex syntactic structures. The result is a new entity which has little affinity with its narrative spoken origins.

Interestingly, it is easy to give each line, each mini-text, a heading which is not simply a paraphrase. This is so in all the texts considered here. That is not a feature of sentences in adult language: it is always possible to paraphrase adult sentences, but not always possible to construct plausible headings. The difference between the child's notion of the sentence at this age, and that of the adult, might be expressed in this way. The child decides what goes together textually, and the sentence has to fit around it. The literate adult knows what a sentence ought to be, and in writing this concept of sentence determines what goes into a sentence, and ideas have to be fitted to suit the form.

This text strongly suggests, then, that, to the extent that they have become aware of them, sentences in early writing are primarily textual units, and that the child's attempt to work towards a definition of the sentence is a textual rather than a syntactic process. It is a matter of handling discourse, text rather than isolated syntactic units. The evidence of the syntax of speech is clearly present in all the line/sentences of 'The Two Poor People'. That presence is generally much more pronounced in most early writing.

Text 8

Going to the Shops

1   When I went to the
2   Shops I saw a train

3   and walk on I saw a
4   King and Queen. I said
5   how do you do they
6   said very well thank you
7   then I lost my money
8   I had to go home agen
9   I got some nwe money and
10   baute a lolly pop

This was written by a six-year-old girl. I have shown the lines of the written text, though they seem not to be significant here (the child had written right to the edge of the sheet at both margins). The chaining syntax of speech is very much in evidence here. The first 'sentence' consists of four clauses. These are either co-ordinated by *and* or simply adjoined. It is likely that *walk* was identical for the child, phonetically, with *walked* (the final consonant *t* can become assimilated with the preceding *k* in casual pronunciation so that it is not sounded and therefore may not have been heard by the child). The first clause, *when I went to the shops*, would, in adult language, be a subordinated clause. In fact it is very common for children to anchor their stories by the use of such temporal indicators. A number of factors may account for this. Children may be asked to write without a specific addressee and without a specific context for their writing. By giving the stories a spatial or a temporal setting children may be able to make up for that lack to some extent, by creating some time and some concrete context. Temporal indicators within a story may provide internal cohesion for the text. In 'The Two Poor People' lines 1, 2, 3, 4, 6, 7, 14, 16, 18, 20 and 21 all start with temporal settings. Many of the texts in this book show this feature. In Text 8 the first clause seems to function more as another independent main clause, signalling the temporal starting point. That is, it could be replaced by 'I went to the shops and I saw . . .' where it is formally treated as another main clause. The second sentence has a similar structure, of co-ordinated and adjoined clauses. The syntactic embedding of the reported speech presents a question: are these, for the child, truly embedded clauses, or does the child know and use them in a formulaic way? Unlike other clauses, *I said* and *they said* cannot appear without a clause (or pro-clause) complement in adult language. However, the child's understanding of the syntax of the verb *say* may be different from that of the adult.

The two sentences do not seem particularly well motivated either from a syntactic or from a topical point of view. While sentence 1 might have 'Things I saw on my visit to the shops' as its heading, sentence 2 is topically too diverse for a single heading. From a textual point of view, sentence 2 could not be interchanged with sentence 1: the sequential structure of the narrative prevents this for one thing; for another, sentence 2 depends, cohesively, on sentence 1, with the link of *they* to *King and Queen*. Within each sentence there is some integration, as both have one instance of the deletion of a repeated subject-noun. Sentence 1 . . . *I saw a train and (I) walk on* . . . ; sentence 2 . . . *I got some nwe money and (I) baute a lolly pop* . . .

Text 9

The Mouse

(1) the mices enemy are cats and owls. (2) the mices eat all kinds of thingk. (3) Mices are little animals. (4) people set traps to catch mouse. (5) mouses liv in holes in the skirting board. (6) Baby mouse dons have their eis opne. (7) baby mouses can't see and they do not have fer. (8) some people are scered of mouses.

Lines are not significant in this text; the child simply wrote to the edge of the sheet. Unlike the previous text, this is not a narrative. Consequently the ordering which, in the narrative, is provided by the sequence of events in the world of the narrative, both for the sequence of sentences in the text, and for the topical connectedness of the clauses within a sentence, is absent here. This poses a dual problem for the child. On the one hand, what is to be the sequence of sentences in the story? On the other, how is the cohesion of clauses within the sentence to be established; what is to be the unifying factor within one sentence? In the event the child fails to solve either problem fully, though the failure leads him a good way in the direction of adult writing. The first problem remains unsolved. If sequence does not suggest the order of clauses, the child has no other mode of ordering available to him — in this story. As a consequence, no significance attaches to the order of the sentences in this text. They could occur in any order. The last sentence could be used as the opening sentence, and vice versa; and all the other sentences in this text could be interchanged. Indeed, for this reason, these sentences hardly form a text at all. The text exists only as a loose collection of facts clustered around a topic. On the other hand, the second problem — what is to be the unifying factor for each sentence — receives a competent answer, namely that each sentence consists of one 'fact'. That is quite close to one adult conception of the sentence as embodying a single idea. The penultimate sentence is the only exception to this rule; it seems that the child regards 'not having fur' and 'not being able to see' as a single fact about baby mice. (Possibly the unifying fact is that the sentence deals with baby mice and lists two attributes of them.)

It is clear from this that narrative (both in speaking and in writing) has a powerful cognitive and conceptual effect on the child. The demands of non-narrative writing are of a different order both cognitively and linguistically from those of narrative writing. It might be said that in narrative writing events control the writer, whereas in non-narrative writing the writer has to control events.

The same writer produced another, shorter story on the same sheet of paper, presumably as part of the same exercise.

Text 21

The Ant

The ~~ants~~ ant have a nest
under the ground.
The nest has many tunnels.
There are different kinds of
ane in the nest.
There is a queen ant and
male ants and worker ~~and~~ ants.

I have shown both the corrections which the child made and the line-layout which the child used. It is interesting that here the child seemed intent on indicating the integrity of the sentence by starting each sentence on a new line; the child has also been careful to use capital letters at the beginning of sentences. In general syntactic terms much the same comments can be made about this text as about the previous one. Textually, however, it is different. Though this is again non-narrative, the child seems to have found a new mode of ordering material here. The text is organized around two principles: one is a general organizing concept, *the nest*; the other is a more abstract though related principle, namely a move from general to specific. This may even be reflected in the child's correction of *Ants* to *Ant* in the title and again in the first sentence, that is, settling for the generic rather than the plural. As a consequence of this order the sentences are structured as a text: the first sentence clearly functions and is structured as a first sentence. The new concept *nest* is introduced in the first sentence with the indefinite article *a*, as an elaboration on the topic *the ant*; it can then be treated as known, and it appears with the definite article *the* in thematic position in the second sentence. Sentence 2 is itself an elaboration on sentence 1. Sentence 3 is an expansion of the topic, and sentence 4 is again an elaboration specifically of sentence 3. The textual structure of this piece is quite accomplished. Sentences 1 and 2 form a unit of statement plus elaboration: 1 ... *a nest* .../ 2 ... *the nest* ...; and so do sentences 3 and 4: 3 ... *different kinds of ane* .../ 4 ... *queen* ... *male* ... *worker ants*. These two sections are linked by *nest*, and by the overall topic *ants*. Cohesion is thus quite noticeably evident: through the repetition of *nest*, the variation in the specificness of *nest*; *a → the → the*, and a similar developed linking involving *ant*; *the ant → different kinds of ane → a queen ant, male ants, worker ants*.

It is intriguing that in this text, which was written immediately following the previous one, as part of the same exercise and on the same sheet of paper, the child has managed to solve both of the problems posed by the non-narrative text for the notion of sentence. Perhaps this is merely coincidence, though the number of factors coinciding here is rather large, starting with the mechanical points of line/sentence coincidence, care over capital letters, and the more fundamental matters of textual structure and cohesion just discussed. One quite noticeable feature of both 'The Mouse' and 'The Ant' is the unspeechlike character of the sentences, a factor which is particularly striking by comparison with a text such as 'The Pioneer Boy' or 'Our Trip to Ayers House', for instance. The effort of producing non-narrative seems to have this effect, among others. Of course, one feature of writing in its fully developed form is its unspeakableness.

The next text, a narrative written by a seven-year-old girl, shows some development of the notion of sentence, both syntactically and textually.

Text 22

Father Christmas

(1) Father Christmas was in the sky one night when he came upon a poor farm house. (2) He went down the chimney and filled the stocking for the little girl. (3) He had a drink then left.

The points made above, in relation to 'The Two Poor People' and other preceding texts, apply here. The sentences are again mini-paragraphs, complete in themselves. Topical connectedness seems the primary motivating factor in the definition of sentence here as in the other texts. Each mini-paragraph sentence is given its own context or setting in that the first of the two clauses in each sentence acts like an adverbial phrase of time or place, providing the setting for the second clause. For instance *Father Christmas was in the sky one night* is both a temporal and a locative description. Even in the case of sentence 3 the first clause has this quasi-adverbial function as *He had a drink* could be replaced by the overt adverbial *Afterwards he left*.

One important kind of evidence for the child's own understanding of what constitutes a sentence comes from the corrections which children make to the sentence structures of their own stories. Here I give one such example; below I discuss another, where the principle used for correction is somewhat different.

Text 13

Birds

(1) I have not got a bird but I know some things about them. (2) ꞁ The have tow nostrils and They clean Ther feather and They eat̸ seeds, worms, bread cuddle fish, and lots of other things. (3) and they drink water. (4) When he drinks he Puts his head up and it gose down. ~~and a~~ (5) A budgie cage gets very dirty and peopel clean it.

There are three obvious corrections to the sentence structure: between sentences 1 and 2, 2 and 3, and 4 and 5. 1/2: Initially the child had ... *things about them the have tow nostrils* ... The correction separates the general statement made in 1 from the detail contained in 2. It is quite like the statement-elaboration structure just discussed in

relation to Text 21. Through the correction 1 becomes a genuine introduction and opening sentence, and 2 becomes cohesive from a topical
point of view. The correction at the juncture of 2 and 3 seems to be
motivated by the child's feeling that sentence 2 is about food (the last
two clauses certainly are), and that 'drinking' is a quite new topic which
belongs in its own sentence. The best example, though, is probably
that at 4/5: here two clearly divergent topics had been included in one
sentence. The child has tidied this up by placing the full stop precisely
at the end of one clause, crossing out the *and* and capitalizing the
following noun. This kind of correction is quite typical of children's
writing at this stage. 'Red Rover' discussed below and in Chapter 7
provides another example.

ii   Towards the adult concept of sentence

Once the underlying motivation of the unit 'sentence' is seen, its
predominantly textual nature understood, and in particular its differing
motivation from the adult's notion of sentence clearly grasped, some
apparent irregularities or 'mistakes' can be seen in a new light. In the
text below, for instance, there are two sentences — 2 and 3 — which do
not conform to the adult language's notion of sentence. However, in
the light of the preceding discussion, they can be seen to be perfectly
well formed and appropriate.

Text 14

Our Trip to Ayers House

(1) On Friday 1st July we all got in the bus and waved to
Miss Martyn. (2) We're off I thought, there was lots of merry
talk in the bus. (3) Tracey was telling some people that the bus
would pass her house 'there it is' said Tracey but it soon went
by. (4) We soon were there. (5) When we had got out of the bus
Mrs. Gilbert said to sketch the frantx frounx front of Ayers
House. (6) When I had finished my sketch I looked at some
of the other sketches. (7) I thought Prue's was the best.

It seems to me that the two sentences are deliberately presented as
single units. The headings would be 'The beginning of the journey' and

'Tracey's house'. If, however, one regards the sentence as a *syntactic* unit, one would want to punctuate these two quite differently. From the child's point of view, which takes the sentence as a textual unit, that is unwarranted. The two sentences each present one coherent fact. This difference between the child's and an adult's punctuation is clearly not a matter of syntactic ability; the story, written by an eight-year-old child, is syntactically complex. The child is able to handle most of the syntactic forms of adult language. As in 'The Two Poor People' speech is brought into the sentence, but now there is a greater flexibility and range of syntactic devices for handling imported speech. For instance in *We're off I thought* the child's 'internal' or 'silent' speech is brought into the sentence. In *'there it is' said Tracey* another speaker's speech is brought into the sentence and handled appropriately (by adult language standards) and adequately. The absence of quotation marks in the one case and their presence in the other may be an indication that the child makes a systematic distinction between 'own language' and 'other language'. In *Tracey was telling some people that the bus would pass her house* the reported speech has become syntactically more integrated into the child's own language, as a that-clause. In sentence 5 *When we had got out of the bus Mrs. Gilbert said to sketch the front of Ayers House*, the other speaker's speech is totally integrated, syntactically, into the child's own text, appearing as the embedded clause *to sketch the front of Ayers House*. The original utterance was presumably something like 'I want you to sketch the front of Ayers House'. One final point about the importation of other language into the text concerns the distinction between *We're off I thought* in sentence 2 and *I thought Prue's was the best*. It seems that the child is making a distinction between her own reported internal speech in *We're off I thought* which is in the present tense, as against *I thought Prue's was the best* in the past tense. The child makes a distinction between thought which has not become speech, not even 'internal' 'silent' speech, but has remained thought - ... *Prue's was the best* - and thought which has actually reached the stage of formulated speech. The child is able to use the formal device of a tense distinction to signal the different status of the two: the proximate present tense to signal the form which is closer to actually spoken speech, and the distant past tense to signal the form which is more remote from actually formulated speech.

There is a textual richness here which ought not to be overlooked. However, in contrast to Text 20, one can begin to see syntax beginning to play a greater part, particularly in the handling of imported speech as well as in the definition of what a sentence is generally. Sentences 5, 6 and 7 are examples of this. Yet at this stage the definition of sentence is still, in the main, a textual one.

A text already discussed makes the same point:

Text 15

The Pioneer Boy

(1) The boy I am writing about is called Sam he lived in the gold fields of Biggs Flat. (2) Well things weren't going to well for the Lam family they were very poor. (3) The night before Sam heard them taking of leaving and Sam didn't like that and went to bed crying. (4) He had lots of freinds in the gold feilds his father had a mine shaft but got no gold. (5) The next day it was Sam's turn to go down the mine shaft. (6) He was told to dig to same place he didn't. (7) Sam soon found his father was sick he had to go down the mine shaft. (8) So Sam did he dug in his place he soon saw a glitter. (9) He saw it was fools gold but that ment gold near. (10) The next day Sam went down he dug he found a pile of gold dust and put it in a bucket he pulled himself up and found he did not only have gold dust but a lump of gold from that day on the Lams were neaver poor again. (11) The piece of gold was called the Sitting Lady.

In many ways the sentences here are reminiscent of 'The Two Poor People'. In sentences 1 and 2 two clauses which report facts which are topically closely connected are simply adjoined to form one sentence, though sentence 1 also contains a relative clause. In both cases the syntax of speech is evident: in speech the two clauses would be intonationally joined in a topic (1st clause)/comment (2nd clause) structure, but of course that structure is not apparent in the written form, though it may well have been audible to the child when she wrote the story. Sentence 3 has three co-ordinated clauses; the first clause contains the embedded clause *them ta(l)king* (and possibly also another embedded clause, *(them) leaving*). On the third occurrence the noun *Sam* is deleted, although it can be recovered from the immediate context. By comparison with 'The Two Poor People' this text shows much greater syntactic development: the relative clause in 1; the clausal complement *them talking* in 3; the of-constructions *talking of leaving*; the syntactically complex conjoining constructions . . . *he did not only have gold dust but* . . . ; passives *He was told*. Speech still provides the overall structural framework, but within that the child uses a more complex sentence syntax, which is not qualitatively different from that of the adult. 'The Two Poor People' uses comparatively simpler syntax.

Textually the story is well developed; each individual sentence is structured appropriately to its context, and this is not due solely to the sequence of events reported in the narrative. Sentence 2, for instance, stands outside the narrative train. Sentence 1 may be taken to be the stage-setting, akin to the when-clauses encountered in the earlier writing of children. In that writing there is, however, nothing akin to sentence 2. Similarly with sentence 4; here again the child pauses, having set the train of narrative events in motion. From there on, the narrative proceeds at a normal pace. However, the sentences which stand outside the narrative train are nevertheless well integrated into the text. So, for instance, sentence 2 could not be the opening sentence; it depends cohesively on sentence 1, which establishes the existence of a family at a particular time and place implicitly, as the family of the boy Sam. These are necessary first steps to enable the writer, in sentence 2, to say something about this family which relates to their existence as poor miners and at the same time provides the narrative motive for the text in that it explains, causally, the sequence of events in the rest of the story. These factors explain the use of the definite article in *the Lam family*, the occurrence of the narrative marker *well*, and the appositional clause *they were very poor*. The textually appropriate placing of sentences 1 and 2 can be demonstrated by inverting their order: 'Well things weren't going too well for the Lam family they were very poor. The boy I am writing about is called Sam he lived in the gold fields of Biggs Flat.' Clearly, the textual structure is broken here. Where inversion is impossible in earlier writing the reason stems from the difficulty of interrupting a clearly marked sequence of events. In these two sentences there is no sequence of events, hence the impossibility of inverting the order of two sentences is due to the syntactically created textual structure: an effect both of conceptual ordering and of grammatical structuring. Many sentences in this text have a topic/comment structure, with the first clause acting as topic, and the next clause(s) as a comment on the first. This is true of 1, 2, 3, 6, 7 and 9 (and of clauses 2 and 3 in sentence 4).

Cohesion is well developed, both within the sentences and across sentences. Names are pronominalized across sentence-boundaries and within them: *Sam* in sentence 5 becomes *he* in sentence 6; *the Lam family* in sentence 2 becomes *them* in sentence 3. There is lexical cohesion across the text concerning lexical items which directly refer to Sam, or do so by association: *boy* 1, *Sam* 1, *he* 1, *the Lam family* 2, *they* 2, *Sam* 3, *them* 3, *Sam* 3, deleted *he* (in *(he) went to bed . . .*), *he* 4, *freinds* 4, *his father* 4, (deleted *he*) 4, *Sam's turn* 5, *he* 6, *he* 6, *Sam* 8, *his father* 7, *he* 7, *Sam* 8, *he* 8, *his place* 8, *he* 8, *he* 9, *Sam* 10, *he* 10, *he* 10, deleted *he* (*(he) put it*) 10, *he* 10, *himself* 10, deleted *he* (*(he) found*) 10, *he* 10, *the Lams* 10, deleted agent of passive (*the piece of gold was called*) 11. In this text, as in Text 12, 'Beaked Whales', the writer pronominalizes only the dominant topic, in this case the name *Sam*.

The sentences in this text still show the influence of the syntax of speech. When asked, some weeks later, why she had placed full stops where she had, the writer said 'Well, you need a second breath for it to make sense', neatly conflating — and confirming — the two major influences here: the syntax of speech, with intonationally marked information units (also called breath-groups or phonological clauses by some writers), and the semantic criterion of topical connectedness. Questioned a bit further, she said 'the teacher says that if you do four lines without a full stop it gets too tiring, you need to take a breath'. It is revealing that 'breath' figures in both explanations.

The most potent factors in the child's *learning* of writing are the models of written language which the school provides, and which it encourages the child to emulate. This point will be discussed in Chapter 5. Here I wish to draw attention briefly to the effect which these models have on the child's developing notion of sentence. First a text, written by the same child, which was produced as part of a local history 'project' at school.

Text 23

Who was Goyder

(1) Most people think that Goyder was the founder of Mylor but he wasn't. (2) He was South Australia's Surveyor General.
(3) The drainage of the South East and the planting of the Pinus Radiata. (4) It was recommended by him. (5) Mr. Goyder lived at Warrakilla an old coaching inn he got it in 1879. (6) He

liked the country so much that he didn't mind taking the daylyx
trip daily. (7) Goyders house is really two in one the oriagnal was
built in 1842. (8) In 1880 Goyder bought the house and named
it Warrakilla.

What is most striking immediately is the much more formal vocabulary
used here: *the founder*, *South Australia's Surveyor General*, *The
drainage of the South East*, *recommended*, etc. The second striking
feature is that this text has noticeably fewer sentences with adjoined
clauses. Sentence 5 is the only clear-cut example of it, though 7 may be
also. Sentence 5 is the very essence of spoken syntax, with its chaining
syntax. Written syntax demands the relative clause . . . *which he got in
1879*. The ratio of sentences with adjoined clauses to other sentences is
1:3. In the previous text, 'The Pioneer Boy', that ratio is 7:4 (sentences
1, 2, 4, 6, 7, 8 and 10 all contain adjoined clauses). This is a dramatic
change. It points to the fact that the child is integrating clauses within
a sentence much more than before. This may be by means of a conjunction, such as *but*, or *and*; by means of complementation: *Most
people think that Goyder* . . . , *He liked the country so much that he
didn't mind* . . . ; or by embedding: *he didn't mind taking the trip daily*.
It is not that these are new devices within the child's grammar (indeed,
they are found well before this), but rather that they now begin to
dominate in the internal structuring of the sentence. The interesting
point is that both 'The Pioneer Boy' and 'Who was Goyder' were written
at the same time, as part of the same social studies project. In one case
the child wrote a story which she created, in the other she was following
a model. This makes the point about the influence of the models which
the school provides all the more strongly. From being a sequence of
loosely joined clauses related to the same topic, the sentence is now
emerging as a structure in which a more restricted topic is treated by
the closer syntactic integration of clauses.

In this instance the adult model can be studied directly. The children
who were doing the project were given two brief local histories, written
by local amateur historians. Here are two extracts, one from each.

Text 24

History of Mylor

Possibly the most outstanding citizen that Mylor had was the then South Australia Surveyor General, Mr. Goyder, after whom Goyder's Line was named; his interest in drainage in the South East and the planting of the Pinus Radiata were also recommended by him.

Text 25

The Story of Mylor

(1) In 1880 the property came into the possession of an outstanding public figure of the day. (2) This man was George Goyder, then S.A.'s Surveyor-General. (3) Goyder's name will always be associated with the delineation of a boundary line for wheat-growing, based on an average 14 inch rainfall.

(4) Apart from his name perpetuating this line of rainfall he also performed invaluable survey work throughout Central and Northern Australia.

(5) In 1860 he was appointed Surveyor General and it was after his return from a mission to England that he took over the Inn. (6) Like William Warland he too was greatly impressed with the natural beauties of its setting. (7) First he changed the name to Warrakilla, an aboriginal name which he acquired during wanderings in the Northern Territory. (8) Then he set about enlarging the original premises.

(9) While religiously preserving the character of the old inn, he added a substantial home built solidly of freestone with walls as thick as a fortress. (10) Around the house he lavishly planted English trees, shrubs and hedges, including the rare Oregan pine and English beech.

(11) To be invited to Goyder's home was indeed an honour, for he entertained in grand style the officialdom and elite of Adelaide. (12) His estate carried a large staff and every day George Goyder travelled to Adelaide in his private coach.

It can be seen that the child has not copied directly from either history. In each case where the child has borrowed she has made the borrowing appropriate to her own text, performing quite complex syntactic operations. The adult version provides the model, for words, phrases and syntax, but the child has to appropriate and assimilate this model into her own conceptual, syntactic and textual scheme. If it were

Model	Child's Text
(1) . . . *the then South Australia Surveyor General, Mr. Goyder* . . .	(1) . . . *Goyder was the founder of Mylor.*
	(2) *He was South Australia's Surveyor General.*
(1) . . . *his interest in drainage in the South East and the planting of the Pinus Radiata were also recommended by him*	(3) *The drainage of the South East and the planting of Pinus Radiata.*
	(4) *It was recommended by him.*

a matter of merely copying the adult model, the effect of that model might be less pronounced. However, the child assimilates and internalizes these forms; they have then become her own.

It would be misleading to assume that no factors other than those so far discussed enter into the definition of sentence for a child. Here I wish to discuss two others which again imply a different mode of conceptualization by the child compared to that of the adult. The two are closely related: 'order' and 'causality'. These too play their part in a child's achievement of the adult notion of sentence. Text 22 provides a good example for the discussion of 'order'. It was written by a child at the age of seven. Clearly the child has imposed an order on the text that she is constructing. The syntactic and textual order mirrors the order of events in the constructed imaginary world of the story. Not only are the three sentences in a strict chronologically sequential order, but within each sentence itself the two clauses are in the order 'early event in the first clause, and later event in the second clause'. In adult language, when-clauses which report an event preceding that reported in the main clause of a sentence do not stand in a predictable sequential relation to the main clause. They may precede or they may follow it. For instance, it seems more usual to say *We packed up our picnic things when it started to rain* (where the later event comes first in the sentence) than *When it started to rain we packed up our picnic things* (where the order of the clauses mirrors the order of the events in the world). A child of six or seven would nearly invariably use the second version. In *Father Christmas was in the sky one night when he came across a poor farmhouse*, the *when* is very much the concrete temporal kind of *when*, and it is used to connect one clause to a preceding clause. In the invented example above, the *when* has a temporal function, but in addition it has a strong causal force, that is, *We packed our picnic things up because it started to rain.* In the child's sentence there is no suggestion of a causal force. Through Texts 22, 14 and 26 (written by the same child at the ages of seven, eight and nine respectively) the development of the *when* can be clearly traced. In Text 14 it begins to get what is perhaps its most usual function in children's writing, a kind of stage-setting function, as in sentence 5 *When we had got out of the bus Mrs. Gilbert said to sketch the front of Ayers House.* While this is akin to the anchoring function mentioned above, it is also quite distinctly a stage setting for something that follows. In the next story, Text 26, sentence 7 *When I visit my family I might let him come out and perform to them* shows one of the more common adult uses of *when*, the hypothetical use.

Text 26

My Ambition in Life

(1) When I grow up I want to be a ventriloquist.
(2) I will have to practise talking without opening my mouth.
(3) I want to travel around in a combination van with a painted sign that will say 'Geraldine and Frank'. (4) Frank will be my puppet and he will wear a top hat and black suit. (5) I will treat him as a child by giving him real school lessons! (6) On my first show I will pretend Frank is shy, but then gradually he will become used to all the people. (7) When I visit my family I might let him come out and perform to them. (8) I will go to university for the first couple of years. (9) I don't want to get married or have children. (10) I want to become a star in about 1990 and I will be 21. (11) I would like to perform in front of the King (Prince Charles). (12) When I am a star I will wear shining clothes with 'I am a star' written on my back.

These texts illustrate the development in the use of *when* from year to year, from the concrete temporal function to an abstract, logical, causal and hypothetical function. In the first of this set of three stories written by the child, Text 22, it is the order of events in the world which provides the order for the text that she produces. The freeing from that order can be seen in the development of the *when*, and more generally in the development of the language as a whole in these three texts.

That freeing from the order of things in the world depends on and derives from the child's ability to substitute a different order. The development of *when* mirrors that freeing, and provides the clue to the alternative order which the child learns to impose. *When* moves from a strictly temporal meaning to hypothetical and causal meanings. These are two of the alternative orders which the child develops in all areas. In the next two texts I wish to look at causality as a factor in a child's development of the concept of sentence. Text 27 was written by a nine-year-old boy.

Text 27

Red Rover

(1) Yesterday when we played Red Rover Jody and Stephen smashed into each other and (a) Jody had a blood ear and she couldn't hear (wer) (w) very well (and). (2) then she had to go and clean her ear.

(3) Then the (we) the (er) teacher said we can't (played) play it again and then we played a nother game.

The syntactic and textual order mirrors the order of events in the world, which this time is the real world. In the first sentence there are four events, *we played Red Rover, Jody and Stephen smashed into each other, Jody had a blood ear, she couldn't hear very well.* A heading for these events might be 'The accident', as all these events relate directly to the accident. The events within the sentence occurred in the order in which they are represented here – the child has made no overt attempt to make a causal connection between the discrete events; there are no 'because''s, 'so''s, 'therefore''s. Nor has the child made an attempt to represent the events themselves in a causal form, that is, in a form where cause (or a causer) and effect are expressed syntactically. The child could have attached a because-clause, thus giving a reason, a cause. However, the child does not do this. Indeed, all the conjunctions are *and* (not *so*, or *therefore*, or *and then*), the least causal of the conjunctions the child might have used. Instead the events are simply presented, and the reader is left to infer the causal connection. A stronger statement would be that the child leaves the sequence to imply or express causality, and perhaps even assumes that causality depends on sequence.

It may seem that this is an over-interpretation of the evidence.

However, the child's own correction of his punctuation suggests that this is not so. Initially the child had written sentence 1 and sentence 2 as one sentence, joined by *and*. In correcting or altering this punctuation, the child must be assumed to have had some rationale, first of all for making two sentences out of one, and second, for making the division where he did. From the point of view of the narrative alone the division could with equal plausibility and effect have occurred in a different place. For instance: . . . *and Jody had a bloody ear. She couldn't hear very well and then she had* . . . However, from the point of view of causality, the correction is well motivated. All the events in the new sentence 1 are events in a causal chain of physical events, one leading to the other. The events in sentence 2 do not, however, belong in that same causal chain of physical events. The *had to* points to compulsion, either from an outside agency, such as the teacher, or the necessity arising from the bleeding. In either case a new type of cause is at work, and the child seems to have taken this as his cue in correcting or altering the punctuation.

If this explanation is correct, we have additional evidence that the child's sentences are highly motivated units. The motivation in this sentence is quite different from the textual motivation of the previous discussion – and indeed, it is quite different from the syntactic motivation of the adult's sentence. It is, however, a highly subtle motivation, cognitively and conceptually. The discussion of causality could be linked to the adult's notion of a sentence containing one idea; here the idea would be the abstract one of causality. Similarly with order, which might relate to the child's felt necessity to present material within the sentence in a coherent form.

To conclude this section I wish to look at some later writings where the effects of the adult models, the genres, have begun to assert themselves decisively. Texts 15 and 23 contained a number of agentless passives. Particularly in the case of the piece of historical writing these are clearly due to this genre. Text 24, for instance, contains two agentless passives in one sentence, even though it was written by an amateur historian: . . . *after whom Goyder's line was named,* . . . *were also recommended by him*. Text 12 moves further in the direction of 'impersonality':

Passives occur in sentences 1: *are found*, 9 *known*, and 10 *is seen, is believed*. The function of the agentless passive in scientific or objective writing is to allow the suppression of the writer from the text, and the deletion of mention of the scientist from the experiment or investigation

Text 12

Beaked Whales

(1) The Beaked Whales live out in mid-ocean, where the tasty squid are found. (2) Squid, it seems, provide most of their meals. (3) Men do not know much about their family because even the scientists who study whales have seen very few Beaked Whales. (4) Generally members of this family have long, narrow snouts, or 'beaks'. (5) They have very few teeth, just one or two on each side of the lower jaw, and these sometimes poke out like small tusks.

(6) The largest of this family is the Baird's Beaked Whale. (7) It grows to 42 ft in length. (8) Most beaked whales range between 15 and 30 ft. (9) The Bottlenose gets to be about 30 ft. long, and its cousin known as Cuvier's Beaked Whale grows to about 26 ft.

(10) Cuvier's Whale is rarely seen, though it is believed that it lives in all oceans. (11) It is unusual in colour, so if you should see one, you should be able to recognize it. (12) Most whales have dark grey backs and pale undersides. (13) Cuvier's Beaked Whales instead has a light back and a dark grey underside, and two small tusk-teeth poke up outside the mouth of the males.

(14) Bottlenose is even more odd. (15) You may possibly see one travelling in a small school of ten or twelve whales.

he or she is conducting. By this method the text acquires an air of impersonality which is, of course, a part of the ideology or ethos of the scientific enterprise. There are other linguistic features of impersonality: *it seems*, for instance, makes no mention of the person to whom something seems. Plural and generic nouns, *men* and *scientists*, are used as the agents by the writer rather than specific individuals. The generalized pronoun *you* (that is, anyone at all, hence no one in particular) has the same effect. Adverbials such as *generally* also belong to this style. The general objectively descriptive style is also due to the tense used here, the universal present.

Textually, and conceptually, this presents an enormous advance on the earlier pieces of factual or 'scientific' writing, 'The Mouse' and 'The Ant'. The organization of the text proceeds according to an abstract schema, from a general statement about Beaked Whales to specific statements about sub-groups of the larger species; it is handled competently in linguistic terms. In terms of cohesion, there is development and continuity both within paragraphs and across paragraphs. I pointed out in Chapter 3 the cohesive features which operate in this text. Here I wish to draw attention to the effect which the development of textual structure has on the sentence. The major textual advance is the paragraph, which in this text has the form and function of the paragraph in adult writing. That is, it is used to encode significant topical segments of the whole text. The child's early sentences suggest that they have a similar function in overall topical development to the paragraph in adult writing, and a similar internal function and structure to the adult paragraph. In this text there is no such ambiguity about the status of the sentence. It seems that one of the consequences of the achievement of the paragraph is that it frees the sentence from paragraph-like functions, thereby permitting the development of the sentence as a linguistic unit with structural, textual and semantic features in its own right.

In the main, the effect is to reduce the content of the sentence. Because the paragraph has emerged as the unit which contains topically connected material, the sentence can now become the unit which contains one topically discrete element. A related effect is that the topical material within the sentence becomes more closely integrated. The syntactic consequence is that the topical elements which do co-occur in the sentence are syntactically (and topically) closely fused, to become single, though frequently complex, units. In Text 15, 'The Pioneer Boy', this process has begun in the subordinating and embedding syntax of sentences. However, the text still has a majority of sentences in which the clausal elements were co-ordinated or adjoined. In 'Beaked Whales' subordination and embedding clearly predominate. There are three sentences with co-ordinated clauses (out of a total of fifteen sentences in the text), 5, 9 and 11. In all three cases there are strong cohesive ties across the clause boundaries, and these cause the sentence to be much more integrated than those of Text 15, for instance; 5 . . . *very few teeth . . ., and these . . .*; 9 *The Bottlenose . . ., and its cousin known as Cuvier's Beaked Whale . . .*; 11 *It . . ., . . . one . . ., . . . it.*

There are a large number of single-clause sentences in the text (six out of fifteen), 4, 6, 7, 8, 12 and 14. This might seem like a return to (or a vestige of) the simpler syntax of early writing. In fact it is the opposite and due, as I mentioned above, to the freeing of the sentence from paragraph-like notions. It is important to understand this clearly, as otherwise the seeming simplicity of this sentence-syntax might be mistaken for an analogous cognitive simplicity. For instance, in sentence 9 of 'Beaked Whales' . . . *its cousin known as Cuvier's Beaked Whale* . . . is a construction of headnoun (*its cousin*) and its modifying relative clause (*known as Cuvier's Beaked Whale*). The combined structure is a complex noun-phrase which acts as the subject of its clause. The relative clause and the main clause each express one element of the text's topical structure: *The bottlenose's cousin grows to about 26 ft* and *The bottlenose's cousin is known (to scientists) as Cuvier's Beaked Whale*. In the relative clause construction the two topical elements have become fused into a single complex topical unit. A similar process operates with nominalizations, nouns formed from full clauses. For instance, in Text 17, sentence 1 . . . *work goes into designing the best possible* . . . , *designing* derives from a clause such as *someone designs panels*. The seemingly simple surface structure therefore conceals a fuller topical and clausal structure: *someone designs panels, and that takes a great amount of work*. In other words as the child attains greater mastery over written syntax much textual complexity and diversity is the subject of syntactic and topical processing, which gives rise to apparently simple structures. In concealing the degree of prior processing, these structures could be misleadingly interpreted as being in fact simple. Hence many of the single-clause sentences are simple due to the prior close integration of material; the simplicity of the clause disguises a complexity of prior linguistic processes of integration. Sentence 4 of Text 12, for instance, contains the following 'propositions': 1 *members of this family have snouts*; 1 *these snouts are narrow and long*, 3 *they are like beaks*; 4 *this is generally the case*. At an earlier stage, for instance that of Text 21, 'The Ant', the propositions would be likely to appear separated out in this fashion. Here they have been processed, compressed, and presented as a single complex proposition. It would be a gross misjudgment of the child's cognitive processes to take this as a sign of simplicity. Indeed, the syntactic complexity (and no doubt this is true of the cognitive processes and the conceptual structures expressed by these sentences) of the remaining sentences — containing quantifiers and comparative constructions, or both — is such that no satisfactory or agreed syntactic descriptions exist of them in linguistic theories.

The transition from paragraph to paragraph is well handled. Each paragraph contains an element (or elements) which is taken up in the following paragraph and further developed there:

para 1 . . . *Beaked Whales* . . . *their family* . . . *this family* →

> para 2 *the largest of this family . . . Cuvier's Beaked Whale*
> . . . →
> para 3 *Cuvier's whale . . . two small tusk-teeth poke up*
> (which is odd) . . . →
> para 4 *Bottlenose . . . even more odd . . .*

Although the development towards the written language is remarkable, traces of the interactive, interpersonal contexts of speech remain. These are not now expressed syntactically, through the structure of speech, but through the interpersonal component of language. That is, those components of the grammar which express aspects of the relations of speaker and hearer are utilized to convey the formality of the situations of speech. A lexical example: 5 . . . *these poke out like small tusks*; 9 . . . *gets to be* . . .; 11 . . . *if you should see one, you should be able* . . .; 15 *you may possibly see one* . . .; 14 . . . *even more odd*. The fact that the child lapses into informality, but does so without using the syntax of speech, is possibly the clearest indication of how firmly the syntax of writing is now established.

Text 17, 'The Cockpit', illustrates the points just made, possibly more conclusively. There are no intrusions of (or lapses into) informality. The textual and topical structure is clear; paragraphs are used to mark off topical segments precisely; the sentences are those of fully developed written language, with great syntactic and topical integration, and a high degree of syntactic complexity.

Text 17

The Cockpit

(1) The crew of a modern jet airliner must have all the information they need at their finger tips, so a great amount of work goes into designing the best possible flight deck control panels. (2) The captain and the first officer each must have controls for flying the plane, and there is an automatic pilot for routine flying.

(3) Basic flight instruments are on the panel in front of each pilot. (4) On the panel between them are the engine throttles and gauges, radio and navigation equipment and things like the parking brake.

(5) The flight engineer has his own instrument panel behind the pilots.

Relative clauses, for instance, are completely fused into their headnouns; 1 ... *all the information they need* ... where the relative pronoun *which* has been deleted to increase the degree of fusion. This permits the construction of a new concept, *the information they need* (rather than the discrete concepts of two clauses, 'the crew must have information', 'the crew needs that information'; or the relatively less fused 'the crew must have all the information which they need'). This is quite characteristic of this text: 3 *the panel (which is) in front of (them)*; 4 *the panel (which is) between them*; 5 ... *own instrument panel (which is) behind the* ...; 2 ... *controls (which are) for flying* ...; etc.

This linguistic development has cognitive analogues — postponing here the question whether they are cause or effect. The emergence of the paragraph permits the child to structure arguments in a new form in that it now presents the possibility of a minimal unit of argument, the sentence, and a maximal unit, the text, intermediate to which is the paragraph as a major segment of the overall topical development and structure of a text. The effect on the sentence is to permit greater precision, integration, reduction and compression of content, and greater complexity, both cognitive and linguistic. The effect on the text is to make new modes of cognitive, conceptual and linguistic order available, in which sentences are the minimal units, and paragraphs the significant segments. Paragraphs attain a status derived from the structure of the text itself, rather than (as in narrative) from 'the world'. The development of this textual structure both permits and demands new modes of cognitive and conceptual organization. In this process the receding audience or addressee is highly significant too. The development of the impersonal style has a significant cognitive corollary. The freeing from the demands of the known, single, immediately present addressee is a necessary prerequisite to the development of a conceptual and textual structure which is not determined (however weakly) by the felt demands or needs of the known addressee and his known world. The freeing from the specific addressee brings with it the possibility of a freeing from the dependence on the order and logic of the real world. As the addressee recedes, so the demands (however adequately or inadequately grasped) of the subject matter become foregrounded. The two processes together lead to formality, impersonality, but permit the development of abstract cognitive, conceptual orders, expressed in the textual structures made possible and available in writing.

Chapter 5
Genre

i Genre and reality

Learning to write involves the learning of new syntax, and of the new
syntactic unit, the sentence. It also involves learning of the larger
structures within which sentences occur. Study in text linguistics and in
stylistics over the last two decades has made it clear that there are
linguistic structures beyond the sentence. Their grammar differs from
sentence grammar as they express demands and needs of a kind different
from those expressed in the single sentence. If sentences express ideas,
perceptions, classifications, it is texts which provide the linguistic units
within which these ideas, perceptions, classifications are organized into
larger wholes. These units express the order which the writer wishes to
establish at the largest level. The textual organization embodies the
type of order which the writer perceives, or which he wishes to impose
on that part of reality which he is presenting to the reader in the text.
Textual structures have a world-ordering, even a world-creating function
which is at least as significant as the world-encoding function of the
sentence. To illustrate the point here is a brief extract from Hemingway's
First Forty-Nine Stories.

> Nick sat against the wall of the church where they had dragged him
> to be clear of machine-gun fire in the street. Both legs stuck out
> awkwardly. He had been hit in the spine. His face was sweaty and
> dirty. The sun shone on his face. The day was very hot. Rinaldi,
> big backed, his equipment sprawling, lay face downward against
> the wall. Nick looked straight ahead brilliantly. The pink wall of the
> house opposite had fallen out from the roof, and an iron bedstead
> hung twisted toward the street. Two Austrian dead lay in the

rubble in the shade of the house. Up the street were other dead. Things were getting forward in the town. It was going well.

Each sentence in this passage encapsulates a perception, complete in itself. Each sentence encodes a piece of the world in which Nick finds himself, either of the physical world or of his mental world. However, Hemingway has left the sentences unconnected, so that they remain isolated and do not make up the orderly integrated account we might expect from a normal perceiver and narrator. So, for instance, *Both legs stuck out awkwardly* is left separated from the first sentence, which it would not be if the writer had used the possessive pronoun *his*, *His legs stuck out awkwardly*. In this Hemingway of course achieves the creation of the world-view of someone in shock: impressions come to him discretely and isolated, and he is unable to assemble them into a coherent whole. *Both legs* ... presents this perception as being about some external reality, much as the twisted iron bedstead. Hence in creating textual incoherence Hemingway is creating precisely the world of someone in severe shock, unable to prevent sensations from reaching his mind and unable to impose any order on these sensations.

The example illustrates what often goes unnoticed, namely that texts have a high degree of internal structure. The structure is so much a part of the whole that it remains invisible to the reader, seeming to be the natural way of saying things. Only when it is disrupted in some way does the structure itself become noticed, in its malfunction or even in its absence. In this we also become aware of the task which the child faces in learning to write, namely the acquisition and mastery of textual structures. Speech has its textual structures too, of course, which I have in some part discussed in the two preceding chapters. However, the textual structures of speech differ from those of writing in most respects, with one major exception, namely narrative. Moreover, most of the situations where the child speaks are interactions with another speaker, so that texts are mutually constructed, in accordance with the demands of the situation and the actions of the other speaker. Consequently the creation of a text (especially an extended text) by the child himself or herself is a quite new task.

Although writers impose the order of a textual structure on their writing, the kinds of textual order which they can impose are pre-determined by the fact that these orders exist in established, conventionalized forms, that is, in the established genres within a given written culture. Just as there is a small and fixed number of sentence types, so there exists a small and fixed number of genres in any written tradition. The individual can no more create a new genre type than he or she can create a new sentence type. The creativity which is permitted to the individual exists in deciding in which type of sentence or genre to encode the idea or the larger world-view.

The child has to gain mastery over the forms and the possibilities of the different generic types, as part of the process of learning to write. The different genres each make their own demands in terms of their formal structures, their ordering of thematic material, their conception of knowledge. These demands have their effects on the syntax at sentence and below-sentence level. All these aspects have to be learned as part of the process of learning to write. The achievement of genre is a necessary and integral part of the achievement of writing; the two are inextricably interwoven.

Inevitably this learning takes place in the school, for the school has to teach genre as much as it has to teach the other skills of writing. But if the teaching of writing has received little attention, the teaching of genre has had even less, with the possible exception of some literary genres. Focus on them has, however, tended to be a feature of writing in the later years of schooling, and it has then become identified with other emphases on writing, concerned much more with psychological and aesthetic than with formal or informal linguistic, social or cognitive questions. The major genres which the school teaches are taught by the way, implicitly: descriptive, scientific, technical, historical writing. This is true also of creative writing: children are asked to write 'stories' — with whatever motivation or purpose — without being given any teaching about the appropriate type of genre, or its main structural features.

Consequently children pick up the requirements of the different genres by osmosis, as it were. They do, of course, have models, but these are presented as models of something else. For instance, the stories which children read are often presented as reading exercises, or else the texts for dictation are presented as relevant to dictation alone; most frequently they are presented primarily for their content, be it brief history, a piece of informative writing or a description of an experiment. The children absorb, together with whatever other purposes there may be, the forms and rules of the genre in which the content is presented to them. Sometimes the teacher's instruction is sufficiently detailed and directed to lead to the constructing of a text which embodies the demands of a genre.

It may be useful at this stage to contrast two pieces of writing, belonging to two generic types. One is a written narrative, the other a descriptive factual piece. The writer of both pieces was seven years old.

Text 20

The Two Poor People
(including the child's corrections)

1   Once upon a time there lived two poor people.
2   They longed to be rich.
3   Onnne day when they were in the woods looking for fire wood.
4   when they met a prince riding through the woods.
5   The prince stopped and looked at them and said Are you poor.
6   A xAt firt they were to scared to answer.
7   But in the end they answer yes we are poor.
8   The prince said would you like to come to the palace.
9   Oh yxxes well come on he said.
10   So of they went.
11   Tkhey arrived at the palacethey were greted.
12   That night they had a feast they were shown to thxeir beds.
13   They hadback had a wonder time that day.
14   Asthe daxsys went by they by they bgan to like it more and more.
15   So the more they bgan to mis their frineds.
16   Just befor they went tobed king said your frneds are coming
     tomorrow.
17   They were so excited that they could hardly get to sleep that
     night.x
18   In the morning they saidto the king when are theyxcoming.
19   They will be coming at lunchtime he said
20   At lunchtime when their frined came they were verey surprisedto
     see them there.
21   One day when they were walking in the woods they met an old
     woman.
22   That old woman happened to be a witch.
23   Shewas beggixng to be helpt home.
24   Sxxo they helped her home.
25   When they got her home the witch gave the king and queen a
     red apple.
26   The king and queen took the apples and went back home and
     eat the appler.
27   Nects day the prince found the king and queen dead.
28   xThe prince knozu a wizard.
29   Thaxat day xxxthe prince went to tel the wizard.

30   The wizard came and made the king and queen aliv agen and
      ciled thxe witch and ~~thxe~~ they live happyly evry erfeder.
      THE END

Text 9

The Mouse

(1) the mices enemy are cats and owls. (2) the mices eat all
kinds of thingk. (3) Mices are little animals. (4) people set traps
to catch mouse. (5) mouses liv in holes in the skirting board.
(6) Baby mouse dons have their eis opne. (7) baby mouses
can't see and they do not have fer. (8) some people are
scered of mouses.

'The Two Poor People' was written outside school, and without any
request by an adult for the child to write a story. The child had not
been taught the genre of 'story' or the specific (sub-)genre 'fairy-story'.
Yet it is quite clear that the child has learned some of the essential
structural and textual features of a fairy-story, as well as some of its
typical contents. The story has a conventionalized opening, a motive/
conflict, *They longed to be rich*; several climaxes, *when they met a
prince . . . at lunchtime when their frined came . . . the witch gave the
king and queen a red apple . . . the wizard . . . made the king and queen
aliv agen . . .*; and a resolution, *they live happily evry erfeder*. Clearly
the child has not fully mastered the formal structure of this genre,
though he has mastered one other significant feature, namely the
convention that it must be in the past tense. In terms of the content-
structure the child knows the kinds of characters which can occur in
this genre: a prince, poor people, wizards and witches, a king and
queen, all in an appropriate setting.

   It is the contrast with 'The Mouse', written by the same child at
about the same age, which reveals the degree of mastery of the genre.
'The Mouse' 'lacks' all the structural, textual and content features of
'The Two Poor People', and thus shows up just how much generic
structure the other text has. 'The Mouse' by contrast has no beginning,
end or climax, no 'characters', and is written in the present tense. Of
course, the point is not that 'The Mouse' should have any of the generic
features of 'The Two Poor People', but to show how generically specific
both texts are. The tense usage is significant: the child uses the past

tense for the fairy-story, and the present tense for the descriptive/ scientific story. In the case of the former this may of course be due to the fact that the child has heard many fairy-stories, all in that tense. It is less clear that he has heard as many descriptive/scientific pieces in the present tense. At any rate, however it may have come about, an association of fiction with past tense and factualness with present tense has become established. This lays the foundation for one of the meanings of both tenses, namely their association with fictionality and factualness respectively. The distinction marks the beginning of a formal distinction between forms of knowledge: that which is presented in the present tense is fact plus knowledge; that which is presented in the past tense is fiction plus knowledge. The former is destined to develop into the scientific, the latter into the humanistic genres.

ii   Factual genres

Below I trace the development of narrative writing in some detail. Here I wish to focus on the emergence and gradually increasing specificness of the 'factual' genres. That development is intimately bound up with the curriculum of the educational system. The description offered here is based on specific curricula, and is therefore not generalizable to all educational systems. The principles, however, are generalizable: the divisions of the curriculum (however implicit these may be in the early stages of schooling) will determine both the types of genre which emerge and the order in which they emerge relative to other types.

As far as the development of writing is concerned, the major curriculum distinction in the primary school system I am referring to is between Social Studies and English. The former encompasses all the factual areas: history, geography, science, technology, geology — generally those subjects which are related to the study of humans, but not exclusively so. Within that, the major written work takes the form of 'projects', that is, topics set by the teacher which the child is expected to explore with more or less guidance. Early projects take the form of children collecting much visual material and pasting this into an exercise book or organizing it in some other form. Writing is restricted to one or two sentence headings to indicate the nature and significance of the material, though there may be some brief descriptive texts. The projects I wish to look at here come from later ages, nine and twelve, that is, grades 5 and 7 in the South Australian system. The teacher in grade 5 provides the children with a set of questions which the children are expected to answer, and which therefore organize and structure the project, and the writing.

The first project is 'A Country of Europe'. Here is the set of instructions:

A Country of Europe — Project

1 This sheet must be pasted into the back of your project book.
2 On the cover of your book put these things
   1) The name of the Country.
   2) Your name.
   3) An illustration.
3 On the first page you will set out a Table of Contents.
  These will be in your Table of Contents.
   1) *Position and description of the country*
     a) Maps would be useful
     b) Main cities
     c) Main rivers and lakes
     d) Mountain ranges
     e) Seas and oceans
   2) *Climate*
     a) What are the summer and winter seasons like?
     b) Is it similar to or different from the climate of South Australia?
     c) How much rain falls each year?
     d) Is the country nearer to the North Pole or the equator?
   3) *What the People Wear*
     a) the national dress of the country
     b) the people's everyday clothes
     c) materials used to make them
     d) does the climate make a difference to the type of clothes they wear?
   4) *The Food They eat*
     a) What food is grown in the country?
     b) Is any of it exported to other countries?
     c) Do they have to import any foods?
     d) Do the people eat any special foods because of the type of land they live in?
   5) *How the people live*
     a) What are some of the customs of the people?
     b) What language or languages do they speak?

c) What do their homes look like?
d) What are the important primary and secondary industries?
e) Do the people have an interesting history?
6) *Interesting places and people*
If a tourist was to travel through your country, would he find any of these?
a) ancient cities
b) places where famous people lived
c) famous buildings
d) places of beauty
e) interesting cities and ports.

Here is the written part of the child's project, reproduced in full. There are illustrations throughout the project, which clearly form an integral part of the total text and should be accounted for in a full discussion of children's work. The writer is nine years old.

Text 28

West Germany

Contents Page.

Position And Description Of The Country
1) Towards the east of Germany are Poland and Czechoslovakia, Switzerland and Austria are south of west Germany. France, Belgium and the Netherlands are west of Germany.
2) The main cities in Germany are Berlin, Munich and Hamburg. The biggest river in Germany is the River Rhine, River Aller and River Elde. The islands are the Frisians Islands in west Germany.

3) Germany has only one boarder that faces the sea. The two oceans they are the Baltic Sea and the North Sea.

4) In Munich you can go and see the Nymphenburg Palace, the Hall of fame, the Frauenkirche. If you go to Berlin you can go and see The Branden Gate it is a huge archway you can see The Olympic Stadium. You can also see Alexander Platz it is a city square in East Berlin.

Climate

1) In West Germany the winter is quite mild. The summer is very hot but warm a ocean current stops it been to hot. The west has a more severe climate than the east. In Southern highlands the summer is long and pleasant. The summer is quite like ours. The mountains and the hills get more rain than the valleys. It is a lot cooler on the mountain than in the valleys.

What the People Wear

1) Now-days German people wear much the same clothes as we wear. They only wear their National costumes for special reasons. In the former days they used to wear their National costumes to church. Now-days they only do it some country areas.

2) Boys sometimes wear leather pants called 'lederhose'. The pants are held up by leather straps with a piece across the front. This is often decorated with animals they used to hunt.

3) Girls have a special German dress which look like a skirt with a blouse and a waistcoat top over the blouse. This is called a Dirndl.

4) German sizes are quite different. They don't have sizes like ($\frac{2}{1}$, $\frac{4}{2}$) theres are like this 35, 45, 55,. Das Kleiderschaft means clothes industry. They use much the same materials as we do.

The food they eat

1) The West Germans have two breakfasts one is cake and coffee the other breakfast is of cheese and meat sandwiches. For lunch they have salt ribs, pork and boiled potatoes, for supper they have open sandwiches with mea, sausage and cheese. Germans do not eat pork and mutton so much now.

Now days Germans quiet often take their second breakfast with them.

2) Nowdays people at work get lunch at the canteen so that has changed there eating habits. At the canteen you can get sausage and cheese with bread.

3) In food shops you can get many different foods. In fish shops you can get fish and eels. Bread shops sell many different kinds of bread and bread is shaped in different ways.

4) West Germans like a lot of sausage. You can get a lot of sausage in Hypermarkets.

5) Cake shops sell many different kinds of cake. Germany is famous for cake.

6) In West Germany open air vegetable markets are very popular. They have many different kinds of fruit and vegetables.

7) In west Germany you can get milk from shops but many people get milk from the dairy store to get it.

8) West Germans like a lot of beer. It is called the National drink in Germany they even maek childrens beer.

How the Poeple live

1) In Germany most people live in flats. Some flats are small but a lot are as big as a small one storey house. If you did get a house you would have a fair sized garden.

2) Kitchens are small but have a lot of modern things. In the flats if you had had at least two children and you lived in a flat you would have a double bunk for the children.

3) Very few German flats have caretakers so people tak turns to tidy up the flats. Gardens are quite sunny but have a lot of shade.

4) People who live in flats have a garden lot called schrebergarten. They can grow flowers and trees and vegetables.

5) Customs) People shake hands a lot more in Germany. On the new year people melt a piece of lead in an old spoon then they put the lead in a bowl of water and try and tell their fortunes. If you are the first hear the cockoo it is good luck.

6) Old German houses look like the one the in picture. They have wooden beams to make the house stronger. The old houses had very big gardens but a lot of the land has now got houses on it. Morden houses have a warander and quite large windows.

7) In mordern homes the furniture is quite mordern but some people had old furniture.

Intresting Places and People

1) Karl Benz is very famuos he invented the first morter car in 1885 it three wheels the morter was at the back. Karl Benz was very famuos. Guterburg made the first printing press. He was very famuos the writing was like this . Gutenburg was never rich he died poor. Ludwig von Beethoven was a great composer he went deaf at the age of 40. He was born in Bonn.

2) Berlin has lots of interesting places. In Munich you can see the Frauenkirche, Hall of Fame, Olypic Tower and Hofgarten. The Nymhenburg palace kings of Bavaria lived for the summer. Hofgarten is a lot of forsets and feilds. Frauenkirche is a huge hall. The Olypic tower over 50 feet tall.

3) The Berlin wall is very famous it was made to diveded Berlin into West and east Germany.

It is not difficult to see how the teacher's directions have shaped the writing. Most of the questions are bound to lead to texts which are lists of facts, and to sentences which are mainly 'relational', that is, a theme/noun is related to some descriptive category, either by the verb *to be* or *to have*; . . . *the Netherlands are west of Germany*; *Germany has only one boarder* . . .; *Kitchens are small but have a lot* . . .; etc. Generally where the child departs from the format of the directions the sentence syntax becomes more varied. There, different clause-types emerge, interpersonal forms appear, and the structure of speech reasserts itself: *If you go to Berlin you can go and see The Branden Gate it is a huge archway you can see The Olympic Stadium*; *Karl Benz is very famuos he invented the first morter car in 1885 it (had) three wheels the morter was at the back*. The teacher's directions have a number of effects which are significant in the development of writing and in the learning of genre. The child is forced to construct texts of a non-narrative kind, and from the examples here it is clear that she finds this a problem. Most of the answers remain lists. However, the pressure exerted by the teacher's demands will force the child to attempt a solution of the problem. So, for instance, paragraph 6 under 'How the people live' is showing signs of competent textual structure.

The teacher's directions also draw the child's attention to the category of fact, and its presentation in writing. Among other linguistic features, the distinction between fact and 'story' is marked here by sentence type and by tense. 'Factual sentences' use the verbs *to be* and *to have* predominantly, and use the present tense. The non-factual sentences use a range of verbs, the past tense, and interpersonal forms such as *you*. Hence the directions act as a prod for the child to attempt solutions to a number of textual, and ultimately cognitive, problems. They provide the suggestion for the content of the different mini-chapters; but in providing the content they also act to make content focal in the text, and so both author and addressee recede in the writing. This, of course, is the beginning of typical 'scientific' or perhaps 'academic' writing, where the ideology of objectivity demands that reference to an author or experimenter should be deleted.

The next set of texts includes some which I have already discussed to some extent in Chapters 3 and 4. I introduce them once more to demonstrate the points just made and, in addition, to draw attention not only to the effect of the teacher's instructions (the chapter-headings are derived from or are direct echoes of these) but also to the effect of actual written generic models. In this case the brief histories above act as models. They were themselves written by amateur historians, citizens of this small community of about a thousand people, who in their turn were not trained in the academic discipline of history and are therefore feeling their way in the use of historical writing. Furthermore, in this case the child writer also wrote a piece of relatively free writing. That is, she wanted to include a story which would indicate what the experience and the quality of life was for a child at that time. This text therefore forms an interesting contrast to the solicited and guided writing of the rest of the project.

Text 29

Mylor
(a school project)

1   Mylor was first settled in 1874 when gold was found at Biggs
     Flat originally Gum Flat for its gums. Mylor was originally
     on the route to Melbourn. In 1885 a few blocks of land were
     sold to people. Around 1890 Mylor was a township. A settler
     who came from Cornwall liked Gum Flat so much that he
     changed the name to Mylor in favour of his home town
     Mylor Bridge he was Sir James Boucaut. It was found that
     most of Mylor was settled around the Onkaparingar and
     other rivers and creeks. Dairys, frams, gardens and orchards

were the main ways of getting money in Mylor except gold
minning. The most well known person who lived in Mylor
was Goyder.

2   The earlyestx earliest settlers I know of are:- Messrs. C. Arnd,
A. Aitken, C. Fleetwood, W. Hawthorne, B. Hope, J. Lappidge,
C. Meredith, W. Nicholls, W & J. Porteus. I don't know their
dates but I think most of them are 1880. Most of them were
in the center of Mylor. Onex last ones Mr. Goyder and
Sir James Boucut.

3   A lot of the people came because of gold. The first piece of
gold that I know of was found in 1873 I don't know who
found it though. Another reason was that Mylor had a
beautiful setting and plenty of housing and fencing matrail.
The last reason I know of is it was under Goyder's Line and
had plenty of good land for dairys and faax farms. Mylor was
planned in 1891 by Sir James P. Boucaut. Mylor is an
abbreviation of St. Mellior.

4   Building Material
The building materail was very simple because Mylor has lots
of gold mines they soon found that stone was available in lots
of placese and easy to get.
   Another comonx common building material was wood
because the amount of tressx trees around Mylor most of the
land around was full of tressx trees and they were easy to get.
   But they needed xsomething to lx put inbetween the stone
and wood they found mud but you could only get it in the
winter so they looked harder then they found clay which was
the best.

5   Why did More People Come.
More people cam because of all the gold lots of gold came
from the hills and people needed money.
   Another reason was that Mylor had plenty of water and
building material.
   The last reason was the good land you could grow lots of
good things in the hills and life stock had plenty to eat.

6   Why did so many people die.
Lots of people died in the early days because they didn't
care about cleaness and germs.
   Most children died of coughs, cuts, diarrhoea, scarlet
fever, small pox, chickenpox and mumps.

They didn't have any antiseptic or bandaids so cuts got
very infected and people soon died.

7   The First Church

Earlyx erx Earliest church I know of was built in 1894 it was
built of stone, tiles, glass and clay the altar had a eglax egx
eagle where the book went it could take 50 people it had
two sermons on Sunday. They were able to keep it going
because of the money people gave.

8   Who was Goyder

Most people think that Goyder was the founder of Mylor
but he wasn't. He was South Austrial's surgver genral
Surveyor General. The drainage of the South East and the
planting of Pinus Radiata. It was recommended by him.
Mr. Goyder lived at Warrakilla an old coaching Inn he got
it in 1879. He liked the coachix country so much that he
didn't mind taking the daylyx trip daily.

Goyders house is realy two in one the oriagnal was built
in 1842. In 1880 Goyder bought the house and named it
Warrakilla.

9   The Bx Pioneer Boy

The boy I am writing about is called Sam he lived in the gold
fields of Biggs Flat. Well things wern't going to well forthe Lam
family they were very poor. The night before Sam heard them
taking of leaving and Sam didn't like that and went to bed crying.
He had lots of freinds in the gold feilds his father had a mine
shaft but got no gold. The next day it was Sam's turn to go down
the mine shaft. He was told to dig in the same place he didn't.
Sam soon found his father was sick he had to go down the mine
shaft. So Sam didx hex dug in his place he soon saw a glitter.
He saw it was fools gold but that ment gold near. The next day
Sam went down he dug he found a pile of gold dust and put it
in the bucket he pulled himself up and found he did not only
have gold dust but a lump of gold from that day on the Lams
were neaver poor again. The piece of gold was called the
Sitting Lady.
The
    n
    d

The first 'chapter' in this project clearly illustrates the development of the impersonal style. It contains seven agentless passives, typical of impersonal, academic writing. There isn't a single slip into a personal style, which is not completely so with most of the other chapters in the project. The first sentence is surprisingly complex, both in syntax, with a series of subordinated and embedded clauses modifying each noun in succession, and in terms of its stylistic arrangement of content. The sentence is still a mini-narrative, but now the elements of the narrative are syntactically closely integrated to form one complex single whole: a statement about Mylor. The elements of the 'narrative' are: (i) Mylor was first settled in 1874; (ii) because (?) at that time gold was found at Biggs Flat; (iii) which was originally (called) Gum Flat; (iv) it was so called because of its gums. The constituent elements of this 'narrative' are, however, no longer in sequential order; that is, the writer is here using an order other than sequence to organize her material. This order derives from the relative significance which she has attached to each element in the 'narrative'. The rest of the text is similarly freed from dependence on sequence to provide coherence. All in all it gives a prospect of Mylor 'in the round'. Interestingly, a picture accompanies the text on the opposite page in the project book, and it represents a highly schematic view of Biggs Flat, with the various occupations and major geographical features depicted around the edge of the page, and goldmining taking place in the centre of the picture. The conceptual model which the child had in mind here was quite clearly to provide a bird's-eye and all-embracing view of the little settlement.

The second chapter in this series clearly provided some problems for the writer. She does not seem to have command of the appropriate genre for presenting 'lists'. She feels that an answer to the question 'Who were the earliest settlers of Mylor?' should consist of more than a mere list of names; but she is not sure how this could or should be organized. Chapter 3 seems to have presented similar problems: 'Why did people come to Mylor' does not seem to call for a 'story', and yet it seems to call for more than a list. In the teacher's mind the question may have been similar to 'When was Mylor first settled?'; that is, she expected a similar kind of response from the child. However, while the child seems to have no problems visualizing a range of activities and events around the question of settlement (a question implicitly about 'living in a place'), she seems to have some problems finding an organizing order for the question 'Why did people come to Mylor?' Her answer therefore becomes a list, items being dragged into the list with a some-what cavalier disregard for their relevance.

The implications are important: three questions which seem, on the face of it, similar in content, implication and evocativeness, 'When was Mylor first settled?', 'Who were the earliest settlers?', 'Why did people come to Mylor?', produce quite different responses from the child. In retrospect, it can be seen that the first of these lends itself to a fuller, more discursive treatment. The others produce lists, and while a more accomplished writer would have been able to disguise the list, it would have been more difficult to produce a text that wasn't in some essential respect a list. The teacher's questions therefore guide, and to a large extent determine, the kind of text the child can or will produce. As with the project on West Germany, it would be quite wrong to see the teacher and her set of instructions as being at fault. For the teacher is attempting precisely to produce something quite like this effect: she wants to confront the child with the problem of writing objectively, factually, descriptively, to produce an expository genre. If there is 'fault', it lies in the absence of any direct teaching of the generic forms. But here the fault lies with linguistics rather than with teachers, for linguistics has only very recently begun the task of providing characterizations of genres.

'Building Materials' is more personal in form; this is due to the absence of agentless passives. Instead of these the child prefers to use the unspecified agent *they* (*they needed something to put* instead of *something was needed to put* . . .) and the indefinite unspecific pronoun *you* (*you could only get it* . . .). The latter is a more personal form in that *they* refers to the first settlers specifically, while *you* refers to anyone faced with this problem and consequently includes the con-temporary reader as an addressee. Chapters 5 and 6 have similar features to those of 4. Chapter 6 contains an explanation directed at the con-temporary reader, *They didn't have any antiseptic* . . ., aimed at convincing the reader. The focus of the text therefore shifts from the topic under discussion to the reader. This uncertainty and shift in focus is still a characteristic of writing at this stage in the learning of genre. By the age of twelve or so that has become less marked, though in Text 12, 'Beaked Whales', that characteristic can still be noticed.

Text 15, the piece of imaginative writing, shows no such problems. The writer establishes her authorial position, *The boy I am writing about* . . ., and from there she simply tells the story, focusing on the topic, the boy, all the time, without betraying her role as narrator or addressing the audience overtly. It seems therefore that the problem for the child is not that of being able to keep one topic in focus; clearly she can do that. The problem seems rather that she is highly conscious that the task is to focus on the topic under discussion, and it is the consciousness of the task of writing objectively that causes her the problems.

Although these chapters show the development towards objective writing, being 'historical' they have many affinities with narrative. For one thing, the texts are written throughout in the past tense. The use of the past tense makes an event specific and particular; because it has happened (no matter how many times) it is not happening now, consequently it is not general, not the case at all times. The past tense is therefore not suitable for establishing general, universally applicable cases or rules. In the texts just discussed the child is showing signs of achieving generality, not by the use of tense, but by the use of the generalizing pronouns *they* and particularly *you*. That is, an event may be general either because it happens at all times or because it happens to everyone without distinction. The former demands the use of the so-called universal present tense; the latter demands the use of the most general pronoun, *you*. In Text 12, 'Beaked Whales', both the universal present tense and the general pronoun *you* are used.

Text 12

Beaked Whales

(1) The Beaked Whales *live* out in mid-ocean, where the tasty squid *are* found. (2) Squid, it *seems, provide* most of their meals. (3) Men do not *know* much about their family because even the scientists who *study* whales *have* seen very few Beaked Whales. (4) Generally members of this family *have* long, narrow snouts, or 'beaks' . . . (11) It *is* unusual in colour, so if *you* should *see* one, *you* should be able to recognize it . . . (15) *You* may possibly *see* one . . .

In addition, agentless passives are prominent in this text, which fits into the generalizing tendency of the text, as the agentless passive implies (among other things) that the event happens irrespective of the agent who performs the action. The child here uses three generalizing strategies: (i) universal present, which implies that the actions or events happen at all times; (ii) the general pronoun *you* (usually as experiencer or object of the action), which implies that the actions or events happen irrespective of the involved participants; (ii) the use of agentless passives, which implies that the specific causer or agent of the event or action is immaterial to the happening of an event. So while the *you* is not part of the adult genre of scientific writing, the strategy which leads to its use here is certainly quite appropriate. In its final form this genre leads to the complete deletion of (reference to) self, of (reference to) the addressee, and of (reference to) any point of specific detail. The attention is focused solely on the object, whose properties are presented as universally the case and timeless, hence always valid.

It is in these characteristics that the major difference between objective, expository, scientific writing and narrative resides. 'The Pioneer Boy' presents the complete antithesis of what is demanded: while fictional, it is specific from all these points of view.

The cognitive implications of the development and achievement of this genre by a child are immense. The self is quite negated in such writing (as it can never be in narrative, particularly oral narrative) and all attention is focused on the object and its properties. The genre itself encodes a view of knowledge which negates the human producers of knowledge, and indeed reifies knowledge as a timeless, universal category, independent of the human subject/producer. Text 17, 'The Cockpit', already discussed in Chapters 3 and 4, is a good example of such writing.

Text 17

The Cockpit

(1) The crew of a modern jet airliner must have all the information they need at their finger tips, so a great amount of work goes into designing the best possible flight deck control panels. (2) The captain and the first officer each must have controls for flying the plane, and there is an automatic pilot for routine flying.

(3) Basic flight instruments are on the panel in front of each pilot. (4) On the panel between them are the engine throttles and gauges, radio and navigation equipment and things like the parking brake.

(5) The flight engineer has his own instrument panel behind the pilots.

The writer has used the universal present tense as the main generalizing, universalizing feature. There is no addressing of the reader, no *you* or *they*, and the crew have become objects too. Human actions are turned into nominal entities: *designing, controls, routine flying*. All this suggests that real command of this genre lies less in being able to use all the universalizing linguistic strategies and forms than in being able to make do with as few of them as possible.

iii Narratives

The development of the objective, scientific genres implies one extreme of the development of 'point of view', namely where all points of view coincide in the objectively factual description or account, in other words, where the individual viewer has disappeared because he no longer matters. The path to this point leads from the viewerless description (Text 21, 'The Ant'), via the explicit presence of the viewer and the audience (as, for instance, in the Mylor project, Text 29, *The earliest settlers I know of* . . . ; . . . *I don't know* . . . *their dates but I think* . . . ; *the last reason I know* . . . ; or in Text 28, *You can go and see* . . . *if you go to Berlin* . . .), and uncertain mixed stages (Text 12, 'Beaked Whales'), to the viewerless stage. Narrative, interestingly, describes a similar path. Early narratives tend not to have a narrator present: Texts 20 and 22, 'The Two Poor People' and 'Father Christmas', have no overtly present narrator. When children begin to write about their own experiences they do introduce a narrator, usually the child himself or herself, or a *we* which includes the child and some others. (See, for instance, Text 33, 'The Fishing Trip'; Text 8, 'Going to the Shops'; or Text 27, 'Red Rover'.) Such stories necessarily have a single point of view, that of the invisible narrator as in 'The Two Poor People', or that of the present but unselfconscious narrator as in 'Red Rover'. These two types are alike in that the presence or absence of the narrator is not at issue, and is not an issue. The child writer is not conscious of the role of narrator, and so the narrator is absent equally in both types as far as the child writer is concerned. The difference between the two types lies in the fact that the story with the present narrator includes an *I* or a *we* as the *speaker*, and therefore it opens up the possibility of a *you* or *they* as speakers in the story also. It opens the door for the introduction of the 'other' in the narrative. In a story such as 'The Two Poor People' different characters speak; but they are all 'others', so that the role of 'other' does not exist in that text as a conscious opposition to the 'self'.

Consequently the narrative in which the narrator appears is significant from a developmental point of view. Text 14, 'Our Trip to Ayers House', shows the possibilities.

Text 14

Our Trip to Ayers House

(1) On Friday 1st July we all got in the bus and waved to Miss Martyn. (2) We're off I thought, there was lots of merry talk in the bus. (3) Tracey was telling some people that the bus would pass her house 'there it is' said Tracey but it soon went by. (4) We soon were there. (5) When we had got out of the bus Mrs. Gilbert said to sketch the front of Ayers House. (6) When I had finished my sketch I looked at some of the other sketches. (7) I thought Prue's was the best.

In fact this child's use of the narrator's *I* is already quite complex, for she distinguishes between the objective *we* (not a 'speaking' *we* as it is in *Last Saturday we went on a fishing trip*, but a *we* in which the author appears without special status) and the narrator's *I*: . . . *we all got in the bus* . . . , . . . *I thought* . . . The whole event is seen through this *I* of the narrator, which is the reader's viewpoint too. Within this the writer can take a number of stances; from a report of her own mental processes, . . . *I thought* . . . , to the speaking voice of a character in the narrative, Tracey's *'there it is'*, to Mrs Gilbert's request *(to) sketch the front of Ayers House*. The ability to detach oneself from the object perceived and described, and to view it objectively, is of great cognitive significance. It is clear that certain of these narrative skills are quite akin to the skills of objective writing in scientific texts as described above. There is a greater continuity between the two kinds of writing activity than is sometimes supposed on the scientific and the humanistic sides of the pedagogic fence.

The conscious incorporation of others' speech into the child's own text is another significant development illustrated in this text. It occurs in two ways: the speech is either directly taken into the text, and marked off as 'other text' by the quotation marks, *'here it is'*, or it is incorporated conceptually and syntactically into the writer's text, so that its otherness is no longer apparent. In 'Our Trip to Ayers House' the other's speech has become an embedded clause in one case, *Mrs. Gilbert said to sketch the front of Ayers House*, and a subordinated clause in the other, *Tracey was telling some people that the bus would pass her house*. The ability to assimilate other speech leads to the possibility of assimilating other knowledge. Cognitively and conceptually this development has immense implications and potential, for in effect it allows the child to apprehend another's thought or perception and make it her own, as a conscious step to assimilate and make use of someone else's knowledge. With the conscious control over one's own and other people's knowledge comes the possibility of genuine advance not only in personal but in social knowledge.

The affinities between this process in narrative and the same process in the development of scientific modes of work are no doubt obvious, but may, because of their very obviousness, be overlooked. On a somewhat more mundane level the process may help to explain the problems which children experience with the dreaded notion of plagiarism. In narrative it is perfectly acceptable to incorporate others' speech, others' text, others' thought into one's own. In scientific writing it is not, and elaborate devices have been constructed to protect the ownership of text and of idea, and the possibility of their use by others. I am not suggesting that we should abandon the clear distinction between own and other text; on the contrary, I am suggesting that because children are aware of the distinction — as displayed in their narrative writing — we should draw on that knowledge to enable them to cope with the demands of scientific writing. Paradoxically, it is of course the spoken or unspoken demand that children should internalize knowledge, and produce 'their own ideas', which leads to the problems over plagiarism. In narrative writing no such demands are made, and children have no problems with making — and marking — the distinction.

As well as different personal viewpoints, Text 14 also has different temporal viewpoints. There is the narrator's present from which point the story is told, in the past tense. Occasionally the writer establishes further temporal layerings within the past, by means of a step from the past perfective form to the simple past: *When we had got out of the bus Mrs. Gilbert said to sketch . . .*; *When I had finished my sketch I looked . . .* 'My Ambition in Life' (discussed in Chapter 4) shows a different temporal viewpoint, from the narrator's present to a time in the future, or to a predicted state.

An additional complexity is introduced when children begin to separate the two narrative roles of protagonist/hero and narrator. At first the two are joined, but by about the age of eleven or twelve they can begin to separate. In the next story this is beginning to happen: the narrator knows something that the protagonist in the story does not know. The writer is twelve years old.

Text 30

Mystery Story

I was watching T.V. when suddenly the lights flickered and went out.

'Oh, a power failure' I said to my self and went to get a candle.

Our next door neighbour's dog Donna was barking (she thinks that her home is at our place so she lives here all the time except for meals), so I went to see what it was.

When I was outside I found Donna lying on her side not moving at all. At first I thought she was dead, but then I noticed she was breathing, she must have been drugged.

The self/protagonist here clearly does not know 'the truth', which necessarily the narrator does in order to create a mystery story. Cognitively this implies that the child is able to work with different levels of explanation; the implication for work on a theoretical level generally is obvious. Not only does it suggest the ability to consider different explanations held by different individuals, and a hierarchy of adequacy of explanation, it also suggests the ability to deal with phenomena at a meta-level: one order of explanation at one level is accounted for, overridden and explained at a higher level. 'Life in the Goldfields', Text 31, shows the same phenomenon, more clearly displayed through the narrative 'errors' which the child is making in the attempt to keep the two levels discrete.

Text 31

Life in the Goldfields

(1) One day my mum and I went to Ballarat. (2) We went to Ballarat to dig for gold because we were poor. (3) So we started

digging for gold in the goldfields in Ballarat. (4) We didn't
struck gold the first, second, and third day at Ballarat. (5) But on
the fourth day we struck gold. (6) We struck two nuggets of gold.
(7) When we made sure that it was gold we packed our bags and
pulled our tent down and went back to Adelaide. (8) When we
got back to Adelaide and took it home and hid it. (9) I hid it
in the closet where my shirts are and I put it in one of the shirt
pockets. (10) When I was putting the gold in the pocket till
Monday my next door neighbour was looking through the
window. (11) So when I was for an hour she came in and said
'Did you get any gold' I said 'Yes'. (12) 'Where is it'. (13) 'I hid
it'. (14) Then when I went to bed about 10:00 PM I checked
to see if the gold was there and it was. (15) So I went to bed.
(16) Then my next door neighbour came in the house and took
the gold. (17) Then when I got up in the morning I went to see
(the) if the gold was (still) not there. (18) So I called my mum.

Sentence 10 shows the knowledge of the protagonist in the story,
as do 11 to 15. Sentence 16 clearly demonstrates the narrator's knowledge. The two levels of awareness lead the writer into some problems
in constructing the climax and the resolution of the story. Sentence 17
shows a correction he made, deleting *the*: it seems the writer was going
to put ... *I got up in the morning to see the gold was gone.* He realizes
that this implies and presupposes knowledge on the part of the protagonist which he cannot have, and so he changes it to ... *to see if the
gold was still gone.* Of course, this continues the same problem, made
worse by *still* with its presupposition of knowledge of the activity over
a long period. He crosses out the *still* and continues the sentence as it
is in the text. The final version has not resolved the problem, for the
negative calls up in the reader's mind the unnegated form ... *to see
the gold was not there.* This little example demonstrates the two aspects
of the problem rather neatly: how to suppress knowledge held at one
level, that of the narrator, from expression at another level, that of the
protagonist, that is, how to separate levels of knowledge and explanation;
and how to construct the two discrete roles of narrator and protagonist.
The latter is more a linguistic problem, the former more a cognitive
problem, though the two are inextricably interwoven.

As I suggested earlier, an important element in this development is
the introduction, in various forms, of speech (both the narrator's and
others') into the text. Dialogue included in the writing shows the highest

development, and ultimately this leads to a separate genre, drama. The development of ideas in exchange, in dialogue, discussion or confrontation has cognitive and conceptual implications. Here is one brief example, written by a fourteen-year-old girl:

Text 32

Confrontations

Grandmother: You been out with that young boy from down that lane, don't you think you are too young?

Caron: Yes I have been out with that boy down the lane and I don't think I'm too young, my friend started going out with boys long before me.

Grandmother: I don't care about your friend, I'm talking about you, you're getting too big for your boots my young lady.

Caron: I haven't got any boots, I care about my friends, anyway, mum don't mind me going out with boys.

Grandmother: Your mother says she don't mind but she do you know, she don't like you going out with him no more than I do.

Caron: Well grandmother I'm going out with him whatever.

Grandmother: You're out every night, you're never at home with us are you?

Caron: It don't matter about that, mum don't mind.

Grandmother: Mum don't mind, how do you know? You're never here to find out what she mind.

Caron: Oh I see you don't care about people's feelings, at least not mine. I've got to go now anyway, 'that boy' as you say is coming.
(She goes.)

Grandmother: That's right, run off with him, don't mind about me, how left out I feel. They are nice when they're little, but when they're bigger they don't care any more about your feelings. That's right, go, go and leave me, alone.

(The verb-forms are typical of the writer's dialect, Suffolk English.)

It may perhaps be too grand an analogy, but cognitively and conceptually this represents two differing views of the 'same' reality, and a theory to deal with it is being arrived at dialectically. Paradoxically this form represents a return to speech in its full form, though now dealt with in a highly controlled and self-conscious manner. Indeed, this emergence of a conscious and distanced attitude to speech is one of the most significant aspects in the development of narrative. First, by bringing speech into a written text its otherness to writing becomes evident, either because it is brought in directly and appears unlike writing in its structure, or because the writer has to make a conscious effort to adapt and modify speech to make it like writing, as in indirect speech or in syntactically fully integrated speech. By the time a child writer can produce a text such as 'Confrontations' the two forms and their possibilities have become distinct, separate, discrete for the child.

Finally I wish to draw attention to another aspect in the development of narrative, which again has great affinities with the development of technical and scientific writing. In the development of certain forms of narrative one of the major achievements is the effacing of the narrator. The writing is fictional, subjective, but attempts to present itself as factual and objective. Below is such an example; the writer is a fourteen-year-old boy.

Text 19

Kingies!
of the rocks

(1) John cast out his killer lure, Brian and Clive followed.
(2) John's President reel, Brian's Daiwo reel and Clive's Abu reel, hummed as their gears meshed and ratchets clicked, their lures swimming across the white foamy water.
    (3) They swam powerfully towards the small bait-fish, gradually coming closer to the rock wall; the Kingfish were hungry.
(4) Casting out and cranking their reels, the men's arms grew tired. (5) The fish rose. (6) They took off with the lures, jumping, weaving, ducking, diving all in vain to get rid of the lure they had taken so much trouble to catch. (7) They stopped at about 200yds from the rock-wall. (8) The men engaged the reels, gaining line and tiring the fish, the fish being dragged and then in a desperate bid to free the hook, shaking their heads and making pitiful runs. (9) They were exhausted and could fight no more.
    (10) All the fish felt the gaff where it had stabbed them and the sugar bag that was coiled around them hurt even more. ~~but~~

(11) Relief was few and far between when the bag was opened up and another fish piled on top.

(12) Brian claimed the world record and Clive and John world records in line to fish ratio weights. (13) A good ~~sun~~ Sunday's fishing.

In achieving the effect of the absent narrator and of the absent perceiver the writer uses a number of linguistic devices. Generally they all tend in one direction, that is, to make things seem obviously or naturally present and known, without question. For instance, in English one of the uses of the definite article is to indicate that an object is 'known' to both speaker/writer and hearer/reader, either because it has previously been talked about or because it is just generally well known. In this text the writer uses the definite article when the reader does not know the object, either through previous mention or in some other way: ... *the white foaming water* ..., ... *closer to* the *rock wall*, ... *the men's arms* ..., ... *the gaff* ..., ... *the small bait-fish* ... The effect of this strategy is to assume, to take for granted, that writer and reader share the same knowledge, which does not need to be publicly discussed but can be taken for granted. Hence the reader is treated as though he or she were part of the group (to whom the writer also belongs) for whom such knowledge can be assumed. This verbal trick establishes a community of writer and reader, a feeling of being insiders, and of complicity.

The writer's use of pronouns has the same effect: usually a pronoun is used when its referent is clearly known or established: *The tea was cold.* *It had been poured twenty minutes ago.* In 'Kingies' the writer works against the convention: *They swam powerfully* ..., *the Kingfish were hungry. Casting out and cranking their reels, the men's arms* ... The effect is both to draw the reader in and also to make the reader assume, if only for a moment, that he knows what is being talked about even before the pronoun referent is identified. Participles are used in the same manner; these are forms where the verb occurs without its subject – ... *casting out* ..., ... *cranking in* ... – which is identified afterwards. The child writer's efforts go beyond these devices. In causal terms, most of the actions are presented as being self-caused or uncaused (employing neither the powers nor the regularity model of causality, discussed below in Chapter 7): *their gears meshed* ..., *their lures swimming* ..., *they swam powerfully* ..., *they took off* ... In using this syntax the child presents a world where 'things just happen, of themselves'. Men, fish, gear are all treated as being the same from the

point of view of causal powers. The fact that no overt causal connections or original causes are established, and yet these things happen,
again produces the effect of a world where such things are not the
subject of questions, because they are known by everyone who is
inward with the world.

Clearly, the absent narrator has worked very hard indeed to establish
his absence. And he has done the same with his audience: they are
nowhere addressed, and yet they are assumed to be completely known
and therefore present in every facet of the language. This represents an
interesting reversal of the starting point in the child's development of
narrative. When children first start writing, they are quite unselfconscious
of their role as narrator. So while the surface of the text has signs of the
narrator everywhere, from the child writer's point of view there is no
narrator present. When children have learned to write they are fully
conscious of their role as narrator. So while the surface of the text may
show no signs of the narrator, from the child's point of view the narrator
is everywhere present. In the same way, child writers may be quite
unaware of any audience when they first write: the needs of a specific
audience are not an issue, and hence are not met. When children have
learned to write, they are fully aware of their audience, whose needs
are acknowledged and met in the text the child produces. At this stage
the audience may not be addressed overtly, but their presence is everywhere felt in the text; it is constructed for and around the perceived
needs and demands of the audience. On the surface, the starting point
and the finishing point have much in common; underneath, the two are
clear, neat and complete inversions of each other.

iv The mastery of genre and its cognitive and social effects

Learning language is learning one of the most highly developed rule-
systems. Every utterance we make is based on pre-existent rules; the
uses of utterances are also rule-governed. These rules constrain what
may be said, and where it may be said. Learning language can therefore
be regarded as the learning of cliché. Learning genres is no exception to
this — it represents the child's socialization into appropriate and
accepted modes of organizing knowledge, of knowing, and the modes
of representing perceptions and knowledge to others. The learning of
genre is therefore intimately linked with the codification of knowledge
in a society, and with modes of organizing and communicating

information to others. This represents a vast convenience to society and no doubt to individuals. If our modes of establishing, encoding, organizing and transmitting knowledge differed markedly from individual to individual, there is no doubt that society would be quite different, and probably far less efficient. However, it is important to recognize, first, that the genres have this constraining effect and, second, that they are conventions. Other conventions can be imagined; indeed, it is one of the main points of this book that children constantly invent their own modes of organizing and knowing, which do not, however, become recognized as such but rather are categorized as errors.

Society rests on a vast network of conventions, and while these conventions are arbitrary when considered in isolation, they are not arbitrary within the context of any specific society. For instance, the genre of scientific writing, with its insistence on suppressing any mention of the individual, ties into the larger social construct of science, with its vast theoretical, ideological, technological, economic and political ramifications. It is no accident that the scientific texts of Western societies have the linguistic features and characteristics that they do. A recognition of this fact reveals that the teaching of genre has great social and ideological effects. If this seems overstated, consider carefully the language of newspaper editorials, office memos, regulations, instructions, advertisements, bills, and so on. The child is being socialized into the structures and value-systems of his or her society. These value-systems and structures are only weakly implicit in any one genre or instance of a generic type. But the message is so constant in the learning of writing and in reading that it is all the more effective for being subtle, covert, and constantly insistent.

Such a view of genre should serve to give some pause to the demands for creativity often imposed on children in school, explicitly or implicitly. The language forms, the grammar are given; the generic forms in which they join to form larger, organized and integrated wholes are also given. No single individual is likely to create a new genre. Where then exists the possibility for creativity? At what stage can creativity become a legitimate demand anyway, given that the years up to the age of fourteen at least are spent in learning the conventions? Should mastery of the conventions be sufficient?

Genres have ideological and cognitive content. It may be legitimate to ask whether this content should become the focus of teaching. An official memo in itself, a generic type, has specific content quite apart from its overt message. It will say something about the lines of communication in an organization, something about power and its distribution, something about the hierarchical position of the recipient and the sender of the memo in the organization, and so forth. To become proficient in the genre one has to become absorbed into and accepting of these contents, and of the institution itself. Effective teaching of genres can make the individual into an efficiently intuitive, and unreflecting, user of the genre. The genre and its meanings will come to dominate the individual just when the individual feels that he has come to a command of the genre, and this is so whether he be scientist, technical writer, bureaucrat or short-story writer. The genre will construct the world for its proficient user. Is that what we want? The question is bound up with the whole larger question of the aims, purposes, functions of language education in schools. How many school-leavers will be called on to become 'creative' users of language? How many will be called on to become creative users of the genres which are most highly valued in the school, the 'poetic' or literary genres? One might reset the aims of language education more modestly, more realistically and more usefully to give students skills in the use and manipulation of language, to give them a fuller understanding of the manifold meanings of language and of the genres with which they will come into contact.

v   Sources and context

The study of genre has a long history in literary criticism. However, much of the work is so specific — focusing on a particular kind of poem, for instance — that it has relevance to this chapter only at the most general level. I have used the term 'genre' in a quite non-technical and non-specific way: 'mode of writing' might have been a better term. However, these 'modes of writing' are the early versions of what will become the specific genres, and to that extent they *are* the genres at the early stages that I am dealing with. My use of the term 'sentence' is quite analogous: early sentences have little in common with their adult counterparts; nevertheless they *are* sentences for the child at that point.

My discussion is influenced by the developments in discourse analysis, text-linguistics, and in French structuralist work. An example of the former is Malcolm Coulthard's *Introduction to Discourse Analysis* (1977). The foremost exponent of text-linguistics has been Teun van Dijk, whose *Text and Context* (1977) provides a statement of the position. Michael Halliday and Ruqaiya Hasan's *Cohesion in English* (1976) has been of fundamental importance in the study of discourse. M. Foucault's *Archeology of Knowledge* (1974) includes a paper, 'Orders of Discourse', which provides fundamental insights into the status, functions and effects of discourse.

Chapter 6
Linguistic and conceptual development: conjoined sentence structures

i Linguistic form and its cognitive implications

In the preceding chapters I have assumed more or less implicitly that there is a link between linguistic form and cognitive processes. There is nothing new about this assumption, though normally the link between language and thought, or language and cognition, is discussed at the level of word-meanings, through concern with topics such as concept-formation, rather than at the level of syntax or of genre. While the importance of the link has never been in question, its status has always remained hypothetical, for it has been possible to interpret the evidence either way. Over the last two decades the significance of the putative link has become heightened because of the shifting of this question into the social domain as a question about possible links between socially differentiated forms of language — social dialects — and cognitive processes.

Consequently two questions now remain to be answered: the initial question, 'Is there a link between language and cognition?', and the other, more urgent question, 'Do socially differentiated forms of the one language give rise to distinctly differing cognitive modes?' In other words, do social dialects have their own distinct grammars, or do they share the one grammar with merely insignificant alterations?

Two distinctly different answers have been put forward. One, associated with the work of Labov, suggests that while the dialects do show surface differences in form, they draw on the same underlying set of rules, and it is these rules which carry meaning. The other answer, associated with the work of Bernstein, suggests that the differences in form displayed by social dialects are significant at every level, both at the level of the form of the utterance, and at that of the grammatical system. For Labov the theoretical underpinning derives from the deep structure/surface structure distinction of a version of transformational grammar current in the mid-1960s. (For documentation see Section vi of this chapter.) In such a grammar, surface differences of related syntactic forms can be taken back to a common underlying deep structural origin. The transformational rules which account for the difference in surface form are regarded as making no contribution to meaning. Hence there are two sets of rules: rules of formation (of the deep structure), which create meaningful forms, and rules of transformation, which lead to the varying surface forms and do not contribute to meaning. Social dialects can then be seen to share the sub-set of rules of formation, and to differ in the rules of transformation (both syntactic and phonological) which lead to the differing surface forms. To the extent that they do not contribute to meaning, the transformational rules would have no cognitive effect or implications; such effects remain with the rules of formation. Speakers of different social dialects are therefore seen to share the same (significant) grammar, and, by implication, the same cognitive processes. To put it in terms of an example: the two different social dialect forms *He done that real good* and *He did that very well* would derive from the same underlying set of grammatical rules, which had generated the one underlying form (something like noun-phrase + verb-phrase [consisting of: [verb + modifier] + noun-phrase]). Differing rules of transformation would then lead to the respective surface forms.

What implications does such a position have for the language of children, and for their learning of writing? Either we can assume that the same theoretical principles apply to the differences between the language use of children and that of adults, or alternatively we can assume that the child's learning of language constitutes a quite different theoretical field, where this theoretical assumption has no application. To my knowledge, the latter position is not seriously advocated. The former is, however. Clearly it is the case that children do, at different ages, use different forms of language, both in speech and in writing. According to this theory we would be unable to draw any inferences from their language about differences between their cognitive processes and those of adults. The difference in language form might be, like the social dialect difference, merely of the surface and based on the same deep grammar. It might be, for instance, that children have not yet learned all or some of the rules of transformation. But as these contribute no meaning to the linguistic form, this would not point to a cognitive difference between adult and child.

A major problem with this view — and indeed with the theory on which it is founded — is that it posits a set of rules in the grammar which have no meaning, or no semantic effect. That is, the application of such rules may lead to different surface structures from one underlying structure, but no significance attaches to these differences in form. Cognitively, the implication is similarly that the learning of a set of (highly complex) rules which operate on structures to transform them into different structures has no effect. This seems counter-intuitive. Pragmatically it is the case that the application of a particular transformational rule is motivated on textual or contextual grounds, so that the meaning of the rule can be said to be that contextual meaning which the speaker needed to express over and above the meaning of the untransformed structure.

At any rate, within this view, differences in cognitive mode can arise on the basis of a different grammar, of the rules of transformation and formation taken together. In children's learning of language this would apply, for instance, where the child learns a new rule of formation, a rule which had not previously existed in the child's grammar. So if adult grammar contains n rules, then the child's language at a given stage might contain $n - x$. This could and would lead to cognitive differences. For instance, while such a view would see no distinction between the two dialect forms cited above, it would make a distinction between a grammar which had rules for sentence-embedding and one which did not. The distinction between a chaining and an embedding syntax would, for example, be a real and significant difference within this theoretical position.

The second theoretical position mentioned at the beginning of this chapter attributes significance to difference at all levels. Bernstein has not formulated his theories within a particular linguistic framework (although some of his co-workers have worked within a systemic-functional grammar). One theory underlying such a position sees the speaker/writer as commanding (or learning to command) a grammar, which gives him or her the potential to mean and express the range of meaning made available in the grammar. These are coded in systems of semantic, syntactic, phonological (including intonational) and lexical choices. The speaker or writer is thus seen as having systems of options available to him in the grammar, systems which are themselves composed of systems of options. A path taken through such a network of systems, exercising choice at those points where it exists, leads ultimately to the expression of the speaker's meanings in structures. Looking at structure within such a theory means that in considering each structural element one is considering a series of choices (often of different kinds) made by the speaker or writer; that is, the structure is a record of choices exercised by the writer or speaker in constructing a linguistic form.

Social dialects may be seen to differ in one or both of two ways according to this theory. They may contain differing sets of systems or of options within these systems in their respective grammars and in this way make available to the speaker different ranges of meaning options. Or they may contain the same set of systems and of options within systems as other dialects, but facilitate certain options or paths through the network of systems. To take the two examples used above, (a) *He done that real good* and (b) *He did that very well.* We might account for the two forms in this fashion. The grammar of the speaker of (a) contains two choices in the system of tense, namely *past* and *present* (if these are the appropriate labels for the two tenses here). The grammar of the speaker of (b) contains two choices in the system of tense, namely *past* and *present*, but under *past* there is another sub-system of *simple past* and *past perfect*. A diagram might clarify this:

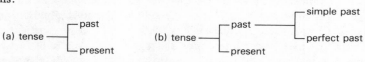

Under the system of modifiers of transitive verbs (i.e. adverbs) the grammar of speaker (a) contains *good*, which appears also as a comp- lement of the verb *to be*. The grammar of speaker (b) would not have *good* as a modifier of transitive verbs. Similarly for *real* and *very*. On this account grammars (a) and (b) are both quantitatively and qualitatively different: in this instance grammar (a) contains fewer options than grammar (b). The qualitative difference arises from the varying range of choices available in the two grammars, or the paths which are facilitated. Grammar (a) may of course contain other options under both tense and verbal complement: the speaker may simply have taken these choices, for whatever reasons. If one assumes that the choices expressed here fully represent the speaker's grammar, then it is the case either that he or she has no other options in these systems, or else that this path is highly facilitated. In either case the speaker's options for expressing tense differentiations are more restricted than those of a speaker such as (b).

The implications for children's language are clear. Differences between the formal structures of their language and that of adults point to the exercise of choices different to those of the adult, either because the grammatical system at their disposal is different, or because they have chosen to exercise different choices in a system which is like that of the adult. In either case differences of form point to differences of *choice*, and these point to differences of cognitive mode and process. Differences of form facilitate qualitatively distinctive modes of thinking.

ii Linguistic and cognitive complexity

The differences in thinking between children and adults are self-evident. However, in practice the two modes are not recognized as different modes; rather one, that of the adult, is regarded as correct, proper, appropriate, and that of the child is regarded quite simply as wrong, inappropriate, deficient. Childish modes of thinking are not regarded as alternative modes; they are simply dismissed. This is no doubt due to the greater power of the adult, the parent, teacher, aunt, neighbour. Children constantly get 'corrected', which of course implies that their actions were not simply different, but 'incorrect'. The assumed link between language and cognition means that children's language and their thinking are frequently regarded as deficient compared to those of the adult. The child may thus be the object of a misjudgment simply as a child; furthermore, as has been pointed out by Bernstein, for instance, the child may be misjudged in school because he or she comes from a social group which speaks a dialect that is qualitatively different from that which dominates in the school.

Because of these factors it is most important to attempt to understand the possible links between language and thinking, and to attempt to understand the cognitive processes which the child went through in constructing the linguistic form spoken or written. I would hope for a situation where the behaviour of children is given the same serious interpretation by adults as that of other adults. In this chapter I wish to make some suggestions about alternative ways of viewing children's writing as a means of gaining insight into a child's mind.

One may ask, for instance, whether the same seriousness of reading (in its fullest sense) is accorded to a text written by a six- or seven-year-old as is accorded to a text produced by an adult; and if not, why not? Of course, the concept of deficiency has been enshrined, theoretically, in various versions of stage-theories of development. These stages are seen as successive steps leading ultimately and necessarily to adult forms of language and cognition.

What follows is an attempt to provide some evidence and material for further discussion in these areas. On the one hand I intend to show that the child's language may be regarded as a window to the child's conceptual world; on the other I intend to draw out certain implications which follows from this approach for the 'different but equal' approach to language difference. The intention is to establish a way of reading the written texts of children which will give insight into their cognitive abilities.

The aspect of language focused on is the development of conjoined sentence structures. If we assume (somewhat loosely) that a simple sentence embodies a single idea, then the development of conjoined and ultimately complex sentence structures is a necessary prerequisite and corollary of the development of certain kinds of complex thought and expression. Conversely, an analysis of these structures may provide one source of insight into the conceptual ability that a child may have at a given stage. An analysis of pieces of text written by a child over a period of time may give insight into the child's developmental process and the stages which the child has followed. In this I do not wish to imply that we can simply 'read off' the child's cognitive structures from the linguistic utterance. Nor, indeed, do I wish to imply an isomorphism between the descriptive linguistic formalism adopted and the putative cognitive structure. This does not imply a rejection of a link between cognitive and linguistic structures. At the very least one may assume the following: (1) If the linguistic utterances are amenable to descriptions which have certain structures — if, indeed, largely similar structures are apparent in the linguistic utterances irrespective of which theoretical framework is used to provide the descriptive apparatus — then we may infer that there exists, at one level of the cognitive process, a mode of organization of (linguistic) material which bears some relationship to the structures within the description. (2) If it proves to be the case that different utterances are amenable to qualitatively distinct analyses and descriptions, then we may infer that the corresponding cognitive organizations differ in an analogous manner. (3) If it turns out that structures which we describe in the utterances of children at differing ages are progressively more complex — on a measure of complexity determined by the theory out of which our description arises — then we may infer that the corresponding cognitive organizations are to that extent more complex. (4) If it turns out that the structures which we describe in utterances show the same patterning for different children, and follow the same path (at some level of generality), then we may infer that we are dealing with a 'structure of structures' which is not arbitrary, and draw some inferences about the corresponding cognitive organization.

There is one further point to be made in this connection. If we assume that linguistic forms do not express meanings in themselves, that is, that the relation between form and meaning is an arbitrary and conventional one, then we cannot infer anything about the quality of the cognitive/conceptual structures which may correspond to the structures described within the linguistic form. That is, we must regard the linguistic form merely as a 'counter' − insignificant in itself − to which a meaning is arbitrarily attached within the linguistic system. This, of course, makes language acquisition into a process whose intrinsic interest is no greater than an interest in the acquisition of other abilities: it will tell us about skills in manipulating counters, from which certain inferences may be drawn. However, if we adopt a view of language which regards linguistic form as carrying significance in itself, we may be able to gain an insight into cognitive processes which goes beyond that of the manipulation view. As an example, we may regard the child's ability to use tense-markers either as an indication that he or she has learned to manipulate the tense 'counter' correctly, without being able to draw inferences beyond that (the 'counter' not having any value of itself) or else as an indication that the child is able to manipulate the 'counter' *and* reality through the concept. To take a different example: in the sentence *The police killed eleven demonstrators* an event is described in terms of causer, process and affected participant. If we assume that linguistic form has a conventional relation to meaning, then no significance attaches to the form *as such*; indeed, any other linguistic form could signal the meaning 'causer-process-affected participant'. The same meaning would be conveyed − according to that view − by a sentence of the form *Eleven demonstrators died (through/of police shooting)*. However, the form may be thought to have significance of itself which is neither arbitrary nor assigned as the expression of an arbitrary relation to a referent. So, for instance, the difference between *The police emitted a roar* and *The police roared* is not a difference signalling a different event in 'reality', but is a difference which arises because of the intrinsic meaning of the two forms. In one case the form presents the event as a controlled, directed action (the police acting as a 'well-trained body of men'); in the other case the event is presented as an uncontrolled, non-direction action (the police acting as a 'rabble'). That is, two distinct versions of causality are at issue here, and these are accurately coded in the linguistic form. The relation between the causer-process-affected form and the 'controlled, directed action' form (or, more fully, 'action initiated and controlled by a causer which directly affects another participant') is not a conventional and arbitrary relation. Hence the user of such a form can be said to do more than merely manipulate a 'counter': the user of that form may be said to perceive reality in that form, and to represent it to himself and to others in that form.

iii   From simple to complex sentence structures

For the purposes of this chapter, a conjoined sentence structure will be taken to be any structure containing two or more clauses. A clause is taken to be a linguistic unit containing one main verbal element (whether in finite or non-finite form) and its attendant nominal participants. For instance, using examples from texts already discussed, in *I went to the shops* there is one main verb, *went*, and two nominal participants, *I*, which is directly associated with the verb, and *the shops*, which is associated to the verb indirectly, via a preposition, *to*. Conjunction may take the form of co-ordination (*I went to the shops and I saw a King and Queen*), producing structures consisting of units of equal syntactic status; or it may take the form of subordination (*When I went to the shops, I saw a King and Queen*, or, *I went to the shops to see a King and Queen*), producing structures consisting of units of unequal syntactic status. A clause may appear fully, or in reduced form. For example, in *When I went to the shops I saw a train and walk on I saw a King and Queen* there are four clauses: *When I went to the shops*; *I saw a train*; *walk on*; *I saw a King and Queen*. In *walk on* the subject noun *I* is understood (or deleted); nevertheless, *walk on* counts as a clause. In another example, *When we had got out of the bus Mrs. Gilbert said to sketch the front of Ayers House*, there are three clauses: *When we had got out of the bus*; *Mrs. Gilbert said to sketch the front of Ayers House*; and the clause embedded in the previous one, *to sketch the front of Ayers House*, which has an understood (or deleted) subject noun *we*. The third clause is itself a constituent of the second clause, a constituent which is syntactically obligatory in this structure as the (clausal) complement of the verb *to say*. On a range of conjunctions, from simple co-ordination with *and*, via the subordination with a when-clause (which is not syntactically obligatory), to the embedded clause, the latter represents the endpoint where two formerly discrete syntactic units are fused into one syntactic unit. To that extent conjunction is handled in a syntactically more mature manner in this sentence than in examples of earlier writing.

Text 22

Father Christmas

(1) Father Christmas was in the sky one night when he came upon a poor farm house. (2) He went down the chimney and filled the stocking for the little girl. (3) He had a drink then left.

The story consists of three sentences, each of which is a conjoined structure consisting of two clauses. In each sentence a conjunction joins the two clauses: *when, and, then*. These three conjunctions seem to function like their equivalents in adult language. However, a closer look reveals that the major principle of conjunction is that the clause which reports the action which is earlier in (real) time should precede (in the linear sequence of the clauses in the written language) the clause which reports the action which is subsequent in time. This earlier-action-followed-by-later-action principle holds for all three sentences. In other words, the three conjunctions - *and, when, then* – have the same function, that of linking sequentially ordered clauses. They are, at one level of description, three kinds of *and*. The point is an important one, for a teacher looking at the story might see three different conjunctions, and infer from this that the child knew the meaning of *and* (simple, 'neutral' conjunction) *as* against *when* (conjunction implying temporal/causal priority, e.g.

> *We packed up our picnic things when it started to rain*
>   later   earlier

where the second clause reports an action which is both temporally and causally prior to the first), and *then* (a conjunction indicating a subsequent action). In fact, the child's use of the three conjunctions indicates that she does not use them in such a fashion. In the child's syntax linear sequence is used to indicate temporal sequence; that is, the order of events is mirrored by the linear order of the clauses in the sentence. In adult usage either the when-clause or the main clause may report the temporally prior event, and the linear order of the two clauses depends on thematic considerations. It is possible that the child can at this age make these distinctions conceptually, but they have not yet come into the language. Adult language is freed from the parallelism between the order of the real world and the order of linguistic structure as the example sentence above shows. In adult language the direct equivalence may be present but is characteristically replaced by a relation based on a level of greater abstraction. Of course, the adult use of *and* is often like the child's: *We got to the picnic spot and put our rugs down.* In other words, this child's use of *and* (and of *when* and *then*) picks up only one of the functions of the conjunctions in adult language. This is not to say that the child has no motivation for using these three types of conjunction. In fact *and* could have been used as the conjunction in sentences 1 and 3, though with a noticeable effect on the conceptual organization of the text. Substituting *and* in sentences 1 and 3 makes it clear that this would obliterate a subtle distinction in the type of events which are being linked. *And* causes the linked events to be read as qualitatively the same. The child has used this kind of equation only in one case, and so the three sentences contain conjoined structures which are finely nuanced as either qualitatively different or the same. These conjunctions are, consequently, in usage neither like their adult counterparts nor necessarily particularly naive. Of course, there is a danger of reading too much into these forms. However, an adult text would receive this degree of interpretation, and, as a working hypothesis, it is useful to assign to a child's text an equivalent degree of interpretation. At the very least this will define what we can maximally assume as the child's meaning and 'knowledge'. Such a reading will supply the teacher with an upper limit for the child's possible ability range and could be the basis for interesting and revealing tests to establish whether this read or imputed ability is characteristic of a child's understanding and performance in other areas.

In each of the three sentences the two conjoined parts retain a significant degree of autonomy, and the two clauses have equal syntactic status within the sentence. That is, the when-clause in sentence (1) is not subordinated. Diagrammatically the relation can be shown as in Figure 1. Nevertheless, there are signs of the child's attempts at constructing an integrated larger structure. In sentence 1 the nominal phrase *Father*

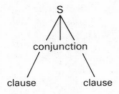

Figure 1

Christmas occurs in its full form in the first clause but is replaced by the pronominal substitute *he* in the second clause. Hence a relation of dependence is established between the two clauses, so that they are not totally independent units; the second clause depends on the first. In the second sentence the process of integration goes further. The two clauses in their full form are *He went down the chimney* and *he filled the stocking for the little girl*. Here the second clause is more tightly integrated with the first because the subject noun-phrase of the second clause is not repeated, it has to be recovered from the context. Instead of repeating the pronoun *he*, the writer can refer the reader to the preceding clause where the subject noun-phrase occurs: the two clauses are so integrated as to form one unit within which repetition is not necessary. The dependence of the second clause is so strong that it comes close to having the status of a dependent subordinated clause. The fusion of the two clauses, conceptually, is correspondingly tighter.

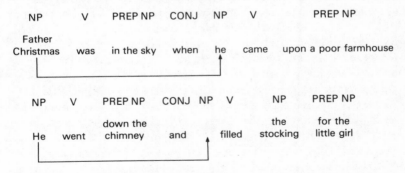

The third sentence, like the second, has the second clause integrated by the unrepeated, 'understood' subject NP *he*. The conjunction *then* may be being used somewhat differently from *and* and *when*: there might have been an *and* in this sentence, i.e. *He had a drink and then he left*. If we assume this, then the third sentence would be a step further on an integration scale, with the conjunction *and* deleted, and the time adverbial *then* introducing the second clause, which is now very much like a dependent clause.

The linguistic rules which this child is following give an interesting insight into her conceptual orientation. It turns out that her use of conjunctions, in this admittedly brief text, is consistently unlike the adult's; and this may point to a conceptual difference. The child does not make a syntactic distinction between temporal and spatial sequence or succession; hence the child may be relying on one mode of order where the adult has several. The child's logic may therefore be quite unlike that of the adult, bound much more to the order of events in the world, and not able to abstract one kind of order from another. We need to see this in relation to the child's attempt to construct complex linguistic and conceptual units, for the two go hand in hand. On the one hand the child is attempting to extend a single idea by conjoining it with another; on the other hand, this has to be achieved within the linguistic-conceptual limits outlined above. On the linguistic level, two clauses are conjoined, and to some extent fused by the two devices of (1) substituting a pronoun for a proper noun and (2) not repeating a shared noun-phrase. On the conceptual level the child is forging a new, complex single unit out of two units which were previously quite independent. In this, two main strategies are at work. The first strategy is that where two clauses share a common overall theme as well as some repeated material, they can be brought together into one linguistic unit. So in the first sentence the common theme is 'temporal and spatial setting of the story'. In the second sentence the theme is 'characteristic Father Christmas activities'. In the third sentence we have the 'concluding activities'. The second strategy is, as I have mentioned, that clauses which are about temporally contiguous activities may be joined according to their temporal order.

These forms of conjunction and integration are appropriate to a stage where the child is tied to a concrete perception and interpretation of events. From a viewpoint such as this it is tempting to draw analogies between this linguistic analysis and the description of the pre-operational stage in Piaget's theory, as well as the phases which are transitional towards the fully fledged concrete operational period. The text strongly suggests, in Margaret Donaldson's words, that 'the symbolic acts are still closely tied to the concrete things [in this case the sequence of events] on which the original physical acts were performed. The child is still mainly thinking about doing things with physical objects: ordering them, classifying them, arranging them in series and so on' (*Children's Minds*, p. 138). The texts (by the same child) discussed below also seem to illustrate the development involved in the transition from the pre-operational to the concrete operational, and from that to the formal operational period: 'The operational thinker has much more interest in explanation and understanding . . . . The formal operational thinker can entertain hypotheses, deduce consequences and use these deductions to put the hypotheses to the test . . . . The formal operational thinker tends to start from the possible' (loc. cit.). The last two sentences characterize Text 26 in this chapter rather well. One important consequence of this analysis is the prospect which it offers for making objective descriptive statements about the type of cognitive activity which the child is engaging in, and its correspondence to the Piagetian developmental stages. A detailed analysis of the types of conjunction which characterize a text produced by a child, or which characterize the writing of a child at a given period, may permit us to make finely nuanced statements about a child's cognitive ability.

It is important to avoid two errors, however. One is a direct equation of the structures inherent in the linguistic description with hypothesized structures of a cognitive kind. The other is an unacknowledged slide into an equation of speech and writing.

As far as the former is concerned, the arguments are clearly presented by Feldman and Toulmin (1975). They point out that the fact that data can be described in terms of formal theoretical systems is not sufficient justification for assuming that these descriptions capture anything more than the theory's own formalism. It is not sufficient evidence for assuming that the formalism corresponds to any cognitive structure. The same point is made in a slightly different way in a recent article by Patricia Smith Churchland: 'There is no doubt that some of the information bearing states of the central nervous system are not a species of sentential attitude; that is, they are not describable in terms of the person's being in a certain functional state whose structures and elements are isomorphic to the structure and elements of sentences. Obviously, for example, the results of information processing in the retina cannot be described as the person's believing that p, or thinking that p, or thinking that he sees an x, or anything of the sort.' Despite Feldman and Toulmin's appropriate caution, three points need to be made: (1) If a number of descriptions, arising out of significantly different theories, produce evidence of similar structures inherent in such descriptions they will be to that extent less arbitrary and dependent merely on the vagaries of one theory. In other words we are likely to be closer to the description of reality as some level. (2) Though linguistic structures derived from such descriptions will give no indication about cognitive structures as such, they do point to a level of organization at some stage in a chain from cognitive to linguistic structure which gives rise to such structures. In other words, while we cannot make any direct inferences about the neurophysiological organization corresponding to given cognitive states, we can say that at some level there is a cognitive organization such that it produces linguistic materials which display given structures. (3) Given the point made earlier concerning the significance of certain types of linguistic materials, (2) above means that we can make legitimate inferences about the nature and content of the level of cognitive organization mentioned under (2).

The second point is equally important, and certainly less acknowledged than the former. As I have stressed in preceding chapters, speech and writing are two distinct modes of language, each with its linguistic (phonetic/graphic, syntactic and textual) characteristics. When children arrive at school they are in many respects competent speakers; they are not, however, competent writers. Competence in speaking and competence in writing have not been treated as distinct competencies. Children's written language has consequently been treated unproblematically as 'children's language', with unfortunate consequences. For instance, in his important monograph *Syntactic Maturity in Schoolchildren and Adults* (1970), Kellogg Hunt discusses speech as distinct from writing, only to collapse them into each other in terms of applying the same descriptive categories to both, that is, T-unit length, clauses per T-unit, clause-length, etc. Similarly in discussing results of analyses: 'On the basis of Hunt's and O'Donnell's studies, and in the absence so far of contradictory data, there is evidence that throughout the school years, from kindergarten to graduation, children learn to use a larger and larger number of sentence-containing transformations per main clause in their writing. . . . *In schoolchildren's speech the same tendency appears to exist up to the seventh grade, and future investigators may find that the tendency continues through the later grades*' (Kellogg

Hunt (1970, p.9); my italics). What Hunt's data do seem to point to is that over time the structure of written English begins to influence the structure of spoken English — as one would expect: 'The number of clauses per T-unit for speech did not increase at every interval; none-theless the number did increase, though in a zig-zag upward path. The values for kindergarten, and grades 1, 2, 3, 5 and 7 were, respectively, 1.16, 1.19, 1.18, 1.21, 1.19, 1.26' (pp. 8-9). To put a gloss on Hunt's findings: the syntax of speech is marked by a relative preponderance of chaining constructions, while the syntax of writing is marked by a relatively greater degree of embedding constructions. My hypothesis is, as I attempted to show in Chapter 3, that as children become more familiar with the syntax of writing, this begins to influence the syntax of speech, and leads to the increase of clauses per T-unit.

One important point is that when children first learn to write, their syntactic ability in writing is well behind their ability in speaking. That is, not only do they draw on the grammar of speech in their writing, but their written implementation of this grammar is partial, due possibly to the need to attend simultaneously to so many various demands which children face in learning to write. This will appear in a number of ways. First of all, intuitively, the child will seem to the teacher to be quite a competent speaker, but will seem quite an incompetent writer (that is, at a stage when the child is beginning to write 'stories'). Second, whereas the child will use some embedded constructions in speech (as shown by Hunt's scores above, which express a ratio of main clauses to subordinate clauses), typically the child's initial writing is characterized by a nearly exclusive use of co-ordinated main clauses, as many texts in earlier chapters, which are entirely typical in this respect, demonstrate. Hunt's figure for grade 4 is 1.739 on an average. He comments, 'The fourth graders make [the sentences] long by excessive co-ordination of main clauses' (pp. 16-17). His 'excessive' shows that children tend to use few subordinating constructions in writing relative to the norm expected by the adult. Third, the child's concept of sentence is, as I demonstrated in Chapter 4, clearly unlike the adult's. In so far as the sentence is the criterial unit of writing, the child's written language will seem deficient in precisely that feature which is most characteristic of writing. Fourth, the fact that, in writing, language *qua* object becomes the focus of the child's attention seems to lead to syntactic simplification compared to the child's spoken language in certain areas, such as modification, use of tense, voice, etc. Slobin and Welsh (1973) make a related point when they suggest that in spontaneous speech the child has an 'intention-to-say-so-and-so' and that this intention sustains and supports the complex utterance. When the intention has faded and the child must process the utterances as pure isolated language — as is the case when a child learns to write — the task for the child is of a very different kind.

Hence the child's written language at first lags behind not only in terms of the adult's (unrecognized hence unacknowledged) expectations about the syntax of written language, but also in terms of the child's competence in certain areas of the syntax of speech. Too frequently these 'shortcomings' all get lumped together and are regarded as an indication of the child's incompetence in language as such. The difference between the child's spoken and written competence is significant in the early stages, so that a six-year-old will produce written texts which match the spoken competence of that same child perhaps at the age of three or four (to the extent that and in areas where such an equation makes sense — see the texts in Chapter 2), and typically the competencies in the two areas tend not to catch up until four or five years on. (See, for instance, Texts 12, 17, 23 and 24). Much of course depends on contingent factors, such as the degree to which a teacher insists on keeping writing 'pure' of the spoken forms, or the child's exposure to written language in reading - or, indeed, on the family's spoken language, which may be closer to the syntax of writing in some families than in others.

In terms of a stage-theory of development it is as though many of the syntactic achievements of speech have to be mastered and achieved again. However, while these were initially learned in a mode more appropriate to the pre-operational period, the second time they are achieved very definitely in the mode of the operational, possibly even the formal operational period. That is, what is at stake in the mastery of writing is the overt, conscious mastery of a symbolic system. It is conceivable that in learning to speak children have learned some forms ready-made, without a full understanding of the syntax of such utterances. The work of Carol Chomsky (1969) points in that direction. It may be that in learning to write children have to learn some of these forms anew, learning them through conscious exploration and understandings.

Hence one cannot assume that the syntax employed in a child's early writing presents a picture of the child's perceptual and cognitive stage overall; but we can assume that the syntax represents the perceptions and the cognitive order which the child has adopted, for a number of reasons, in writing the stories.

The closest this child writer comes to moving away from the concrete level evident in Text 22 is in the third sentence, where the second clause could be thought of as nearly a dependent clause. Hence syntactically this sentence is closer to subordination than to the co-ordinating constructions of the previous two sentences. Subordination is conceptually more abstract, involving order of a hierarchical rather than a sequential (either linear or temporal) kind.

Text 14

Our Trip to Ayers House

(1) On Friday 1st July we all got in the bus and waved to Miss Martyn. (2) We're off I thought, there was lots of merry talk in the bus. (3) Tracey was telling some people that the bus would pass her house 'there it is' said Tracey but it soon went by. (4) We soon were there. (5) When we had got out of the bus Mrs. Gilbert said to sketch the frantx frounx front of Ayers House. (6) When I had finished my sketch I looked at some of the other sketches. (7) I thought Prue's was the best.

Text 14 was written by the same child, approximately one year later than Text 22. The extract reproduced here represents about half of the story which the child wrote, but it is sufficient to illustrate the development which has taken place. The difference between this and the previous text is immediately apparent, simply intuitively. It shows greater variety of structure, the syntax is more complex, the introduction of direct speech gives the text freshness and liveliness. To make the points of difference specific, I will discuss each of the seven sentences in turn:

(1) On Friday 1st July we all got in the bus and waved to Miss Martyn.

As in Text 22, the two clauses conjoined by *and* follow the temporal sequence earlier *and* later. As before, the identical subject-nominal in the second clause is deleted:

(2) We're off I thought, there was lots of merry talk in the bus.

In this sentence two main clauses are conjoined (or, better, adjoined), in the manner familiar from the previous text, the earlier *We're off I thought* preceding the later *there was lots of merry talk in the bus*. However, the *We're off I thought* represents a new structure, where one clause is subordinated to another; that is, *I thought* is the main clause, and its complement is *We're off*. Diagrammatically this can be shown as in Figure 2.

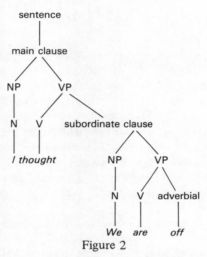

Figure 2

Whereas in Figure 1 (p. 137) the two clauses are of equal status, here one is contained within the other. Cognitively this is a more complex structure than the simple co-ordinated structures seen before. Its structural meaning is: mental process plus the content of that mental process. Clearly, it represents a significant development linguistically and cognitively. Linguistically it enables the child to make any clause a part of another clause and, in particular, to bring into her own text both thoughts and other speakers' speech. Cognitively it allows the child to bring any proposition into another proposition as an integral component of it.

The example raises the issue, discussed in Chapter 4, of the child's notion of sentence itself. The punctuation reflects the child's intention to treat the whole unit as one sentence. We can of course regard this as a mistake, and assume that there should be a full stop between *thought* and *there*. However, as the child uses full stops, commas and capital letters with great care, this would seem an unwarranted step. We seem to have further evidence here of the child's conception of what a sentence is. As before, it is clear that the child's understanding of 'sentenceness' differs from the adult's. (The third sentence below is another case in point.) The two topics — the formation of complex sentences and the notion of 'sentenceness' - are intimately bound up with each other and interdependent. Minimally the child's conception of 'sentenceness' includes facts such as 'what is the conceptual unit of writing', 'what belongs together most closely in sense', 'what provides the internal coherence of the different items to be expressed'. These factors make specific demands on syntax generally, and on the syntax of conjunction in particular. Again, it is clear that the question 'What is a sentence?' does not arise for the child until he or she is faced with the task of learning to write. The concept of sentence then presents itself objectively as a problem. Looking at the seven sentences in this story (as well as the three in the previous one), it seems clear enough that there is, for instance, some such notion as topical connectedness at work (i.e. sentence 1 'the departure'; sentence 2 'the trip'; sentence 3 'an incident on the trip'; and so on).

Sentence 3 contains five clauses:
  (i)   Tracey was telling some people
  (ii) that the bus would pass her house
  (iii) 'there it is'
  (iv) but it soon went by
  (v)   Tracey said ('there it is')

Two of these clauses are complex in the manner of sentence 2: *Tracey was telling some people that the bus would pass her house* and *'there it is' said Tracey*. In each case one clause is subordinated to another. In the first case the writer has processed Tracey's speech, contained in the subordinated clause. It is closely integrated syntactically with the main clause, so that it becomes direct, reported speech rather than the direct speech (and thought) of the previous example and of the second clause here. One point to note is the different punctuation which the child employs in the case of *We're off I thought* and *'there it is' said Tracey*. It may be that the child is simply inconsistent, that is, that she has made an error. However, she puts quotation marks around the other speaker's speech, which she has brought into her text, whereas she does not use quotation marks around *We're off*, which is her own language and thought. It may turn out that we are looking at a mistake;

though it is equally plausible that the child is making a distinction between 'own text' and 'text of other speakers'. Such a distinction is a far from trivial one.

The fifth sentence shows a further stage in the syntactic incorporation of speech:

(5) When we had got out of the bus Mrs. Gilbert said to sketch the front of Ayers House.

Here the (reduced) clause *to sketch the front of Ayers House* represents an actual utterance spoken by Mrs Gilbert. It is now completely absorbed, syntactically, into the main clause, so that it has lost even its status as indirect reported speech. The three stages of this absorption which we have seen so far are represented by these examples:

1   Tracey said *'there it is'* (actual speech is brought directly into the clause.)
2   Tracey was telling some people *that the bus would pass her house* (Speech is syntactically processed, to make it more a part of the writer's own text.)
3   Mrs. Gilbert said *to sketch the front of Ayers House* (Here speech is heavily processed, and has become totally a part of the writer's own text.)

The sixth and seventh sentences illustrate points made above about the order of clauses and, in the case of 7, about the syntactic incorporation of, in this case, a report of the writer's own thought. An interesting comparison can be made between sentences 2 and 6. *We're off*, in 2, is a piece of reported speech, silently spoken, but speech nevertheless. In 6, *Prue's was the best* is not silently spoken reported speech – if it were, it would be *I thought Prue's is the best* – but is a thought, treated syntactically like a thought. This seems to support the earlier assumption that the child distinguishes between 'own text' and 'other speakers' text'. Here the distinction is between 'own speech' and 'own thought'; it is made through the use of tense-forms: the present tense is used for the form which is closer to actual speech, the past tense is used for the form which is more distant from actual speech. Indeed, the range of distinctions available to this child to mark the reality/authority status of 'imported' speech is astonishing: from direct quotation, to indirect reporting, to heavily processed reporting, to the distinction between own and others' text, to a distinction between silently spoken thoughts and real thoughts.

The conjunctions *when*, *and* and *but* are clearly distinct in form and function in this text. Whereas in the first text the clause introduced by *when* came second in the sentence, in this text these clauses come first. They have at least one of the functions which they have in adult language, namely setting the stage, providing the temporal reference-points for the clause that follows. And whereas in Text 22 *when* acted as a co-ordinating conjunction, joining clauses of equal status, in Text 14 *when* is a subordinating conjunction, joining a subordinate to the main embedding clause. The child also uses some other devices for conjoining clauses, namely quotation marks, commas, and *that*.

Text 26

My Ambition in Life

(1) When I grow up I want to be a ventriloquist.
(2) I will have to practise talking without opening my
mouth. (2) I want to travel around in a combination van
with a painted sign that will say 'Geraldine and Frank'.
(4) Frank will be my puppet and he will wear a top
hat and black suit. (5) I will treat him as a child by giving
him real school lessons! (6) On my first show I will
pretend Frank is shy, but then gradually he will become
used to all the people. (7) When I visit my family I might
let him come out and perform to them. (8) I will go to
university for the first couple of years. (9) I don't want
to get married or have children. (10) I want to become a
star in about 1990 and I will be 21. (11) I would like to
perform in front of the King (Prince Charles). (12) When I
am a star I will wear shining clothes with 'I am a star'
written on my back.

In this text embedding, subordinating, constructions predominate over co-ordinating ones. In addition to subordination by the use of *when*, *that* and the to-construction, the child now uses the verbal *-ing* form, *I will have to practise talking without opening my mouth*, to embed clauses.

A new conjunction appearing here is *or*. Its use by the child marks the conclusion of a development which started with conjunction by simple sequence, mirroring the order of real events, and ends with the achievement of an abstract level of logical order. This cognitive freeing from the order of the real world was under way in Text 14 and was indicated there by the use of embeddings as well as by the use of the conjunction *but*. Here in Text 26 *but* again occurs with its logical force of 'partial denial of a presupposition contained in the preceding clause'.

The higher level of cognitive order which is signalled by the use of *or* and *but* is reinforced in the use of conjunctions of an instrumental-causal kind. In sentence 5 *I will treat him as a child by giving him real school lessons* the clause starting with *by* is beginning to have a causal force. A gloss might be 'The fact that I'm giving him real school lessons causes it (brings it about, is a sign of the fact) that he is treated as a real child.' Similarly, the use of *when* in Text 26 is unlike its use in Text 14. Whereas in the latter the clause introduced by *when* reported a completed event, placed in past time, in Text 26 the when-clause is about an event conceived of as hypothetical-potential. Again this signals a move away from dependence on the order suggested or imposed by the real world, to an order of an abstract, hypothetical kind. It is a move, syntactically, from temporal *when* to a hypothetical, concessive, causal *when*. The cognitive implications of this syntactic development are clear enough. Though not quite of the same level of abstractness as the instances just discussed, the use of *with* as a conjunction certainly fits into this pattern: . . . *in a combination van with a painted sign that will say* . . . At the stage of Text 22, 'Father Christmas', the child might have used *I (will) travel around in a combination van and the van will have a sign and the sign is painted on*. In 'My Ambition in Life' the clause *the sign is painted on* has been reduced to the status of a prepositional adjunct. Cognitively, *a combination van with a painted sign* is now a single percept. It shows the process of conjoining in its most developed form, for here we have an embedded clause which has been processed linguistically so that it is now syntactically, perceptually and conceptually totally fused into (a part of) the embedding clause.

iv   Some practical implications

At the beginning of this chapter I mentioned that the child's language might provide a window on his or her conceptual world. I have attempted to illustrate how children's writing may be read to demonstrate the close relationship between language and cognitive conceptual development. The analysis reveals a syntactic and cognitive richness in the three texts which is not apparent on the surface. The syntax points to a specific, clearly articulated cognitive system. At least two questions follow. First, do the linguistic and cognitive structures which children use at different stages point to qualitative rather than quantitative differences between the child and the adult? Second, what should a teacher's attitude be to the child's writing, and to the difference between the adult's and the child's written language?

The answers depend, as I suggested in Section i, on the kind of theoretical framework one uses in approaching these questions. Differing conceptions of the process of language learning entail quite different answers. For one thing, the assumption which I make throughout this book that linguistic form reveals cognitive structure and content is not only open to the objections mentioned earlier, but may also be rejected at once by linguists who hold that the relation between form and content is an arbitrary and conventional one. If that is the case, then any form may represent any content, and nothing of real consequence follows from differences in form. For another, the various currently held theories of language learning differ in fundamental respects. One highly influential theory, deriving from Noam Chomsky's work, regards the process as the unfolding and development of the child's innate ability, in response to the specific constraints of the native language. A second approach sees the process as the gradual and partial 'acquisition' of fully fledged adult language. On such views the language system exists outside the child and has to be 'acquired' through a gradual process. Behaviourist theories are clear examples of this approach. Both tend in a similar direction, for necessarily both regard the stages prior to the achievement of full adult language as unfinished, partially achieved and not fully developed versions of the language to be learned. Consequently both lead to a devaluing or an undervaluing of the language of the intervening period, and of the cognitive models which are expressed in the linguistic forms. This is not to dismiss the total divergence of these two views in other respects, such as their conception of the nature and role of the mind engaged in the learning process. A third approach sees the child as an active participant, a 'constructor' of language, acting in response to the demands of a varied environment, including the language of the social group in which the child grows up. The work of Michael Halliday is the best known and most fully articulated contemporary example of this approach.

Against the first two views I wish to argue that the written texts discussed here embody adequate — indeed, the correct — syntactic forms for the cognitive/perceptual stage of the child at the time. The first of these views argues that an acorn can only develop into an oak: the oak may be stunted or majestic, depending on circumstances, but it will be an oak. Its 'oakness' is there at every point, in essence. Consequently, no real interest attaches to the developmental process *per se*; it is predictable and known. According to this view the grammars of the intermediate stages in the child's language development are both akin to the adult's, as mentioned earlier, in displaying fundamental similarities (the types of rules, the rule-governedness of utterances, the strategies employed in constructing grammars) and unalike in being but partial versions of the full grammar of the adult, lacking, for instance, the rules of transformation which lead to differentiated surface structures. The second view also disvalues intermediate stages, as these are merely stepping stones established under a (more or less complex) stimulus-response system towards mastery of the full adult form. The third view regards the intervening stages established by the child as a response by the child to its perceived needs in relation to a given environment. Therefore the intervening stages are adequate, in an important sense, to the child's physical, social, cognitive needs at a given time. Inevitably the socialization process causes the child to move towards an endpoint which is identical with that of the group in which he or she lives. The important point is that according to this view the intervening stages have a validity of their own, and do not exist merely as more or less fully realized versions of full adult language.

The conjunction of this third view of language development and the assumption that linguistic form in itself expresses conceptual/cognitive content, points in the direction of qualitative cognitive differences between child and adult being encoded in the respective linguistic structures of child and adult.

I mentioned earlier the syntactic gap between spoken and written language in this age-range. In the same way that a concept such as the sentence becomes problematic for the child when he or she learns to write, so notions of order, causality, become problematic when the child is asked to 'write a story'. In learning to speak, the child has learned some of the structures and contents of adult language unreflectingly. That is, the major context of pre-school children's use of language is in interaction, often with adults. The interaction itself provides both the stimulus and the constraints for language use. In such a context a child may learn syntactic forms as ready-made and unanalysed units. In learning to write, this interactive motor for language use is absent, so that language has to be produced from scratch, as it were. Furthermore, linguistic structures present themselves in an objective and therefore problematic fashion — and the child responds to the possibility and opportunity of exercising choice in the selection of linguistic form. This discussion may go some way towards suggesting what a teacher's attitude towards children's writing can be: at this early stage an awareness of the qualitative difference between the syntax of speech and writing, and between the child's and the adult's syntax, coupled with a recognition of the appropriateness of the form of the child's expression, can provide the first stage in the teacher's response. Any positive intervention on the teacher's part would need to proceed from that basis.

If this hypothesis of linguistic and cognitive adequacy and appropriateness is rejected we are left with the more puzzling problem of why an eight-year-old, say, does not use a range of syntactic forms in writing which are commonplace in his or her spoken language several years earlier. In terms of the mere mechanics of writing, *When we left our house we went to the beach* seems as 'difficult' or 'complex' as *we left our house to go to the beach*. Given this, and the fact that five- and six-year-old children constantly use constructions of the second type, the better hypothesis at the moment is the one which attributes significance of a perceptual/cognitive kind to the syntax of the child's written language. That is, in writing a story, the child has to concentrate on so many varied factors that he or she uses that syntax and that textual structure which comes most readily to mind, which imposes least additional cognitive load. That form may be one which uses sequential textual structures. And these structures are drawn on in 'visualizing' and 'creating' the event and its representation in writing.

In the discussion of Text 22 it emerged that the child's use of con-junctions, and of the sequence of clauses, is tied to the order of things in the world. The adult's language is freed from this order in as much as the adult has the choice of either representing the order of events in the world or presenting them in some interpreted form. In this respect alone there is a fundamental qualitative difference, and the discussion of Texts 14 and 26 reinforces this conclusion. How are we to evaluate this difference? Freedom from dependence on the order of things in the world may be an absolute prerequisite for control of that world, both physical and social. The individual/speaker who does not have this freedom is tied to the order of things in the world. Yet the freedom is achieved through an interpretation of events, and consequently such linguistic forms present skewed images of the world to the speaker and hearer. The early writing of children presents models of causality, for instance, which are simpler than those of the later writing of children or of adults, in at least two senses: (1) the order of events in the world is taken over by the child (or imposes itself on the child?) and is used to provide the structure of the narrative; (2) versions of causality in the early writing of children tend to be predominantly dependent on temporal sequence. That is, there is typically much less theoretical interpretation in children's early writing than in their later writing. This simplicity may indicate a directness of perception without the heavily distorting filter of the more interpreted, more complex and distanced adult language.

Nevertheless, it is the case that to function effectively in adult society, the child needs to learn the adult forms, to acquire the tools necessary to interpret the world. The question of the teacher's role thus arises yet again. If we accept that any given syntactic form (and any resulting differences between child and adult) are appropriate to and an indication of a specific cognitive stage, then it is clear that 'correction' becomes a problematic concept. For instance, if the teacher decides to insert a full stop between two clauses in the child's text, then the teacher has in effect imposed the cognitive/linguistic form appropriate to a cognitive stage which the child has not yet reached. The child will notice the imposition of the rule, but will have no way of understanding the meaning of that rule.

Certain kinds of intervention are therefore likely to be ineffective, and are bound to be puzzling to the child. (This, of course, ignores the social control function of corrections, where it might be argued that they are more effective the less the child understands the grounds of the intervention.) However, in the light of the preceding argument and the well-understood fact that passive language knowledge is always well ahead of active performance (whether in foreign language learning, first-language learning, hearing compared to speaking, or reading compared to writing), it should be possible for the teacher to make interventions which are based on and represent the child's passive knowledge; in this way 'corrections' become appeals to the child's knowledge of the syntax, textual structures and the generic forms of spoken language in particular, and attempts to activate that knowledge for the learning of writing. Furthermore, once it is realized that the child is using specific linguistic, cognitive and conceptual models and the nature and content of the models are understood, these can become the subject of discussion at a level which the teacher knows to be appropriate. Alternative linguistic and cognitive models can be brought into such a discussion, more or less overtly, by comparison or contrast. For instance, the teacher, realizing the mode of perception and form of order underlying a given story, might discuss with the child writer how else the event might have been perceived, ordered and presented, and suggest to the child a rewriting which aims to present the events in that different form. The level at which such a discussion could be conducted depends on a large number of variables, of which teachers are, of course, intuitively aware. (These ideas are further elaborated in Chapter 7.) In this way the child's whole range of passive knowledge becomes much more overt and explicit, is articulated for the child, and becomes the focus and starting point for continuous movement in the process of learning.

All this presupposes adequate descriptions of the syntax of speech, and, drawing on that, a building-up of the child's knowledge of the syntax of writing, both sentence-internal syntax (modes of conjunction typical of each form, for instance) and sentence-external structures (for example, the types of cohesion typical of each form). It also assumes that the cognitive import of the linguistic developmental stages is understood by educators and adequately described by linguists. In the case of writing, the latter task has in the main yet to be undertaken.

v   Stages in the development of conjoined sentence structures

As a first attempt towards such a description I offer the following tentative description of stages in the development of conjunction in children's writing. Although in my scheme each stage is represented by

Stage I   *Pre-conjunction* (sequence alone)
(not discussed in this chapter)

Structure	clause	full stop or not	clause
Example	*We go to the beach*		*My daddy caught a fish*

Stage II   *Rudimentary conjunction* (conjunction + sequence)
(not discussed in this chapter)

Structure	clause	full stop or not	conjunction	clause
Example	*We go to the beach*		*when*	*my daddy caught a fish*

Stage III   *Conjunction* (conjunction, sequence and
substitution/cohesion)

Structure

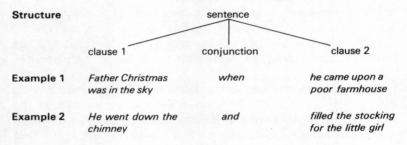

	clause 1	conjunction	clause 2
Example 1	*Father Christmas was in the sky*	*when*	*he came upon a poor farmhouse*
Example 2	*He went down the chimney*	*and*	*filled the stocking for the little girl*

Stage IV   *Sub-ordination* (linear sequence beginning to be replaced
by hierarchical order)

Structure

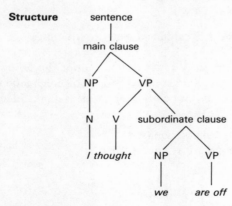

Example 1   *We're off I thought*

Example 2   *Mrs. Gilbert said to sketch the front of Ayers House*

Stage V *Embedding* (hierarchical and 'logical' order predominant)

Syntactic structure

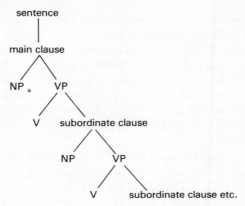

Example 1   *I will have to practise talking without opening my mouth*

Example 2   *I don't want to get married or have children*

Example 3   *I will treat him as a child by giving him real school lessons*

one syntactic form only, in fact a number of different kinds of conjunction types may be available to the child at each stage. For instance, at Stage IV the child uses, in addition to the two forms mentioned here, subordination with *when*, embedding with *-ing*, direct quotation, etc.

vi   Sources and context

The modern debate on the connections of language and thinking stems from the writings of Benjamin Lee Whorf (*Language, Thought and Reality* is a collection of some of the most pertinent articles), and in a somewhat different direction from L. Vygotsky's *Thought and Language*. Bernstein transposed Whorf's argument from one about the cognitive implications of differences between distinct languages to one about cognitive implications of socially determined differences of use within one language. This has sparked off a huge debate. A major protagonist in the debate has been William Labov, who has maintained that these differences cannot be so interpreted, as they are founded on the same underlying set of rules (Chapter 1). The theoretical position of Labov is based on the earlier theories of Noam Chomsky; Bernstein is not based on a linguistic theory, though Halliday's systemic-functional grammar would lend strong support to such a position, as it views the speaker as making significant choices from systems of options which are the grammar of the speaker's language. If certain sets of choices — paths through the network of systems — are strongly facilitated, they may become habitual and then form the linguistic experience of these speakers. This would give rise to distinctive codes. The formal linguistic theory is set out in G. Kress (ed.), *Halliday: System and Function in Language.*

Outside linguistics the theories of Jean Piaget have probably been most significant in approaches to cognition. His writings are readily accessible in most libraries, and the titles of some of his books are provided in the Bibliography. Margaret Donaldson's *Children's Minds* is an excellent introduction to the topic; it includes a useful summary of major concepts in Piaget's work. A formal treatment of the relation of behaviour and cognition is Feldman and Toulmin's 'Logic and the theory of mind'. They are sceptical of attempts to draw inferences about cognitive processes from the theoretical descriptions which have been given of different forms of behaviour — language, for instance.

A linguistic approach which assumes an intimate connection between linguistic form, linguistic processes which give rise to that form, and their expression of cognitive processes may be found in Kress and Hodge, *Language as Ideology*.

Chapter 7
The expression of causality in children's language

Gunther Kress and *Michael Rowan*

i The adequacy of a child's grammar

Through all the chapters so far the cognitive implications of linguistic forms and linguistic processes have been stressed, sometimes more prominently, sometimes less so. In Chapter 6 the link was made explicit through the exploration of the development of the linguistic process of conjunction and its simultaneous cognitive effects or causes. In this chapter an abstract concept — causality — is the focus, and the attempt is made to show the linguistic forms which may be being used by the child to code the different causal models which the writer may wish to express.

Text 27

Red Rover

(1) Yesterday when we played Red Rover Jody and Stephen smashed into each other and (a) Jody had a blood ear and she couldn't hear (wer) (w) very well (and). (2) then she had to go and clean her ear.

    (3) Then the (we) the(er) teacher said we can't play it again and then we played a nother game.

This story was written by a nine-year-old boy as a routine class exercise. We know little about the purpose of the child in writing the story or the teacher in asking for the story to be written. The child may have been attempting to meet a number of expectations which he felt the teacher had; the teacher may have had a range of motives in asking the children to write the story. However, we can imagine the teacher looking at the story, attempting to make something of it. The most frequent manner in which this occurs is that the teacher feels that he or she needs to correct the child's writing or to comment on the text in some way. That is normally a part of the exercise. But how should the text be corrected? Apart from the obvious corrections at points where rules of the grammar of adult writing have been straightforwardly violated, any further alteration assumes a certain model – a model both of what the teacher expects and of what the child was attempting to say. Quite clearly, corrections can then be seen as attempts to shift the child's model in the direction of the teacher's, or to impose the teacher's model on the child. It may be that a teacher assumes that no model underlies the child's text; in that case, the teacher's corrections may be seen by him or her as having the function of providing a model for the child.

In this chapter we wish to draw out one of the models inherent in children's writing, in this instance focusing on models of causality. We wish to show that such models have their own consistency, coherence and plausibility; and in doing so we wish to make some comments implicitly about the covert effects and assumptions of 'corrections'. This may reveal the strategies which teachers are likely to adopt in correcting or commenting on stories and, at the same time, may prove useful to teachers as they reflect about their own strategies in such cases.

In looking at this story, a teacher might quite easily have something like the following in mind as the child's intended meaning. The teacher would carry out small-scale corrections in order to bring the text a little more into line with this version, though not necessarily completing the task with children of this age level.

Text 27(a)

Yesterday while we were playing Red Rover Jody and Stephen collided, and therefore Jody's ear began to bleed, impairing her hearing. With the intention of restoring her hearing, the teacher told Jody to clean her ear.

In an attempt to prevent another accident, the teacher said that we could not play the game any more, so as a result we chose another.

We are not suggesting that the teacher would have expected the child to have written the story in this form, or a story with this degree of elaboration; nor are we suggesting that the teacher or any other adult would write the story in this way. We are suggesting that the teacher might consider that this represents the full elaboration of the idea which is partially expressed in the child's text. While the child could not have been expected to produce a story of this kind — indeed, stories are not at all like this — the child could have produced a story, or might be encouraged and taught to produce a story, which comes closer to this schema than the story which the child actually wrote. In any event, it is clear that corrections by the teacher to the original text presuppose a standard of appropriateness and correctness, and a notion of the child's conceptual schema, which consists both of the rules of grammar and of some decision on the teacher's part as to what the child is intending to say.

We wish to pose some questions about this teaching strategy and about the whole notion of correcting children's writing. We will do so by clarifying some of the ideas which seem to underlie this teaching strategy and by questioning their validity. In this way we seek to undermine the accepted methods of teaching by correction or at least to render them problematic. Beyond this, we wish to show that corrections may amount to the imposition of one cognitive system, that of the teacher, on another, that of the child. Some of the terms we use in the course of our analysis are briefly described below.

In common with current linguistic practice, we take a grammar to be a system of rules which govern the arrangement of syntactic units into larger syntactic units: in the case of writing, sentences and texts, the meaning of which can be understood by a user of that grammar. The function of a grammar is to allow a speaker to express a range of thoughts and a complexity of thought greater than is possible by the use of single words. A grammar may be adequate or inadequate to the needs of, and demands made on, the speaker. The larger structures stand in given and determinate relations to the meanings which they express. We say a grammar is adequate if that grammar allows a speaker to express the range of meanings which that speaker needs to express in such a way as to be understood in a regular and predictable manner by a fellow user of that grammar. A grammar might be inadequate either because the range of utterances made possible by the grammar is too restricted to permit the expression of meanings which the user needs or wishes to express, or because it does not allow meanings to be clearly and appropriately expressed. A grammar is inadequate if it is either insufficiently precise, or insufficiently comprehensive, relative to the needs of the user of the grammar.

Employing these definitions, we might say that a grammar can be legitimately criticized because — but only because — it is inadequate. That is, there are many grounds on which grammars can be criticized, such as social grounds, where speakers of a lower status form are criticized for debasing the language, or aesthetic grounds, which are most frequently also social grounds but need not be. However, such judgments are based on inequalities of the social system, or on subjective assessments on the part of one person or group, rather than being based on linguistic factors. Therefore the whole idea of correcting a child's grammar assumes that the child's grammar is inadequate to the expression of the child's meanings. This is not the manner in which such corrections are ordinarily thought of, and consequently justified. Rather, it seems to us, the child's grammar is commonly thought to be inadequate, when compared with the adult's grammar. The latter is thought to encode meanings and systems of ideas which seem common-sensical and natural; and to do so adequately, in our sense. Hence, by contrast, the child's grammar and the meanings which it expresses are commonly thought to be an imperfect or underdeveloped form of adult grammar. In this view, the process of learning to write (and, at an earlier stage, to speak) is regarded as a process of gradually developing an appreciation and grasp of adequate, adult grammar. We will call this notion the 'received view'.

The received view sees the child's grammar not simply as different from the adult's but as deficient in specific ways. Were this the case then the teaching strategy sketched above would be straightforwardly justified on both philosophical and pedagogic grounds; the child should adopt adult grammar, for the child's is deficient. The child needs to be brought to understand adult grammar because this is a better grammar and the child, recognizing this, will willingly adopt the self-evidently superior grammar which the teacher seeks to instil in him or her. It seems to us, however, that 'better' and 'deficient' when used in this connection rest on the thesis that the child's grammar is, by comparison with the adult's, not adequate to the needs of the child. At least, that is the only sense of these terms which gives some justification of the received view. It is this thesis we wish to challenge by pointing to the fact that adequacy must always be defined in relation to need, and not taken as a given.

A grammar is inadequate if it does not permit the user's thoughts to be normally conveyed in a precise manner. If we are to criticize the child's grammar as inadequate we must therefore show that it does not allow the child's thoughts to be commonly so conveyed. It might be thought that this is easily established – for example, by the evident superiority of Text 27(a) as compared to Text 27. This assumes, however, that in Text 27 the child was actually seeking to express the meanings contained in Text 27(a). Although it is widespread and commonplace we think that this assumption may well be wrong.

ii   Two models of causality

In order to challenge this assumption we will sketch two rudimentary models of causation and then show how these appear in the stories. We need to distinguish between two theories of causality: the 'powers' theory of causality, and the 'regularity' theory of causality. The powers view appears, in English, as the commonsense view. It embodies the idea that one thing causes another by making it happen: that a causal connection is a real, active process, by which one thing produces another. We might say, according to the powers view, that a cause has some real, active causal power, the exercise of which brings about the effect. The regularity view, on the other hand, sees causal processes as merely the regular succession of states of affairs; a cause and an effect are things which happen together in sequence, and there is no more to causality than this togetherness. The regularity view does not recognize the existence of actual causal powers. These two theories of causality – or rather, sophisticated near-relatives of these two theories – have been major contenders within philosophy, ever since Hume carried out his famous attack on our claims to knowledge of causal powers. Now our contention is that while the powers view tends, in English, to be reflected by adult grammar, the regularity view tends to be expressed more often in the grammar of children. In terms of the discussion in the preceding chapters, the chaining syntax of speech tends towards the expression of the regularity view; the embedding and subordinating syntax of writing tends towards the expression of the powers view. As children are users of the chaining syntax in both speech and early writing, the regularity view may, for that reason alone, be characteristic of children. As adults are more likely to be users of the embedding syntax (certainly in more formal situations), this fact alone might lead to their being more disposed to the powers view. As the socially most prestigious form of the language, the form which defines the 'standard', is the language of the embedding syntax, the adult's grammar 'naturally', though not necessarily or exclusively, seems to express the powers view. Thus this view may be said to be idiomatic of adult grammar, while in the child's grammar the regularity view holds this privileged position. It is important to note that this is a tendency; adult language will frequently be found to show the syntax of the regularity view, in particular wherever the syntax of speech asserts itself, or where causal relations in the sense of the powers view are not understood or perceived and therefore cannot be, or are not, either claimed or expressed. Interestingly enough, much scientific writing shows this tendency. A similar preference for the regularity view holds for the language of children — spoken or written — particularly at the early stages of the process of learning to write.

It would be a grave mistake to consider the regularity view naive, childish, immature or anything similar. Indeed, the body of philosophical opinion since Hume would probably take the opposite position if a choice were to be made. Thus if one significant difference between the child's and the adult's language is the theory of causality expressed by the grammar, the child's language cannot unproblematically be described as naive, immature or underdeveloped. Rather, if the child were to employ the regularity view, and if the child's grammar were to be adequate to this, then the child's grammar would have to be seen as adequate. This would undermine the idea that the child's grammar is an impoverished or underdeveloped form of adult grammar, and in turn put in question the teaching strategy described above. Evidence for this view can be found in a detailed analysis of Text 27. This text, we argue, can be explained as an adequate expression of the regularity view. Indeed, we argue below that the narrative or textual structure of Text 27 overall seems to be based on the child's adherence to the regularity view of causality. It reports a collection of acts and times and people brought into contact with one another, but not to affect each other in such a way as to form a unity.

In the story a time-setting is established first, *Yesterday when we played Red Rover*, both as a reference point for the whole sequence of acts and to establish the temporal contiguity of the events constituted by Jody and Stephen coming into contact, *Jody and Stephen smashed into each other*. However, we need to note that two temporal reference points are in fact established, *Yesterday* and *when we played Red Rover*. The former not only places the story in the real world but provides a frame of reference within which the acts are to be interpreted. The when-clause (*when we played Red Rover*), on the other hand, marks the beginning of the causal chain as well as giving a specific frame for the series of actions. *When* seems to be vague, functionally, having both a temporal and a causal sense, which at this stage seems to be functionally undifferentiated. In this clause there is no causal activity in the powers sense of cause. Syntactically, the difference between *Jody and Stephen smashed into each other* and *Jody and Stephen smashed each other* is clear. In the former example, the syntactic participants which are related to the verbal process by the preposition *into* are just incidentally there, they are not causally active; and nothing is implied about the consequent state of the two participants. Compare *Jody smashed into the wall* as against *Jody smashed the wall*. In the second example *Jody* is causally potent, and there is an implication about the consequent state of the wall. A passive can be made from the second - *The wall was smashed*; and the verbal part can become an attributive adjective, *the smashed wall*, showing clearly enough the consequent result and the close relation between effect and affected entity. The same is not true of the prepositional form. *The wall was smashed into* is not only an awkward passive, it says nothing about the consequent state of the wall. It is possible to conceive a situation where someone might say *that's the wall the car smashed into, and you can't see a mark on it*. The grammar used by the child makes no assertion about the causal potency of either Jody or Stephen; nor does the grammar make an implied statement about the effect of the action. The grammar expresses, noncommittally, that an event took place. Jody and Stephen remain grammatically simply two children who came into contact.

The first sentence, that is, the linguistic unit to the first full stop, consists of four clauses, each reporting a discrete event. The four clauses are conjoined by *and* in a sequential order which mirrors that of the events in the world, and which indicates causality by succession. Interestingly, there is no expression of causality within each clause. That is, within a fully transitive clause causality is expressed via the relation actor/causer → (verbal) action → affected entity. In an intransitive clause events are portrayed simply as happening. *Tomatoes grow* says nothing about who, why or how; *John grows tomatoes* specifies a causee, or causer, namely *John*. With intransitive clauses causality has to be expressed by other, additional means, either through some adverbial adjunct (*Tomatoes grow with the application of fertilizer*) or through the sequence of clauses (*The rain fell and the tomatoes flourished*). Here each of the three clauses is intransitive, so that structures of the type *X cause / affects Y* do not occur. The first clause, *We played Red Rover*, is no exception as *Red Rover*, while seemingly the object of a transitive verb, is not an affected entity, but rather the expression of the semantic content of *play* in noun form. That is, it names the kind of game that was being played. (Similarly *sing a song = singing, dance the waltz = waltzing, give a kick = kicking*.) The second clause is a conjunction of two intransitive clauses, *Jody smashed into Stephen* and *Stephen smashed into Jody*. The third clause, *Jody had a blood ear*, is presumably the effect of the previous clause, but it is significant that in itself the clause is non-causal, Jody *had* rather than *got a blood ear*. *Got* is perhaps the most frequently used verb in the speech of children at that age. *Got* clearly refers to the resultant of a process, and hence belongs to the powers view. (Interestingly, the use of *got* is regarded by many teachers as stylistically undesirable.) Hence the use of the non-causal *had* is all the more noteworthy. The effect simply follows in time; to Jody's ear is added blood. The ear itself does not bleed, that is, the child does not write *had a bleeding ear*. In that form the *ear* would be doing something. This writer seems bent on avoiding any suggestion of the powers view, of action done or caused by some specific active power. So instead the writer prefers a descriptive or classificatory form: he is concerned to show that *is*, and in this case to show not what ears do but what they *are*. Hence he does not use *she had a bleeding ear*, for that is not what ears *are*. The fourth clause is also non-causal, intransitive, simply describing a state of affairs.

Within the first sentence we have an aggregate of events, and causality is suggested only through the temporal sequence in which the events are placed relative to each other: first the statement that *we played Red Rover*, then Jody and Stephen *smashed into each other*, then the *blood ear* added to Jody. A new aspect, Jody's impaired hearing, is added on to this. The only causal connection of this last event with the bleeding of the ear, hence with the accident, and hence with playing Red Rover, is the temporal relation of contiguity established initially by *Yesterday when we played Red Rover*, and the fact that it is the last event in this sequential/causal chain.

The child's own correction, crossing out the *and* and putting a full stop instead, needs to be commented on. Initially, the child had included the next two clauses, *then she had to go and clean her ear*, within the first sentence. The correction is therefore a significant act. Instead of including these two clauses in the same causal chain, conjoined as before by *and*, the child has decided to end the sentence there. This decision is indeed well motivated, for the first sentence now becomes one coherent unit dealing with all the events and only those events involved in the accident, and leading up to a specific state, *she couldn't hear very well*.

The separateness of the second sentence is marked formally by the fact that it begins with a new temporal marker, *then*. This in itself seems to show that the preceding clauses were tightly connected internally without needing any specification of connection. Even before the writer decided to put the full stop there, thus formally making it a new sentence, a statement of the connection was needed as the internal coherence was broken. Structurally the second sentence differs from the first in a number of ways. The two clauses of which it consists are more integrated; that is, the subject and the auxiliary verb of the second clause in this second sentence are identical with those of the first clause and have therefore been deleted. The full form of this sentence would have been *She had to go and she had to clean her ear*. Another way of putting this is to point out that in the first sentence each clause has its own subject-verb structure, marking them as having the status of independent events in their own right. This is not the case with the two clauses in the second sentence. In *she had to go and clean her ear* the two clauses report aspects of the same event; *go and clean* can nearly be regarded as a special aspectual form of the verb *clean*, while *had to* acts as a modal auxiliary, like *must* (*had to* can be regarded as the *must* of reported speech). The second clause in the second sentence is transitive, structurally, and hence represents an example of the powers view of causality, Jody being the potent causer of the action of cleaning, which directly affects the object, *her ear*.

The two clauses are further unified in that both report actions for which an identical causal source is given, through the modal *had to*. An external, social cause is cited, and the actions of both clauses are equally subject to that same cause. In fact there is no implication of a sequential causal relation between the two clauses; that is, Jody did not clean her ear because (or as a result of the fact that) she had to go. In other words, a different type of causality is at work here, not the physical causality of events happening in the natural world, but the social causality of events happening due to the social power of an actor in the social world.

The child's correction in making a new sentence of the last two clauses is therefore well motivated. Sentence 1 and sentence 2 are distinctively different in terms of the causal models. Sentence 1 is composed of clauses which each report independent events, in a sequence which mirrors that of the external world, and suggests causation by sequence. Sentence 2 contains two clauses which do not stand in that sequential relation to each other; and furthermore, here an external cause is alluded to through the modal verb *had to*, suggesting some external socially superior cause. (While *had to* in adult English is ambiguous between 'self-caused necessity' and 'external compulsion', in children's language, up to the age of ten or eleven, it tends to have only the 'external compulsion' meaning. This may be a revealing — and damning — insight into their experience of the world. For 'self-caused need' these children tend to use simply the past tense of the verb in question, e.g. *she went and cleaned her ear*.) Moreover, the second clause in that sentence expresses within itself the powers view of causality. The level of complexity of the judgment implied by the placing of the full stop is quite astonishing. From the point of view of simple narrative structure or narrative flow the full stop is not particularly functional, because from that point of view these two clauses belong to the one little story, they are part of the same incident, the consequence of which is reported in the third sentence. Judging from the evidence of the lower-case letter *t* on *then*, the child seems to have written these six clauses as one sentence initially, and then on rereading made the correction. We assume that he did so because he intuitively felt that two distinct causal models were operating there.

The third sentence contains three clauses, two of which are syntactically subordinated to or embedded in the first clause. The sentence begins with the temporal marker *then*. Clearly the actions reported in the three clauses of the third sentence are distinct from those of the first two sentences. They are not events which are integrally connected with the accident, though of course they are linked to the preceding two sentences, as the 'consequence' of what has gone before. The causal link is established by sequence (succession) alone, hence the causal connection is that of the regularity view. The temporal marker *then* in children's writing of this stage seems to have the function of marking a temporally subsequent event, but an event which is closely linked by dependence on the preceding event. The three clauses are intransitive. Unlike the first sentence there is no unambiguous sequential causal chain established. The two indicators of external social causation are causally ambiguous. The verb *said* in *the teacher said* is ambiguous, in adult English, between 'he stated' and 'he commanded'. The latter is the more plausible, as statements made by powerful speakers which entail actions or prohibitions on actions by the addressee tend to have the force of commands. This is, again, notably so for children, e.g. 'Why do I have to do it?', 'Because mummy/daddy said so!' The modal verb *can't* is similarly ambiguous for adults between an 'ability' and a 'permission' reading. Hence a number of interpretations are theoretically possible, e.g. 'the teacher stated that we are unable to play it again', where there is no active causal link between the two clauses. But in the language of children of this age the 'command + permission' is by far the most plausible reading. And an interpretation of this kind, 'the teacher commanded (us) that we are not permitted to play it again', has a strong causal link. The third clause is linked by *and* and introduced by the temporal marker *then*. Here the sequence between clauses 2 and 3 does not imply an active causal connection. Indeed, the *then* seems to act here as it does at the beginning of the second sentence: it marks the beginning of an event which, while it is part of the narrative and dependent on what precedes, is a thematically discrete unit and not strongly part of a causal chain. The child could easily have made a tighter link between the second and the third clause: by leaving out *then*, or by using *so* instead of *then*, all of which would be within the linguistic competence of the child.

As the third sentence does not contain a clearly articulated causal chain, there is also no need for the child to adopt the punctuation which he used to separate sentence 1 from sentence 2. It would have been perfectly all right to cross out the *and* and put a full stop before *then*, as the child did with sentence 2. This would leave two good sentences. From the point of view of causality, however, there is no motivation for such an alteration. Hence the absence of the change here is as strong an argument for the child's operation with a causal model as the presence of the change in the previous sentence. Here we simply have a narrative train, and the three clauses are appropriately accommodated within the one linguistic unit.

To sum up briefly: the child uses a number of causal models – the regularity model, the powers model – and he seems to make a distinction between social and non-social causation. Causation (of the regularity kind) is most clearly expressed between conjoined clauses within a sentence. The concept of sentence itself seems to be at least in part justified or defined on the basis of causal models. Causation is not expressed within clauses, with the one exception *(she had to) clean her ear*. Whereas causation in the physical world is clearly handled within a regularity view of causality, causation in the social world is expressed vaguely or ambiguously. This vagueness, to an adult reader, may reflect the child's experience of the teacher as an active causal power of such magnitude that he needs no explicit mention in the story. (It could, of course, be the child's mode of subversion, with the teacher existing on the periphery of the child's world, rather than being an implicit expression of the teacher's power.) The connections between the sentences in this story are temporal/sequential rather than causal. Hence we get a picture where some events are tightly connected within one sentence/causation unit through a regularity model of causality, while these larger units themselves are weakly connected by temporal succession.

It is important to note that the child has the different models available, including the powers model. He or she can make a choice, and hence the significance of having chosen attaches to the choices made. We are assuming rather that in this instance the child perceived the events as being of a type which were best described or represented by the regularity model of causation; or more strongly, that the child saw these events in that way. In a different context, with different events, the child might well have used a different model.

It is equally important not to draw inferences from an implicit equation of the child's spoken language and his ability to write the language. On the one hand, as we have pointed out, speech is more disposed, by its very structure, to an expression of the regularity view of causality. But further, the spoken language of children at this age is well in advance of their writing ability, and what we need in part to explain is the cause and nature of that gap. It may be that in writing the child is faced with the task of seeing the world objectively, and uses the syntax which expresses his or her objective view of the world.

As a comparison we will briefly discuss another story written by a child in the same age group, and in the same class. The task set was the same for both children; the stories were written as part of the same class exercise.

Text 33

The Fishing Trip

(1) On the weekend, we went out fishing and I caught two sharks. (2) When we came back we had 100 whiteing. (3) When it was tea time we (cleand) cleaned the boat. (4) Then we (aet) (eat) ate the fish. (5) (a) After that we went to sleep.

Some similarities are immediately apparent, for instance the temporal setting at the beginning of the story, and the conjunction of clauses with *and*. However, the differences are perhaps more marked. Three clauses are transitive - *I caught two sharks, we cleaned the boat, we ate the fish* - so that the powers theory is more markedly present in this story. The events reported by the clauses within the sentences are not in a sequential relation, with the possible exception of *we went out fishing and caught two sharks*. In fact all the sentences have the structure 'adverbial phrase of time plus main clause'. The adverbial phrase is not causally prior, but acts as a reference point for the event reported in the main clause.

While the clauses *within* the sentences are not in a sequential order which mirrors the order of events in the world, the sentences themselves are, in general, in such an order. Sentence 1 is the exception, in that it provides the frame and reference point for the whole story. To some extent therefore one kind of topical-textual structuring is taken out of the sentence, and becomes a feature of the whole text. The time adverbials provide, in each case, the sequential and cohesive link with the preceding sections of the text.

Two sentences have an adverbial clause beginning with *when*, and the difference between *when* and *then* may have a significant relation to causality. We said that *then* in the first story marked a new topic, or causal unit; additionally, *then* established a temporal reference point in relation to the preceding temporal reference point and a dependence in terms of content. It is therefore more conducive to a clearly articulated sequential order. *When*, on the other hand, establishes a temporal reference without a clear (or any necessary) relation to the preceding temporal reference point established in the text; it acts internally to the sentence. Hence temporal sequence and, consequently, causal sequence between sentences, are weakened. This may have implications for theories of causality in so far as the regularity view depends on articulated notions of sequence whereas the powers view does not. This hypothesis seems to be borne out by the two stories. The first shows a strongly developed sequence of clauses within sentences, and between sentences, and does not draw significantly on the powers view. The second story has a weakly developed sequence, certainly within but also between sentences; however, it draws more strongly on the powers view of causality.

Our analysis is little more than suggestive. But it does suggest that the child's grammar can be consistently interpreted as a genuine alternative to, and not merely an underdeveloped form of, adult grammar. This is sufficiently interesting to merit discussion, for if our analysis is correct, the implications for teaching are particularly noteworthy. Some aspects of established teaching methods are not justified if the thesis of underdevelopment is false, as we suggest it is. Rather, what is indicated by our analysis as an appropriate method of teaching adult grammar, and the conceptual/cognitive model encoded in it, to the child — an aim which we in no way dispute, given the greater comprehensiveness of the adult form — is not the accepted method of teaching by correcting according to the standards of adult grammar, but a method of teaching which aims to give the child experiences which cannot be adequately expressed in the child's grammar.

If our thesis is correct, it would seem that children, at given stages, have the grammar they do because this grammar is adequate to their cognitive and social needs at that time. To teach children adult grammar, therefore, a justifiable teaching strategy would need to be centrally concerned with broadening their experience. They might then experience the need for specific aspects of adult grammar. With respect to causality, such a strategy would require that children have the experience of being active causal agents or manipulating real things and of seeing their acts as the generative causes of real-world situations. Without such experience children must see adult grammar as not only foreign to their world but irrational, since it makes claims about actions and forces when only events in sequence are experienced. With such experience they will see the sense in adult grammar, or — if the Humean analysis of causality is correct — come to share our adult delusions.

iii   Non-causal sequence

It may·be thought that all sequences necessarily express causality, and that therefore, conversely, we cannot attach any special significance to the expression of causality by sequence. That is not the case, however. There are many instances of either temporal sequence or sequential conjunctions which do not express causality. Below are a few such examples. The first text, 8, 'Going to the Shops', was discussed in Chapter 3. It contains sequences which express causality, sequences which can be construed in a causal fashion, and sequences which are non-causal.

Text 8

Going to the Shops

(1) When I went to the Shops I saw a train and walk on I saw a King and Queen. (2) I said how do you do they said very well thank you then I lost my money I had to go home agen I got some nwe money and baute a lolly pop.

Examples of causal sequences here are: *When I went to the Shops I saw a train, I got some nwe money and baute a lolly pop* and *I said how do you do they said very well thank you.* A sequence which can be construed in a causal fashion is *and walk on I saw a King and Queen.* A non-causal sequence is illustrated by *they said very well thank you then I lost my money.*

An example *par excellence* of non-causal sequences occurs in Text 9, 'the mouse'. Not one sequence there has causal implications. Of course, as I pointed out, that may be due to the fact that it is not a narrative. But as 'Going to the shops' illustrates, narratives need not be fully causal. Indeed, another text discussed earlier, 14, 'Our Trip to Ayers House', is a straightforward narrative, but none of its sequences imply causality.

Text 14

Our Trip to Ayers House

(1) On Friday 1st July we all got in the bus and waved to Miss Martyn. (2) We're off I thought, there was lots of merry talk in the bus. (3) Tracey was telling some people that the bus would pass her house 'there it is' said Tracey but it soon went by. (4) We soon were there. (5) When we had got out of the bus Mrs. Gilbert said to sketch the front of Ayers House. (6) When I had finished my sketch I looked at some of the other sketches. (7) I thought Prue's was the best.

Temporal sequence is the dominant organizing principle in this text though, as I pointed out above in the discussion of the text, there are other principles and modes of order at work. But the temporal sequence here carries no implication of causality; that is, it is not the case that *and waved to Miss Martyn* is presented as causally dependent on *we all got in the bus.* (The fact that it may do so in reality is not at issue here; what is at issue is what causal model the child chooses to present that reality.) The only instance of causality, involving this time the powers model, occurs in 5 ... *Mrs. Gilbert said to sketch the front* ... where a clause (in its full form), *we sketch the front,* is embedded to the clause *Mrs. Gilbert said.* This latter agent therefore seems to be causally responsible for *we sketch the front* ...

Hence neither sequence in itself nor sequence in a narrative necessitates the presence of a causal model, or a causal implication in a story. Nor is content the determining factor; many stories written by children seem to demand causal models for their organization and presentation. Text 34, 'The Egg Hatched By A Dog', is one such story. One would assume that the content here demands causal connections, causal chains. But that is not how the writer, a twelve-year-old boy, chooses to tell the story.

Text 34

The Egg Hatched By A Dog

(1) One day I went for a walk to the river. (2) Down at the river I found an egg. (3) I took it home and I gave it to my dog. (4) My dog sat on the egg for two weeks. (5) At the end of the two weeks I was surprised because the egg had hatched. (6) I called my Dad and he ran out to me I said 'Look at this chicken'. (7) It had a head like my dog and a body like an ordinary chicken. (8) I ran inside and called the news the news came and took pictures. (9) My dog was happy with the chicken the chicken could do any thing a dog could do. (10) It could bark and it could lay bigger eggs than any other chickens.

In 3, for instance, the *and* conjoins two clauses which do not stand in a causal relation; such a relation could have been established by the child through the use of *to* (*I took it home to give it to my dog*) or *so* (*I took it home so that my dog could hatch it*), etc. In 5 there is a causal relation between two events; interestingly, it does not involve the process of hatching, but it involves the narrator's subjective response 'That the egg hatched caused that I was surprised'. The egg hatched itself, as far as the linguistic model is concerned. We know, of course, that the dog sat on the egg for two weeks, but that is not linked causally to the egg's hatching. That is, one would have expected either a weak causal link, 'My dog sat on the egg . . . and at the end of two weeks, the egg hatched', or a stronger expression of causality, 'At the end of two weeks my dog had hatched the egg'. The narrator's mention of his surprise reinforces the non-causal interpretation. Of course, the child is having a joke here, he is writing a funny story. However, it is doubtful whether his joke actually extends to the manipulation of causality. Rather, the somewhat magical, mysterious nature of the process seems to demand expression in a non-causal model, so that the details can be left somewhat obscure. (The child's sentences also seem to point to a relatively early stage in the learning of writing; that is, they are still very similar to sentences in, for instance, 'The Pioneer Boy'.) More significant than this is the fact that many stories written for children present events in such an a-causal fashion (note, for instance, the sequence of events in Vera Southgate's *The Enormous Turnip*).

The significant point is that the writer's decision to use one causal model rather than another, or no causal model at all, depends very much on the writer's felt needs or wishes, and far less — if at all — on either the genre, or the content, or the available syntax. At times the nature of the task — set by the teacher, or derived from some other source — acts as an important determining factor. In the text below, 'The countryside around school', 'the children were asked to write a short essay on the countryside around the school. No further instructions were given' (Burgess et al., *Understanding Children Writing*, p. 130).

Text 35

The Countryside Around School

(1) The countryside around school is very nice. (2) There is a farm about twenty yards away and the main crops are potatoes and barley. (3) On the front of the school we have five Chesnut trees and a big garden with a tennis court at the bottom, next to the front garden is a main raod and the busses go past every half hour, lots of the big lorries pass by every day. (4) Next to the road there is a railway track and the trains go past every half hour. (5) In the back garden there are two greenhouses and one tin shed, we have quite a lot of apple trees and one plum tree and a big vegetable plot.

(6) There is a little beck that flows at the bottom of the back garden and at the side of the front garden. (7) Our school is the shape of the letter L. (8) Our playing field it is about five acres

and we have a cricket pitch and three rugby pitches and three hockey pitches and two tennis courts. (9) We have a net ball pitch and we also play in the Net ball pitch. (10) When you go out of the playground and walk down the back garden path there are two trees planted two yards between each other and now they are fully grown they have made an arch way. (11) If you look out of our form window you can see Skiddaw. (12) The front garden has a drive from the bottom to the front of the School.

(13) Beside the Chesnut trees there is a new art room which has just been built. (14) It is near Wigton and in Cumberland.

The sentences in this text are, with very few exceptions, non-causal. The child (an eleven-year-old boy) has presented his perceptions in terms of static descriptions, with *is, are, have* as the main verbs: 1 *The countryside . . . is very nice*; 2 *There is a farm . . . the main crops are . . .*; 3 *On the front . . . we have five Chesnut trees*; etc. The sequences of clauses within sentences and across the sentence-boundaries do not imply or express causality: 2 *There is a farm . . . and the main crops are . . .*; 3 *. . . we have five Chesnut trees and a big garden . . .*; 4 *. . . there is a railway track and the trains go past . . .*; etc. Causality is expressed in a number of clauses and conjoined clauses. The powers model of causality is encoded in the agentless passives in sentences 10 and 13 (*. . . there are two trees planted . . .*; *. . . which has just been built*) and in the transitive clause in 10 (*. . . they have made an arch way*). In each of the three cases there is an agent, either named, *they*, or deleted as in the agentless passives. The regularity model is encoded in the sequence of clauses in sentence 11: *If you look out . . . you can see Skiddaw*. However, the major part of the text by far is in a non-causal form. This suggests that while the child is perfectly aware of and able to use causal models, the type of task demanded of him strongly influences which model will be most prominent for him. This point relates to the suggestion made earlier on, that if one wishes to intervene in a child's cognitive processes, one way of doing this is to construct experiences or tasks for him which demand the use of certain models, or which make available the experiences which will lead to the development of those models.

iv   Causality and writing

The two models of causality – power and regularity – clearly exist in both speech and writing. However, the two forms of language differ in the degree to which causal models are present, and in the extent to which the two forms favour one or the other of the two models of causality. Speech, with its chaining syntax, clauses co-ordinated in sequences, tends by its very structure to favour the regularity model. Writing, with its greater preponderance of subordination and embedding, leaves the regularity model as an option, but tends to favour the powers view. So whereas speech might be typified by a form such as *we stopped and had our picnic*, writing might be typified by a form such as *we stopped to have a picnic*. The spoken form implies causality, but does so weakly; in the form of the written syntax the causality is much more explicit.

The powers view is strongly encoded in real (that is, semantic as well as syntactic) transitive clauses; and to the extent that transitives and intransitives both occur with equal frequency in speech and in writing, the two modes of language are not differentiated from that point of view. The regularity view is, as pointed out above, expressed through certain clausal sequences. These sequences are linked by co-ordinating and subordinating conjunctions such as *and*, *when* and *then*. Conjunctions such as *because*, *so*, *therefore* and *thus* are explicitly causal and belong to the powers model. All of these, with the exception of *therefore*, occur commonly in both speech and writing, though it may be that *because* and *therefore* are more frequent in writing than in speech. There may thus be a tendency for one group of conjunctions to occur with greater frequency in speech and another group in writing. In the developing writing of children this certainly seems to be borne out. The earliest conjunctions used are *then*, *and* and *when*; Later *because* appears, followed by *so*, with *therefore* later still. In this the development of causality is closely linked with the development of modality. The change of *when*, for instance, from a purely temporal conjunction to a more explicit causal conjunction is accompanied at the same time by a change of *when* to a conditional. Indeed, in some instances the two are indistinguishable. Complex conditional conjunctions such as *if ... then* are at the same time used to carry causal implications, directly or covertly. Indeed, it seems that the recognition by the child that there are direct causal links between events is at the same time accompanied by an awareness that conditions attach to the fulfilment of the causal connection and events exist in different modes.

Adverbial phrases can be used by the writer or speaker to express causality; again, both the regularity and the powers model can occur in prepositional phrases, though the powers model is, on the whole, the predominant one. Prepositions such as *with*, *by*, and *through* express the powers model, more or less strongly: *he lost his life by his own carelessness* seems more causally direct than *he lost his life through his own carelessness*, though both forms express the powers view. *In*, on the other hand, tends to express the regularity view: *he lost his life in the floods*. Again, the prepositions which express the powers view tend to be more frequent in writing than in speech; though *in* is probably as frequent in writing as it is in speech.

All in all, there seems to be a closer connection of the powers model of causality with writing than with speech; and a closer connection of the regularity model with speech than with writing. This tendency finds expression in a number of linguistic features: in sequence, in transitivity, in conjunctions, and in prepositions. To some extent the syntax of speech and writing each facilitates one model more than the other; and though it would be an exaggeration to maintain that the powers view depends on the syntax of writing, it is clear that writing speeds up the development, use, and frequency of occurrence of the powers view. The very overtness of linguistic activity may be an aid in this process; that is, ideas find a seemingly concrete manifestation in writing, and may be manipulated and disposed with greater deliberation. The necessary sequential unfolding of speech may make one form of causality seemingly more natural and inevitable; in writing this sequentiality can be interrupted at any stage, and a reordering of ideas and conceptual materials made. The major textual modes of speech – narrative, monologue and dialogue – all have an inbuilt directionality and sequentiality which may 'naturally' suggest one mode of causality rather than another. Certain genres exist only in either speech or writing: while narrative is typical of speech, the scientific report is typical of writing. Sequence typifies speech; hierarchy typifies writing.

In short, speech and writing tend toward their own preferred models of causality; inevitably, therefore, the learning and development of writing has cognitive implications and effects. Hence writing has much to do with models of causality.

v   **Sources and context**

A discussion of the two views of causality, conducted as part of a critique of the regularity view, is to be found in Harré and Madden,

Causal Powers (1975). Chapter 3 of Kress and Hodge, *Language as Ideology*, 'Language and processes: models for things that move', contains an analysis of causal models contained in children's stories, in particular *The Enormous Turnip* by Vera Southgate.

Chapter 8
'Errors'

i   Convention and correction

From early on children find themselves corrected. This happens in all aspects of their lives, from being told not to pull books out of bookshelves or saucepans out of cupboards, to being prevented from pulling out handfuls of little Joanne's hair. Children learn through constant negation and prohibition of (parts of) their actions: don't do this, don't do that! The learning of concepts is no exception. A child sees an animal, and says (in some phonological form): 'That's a dog.' The parent, uncle or neighbour responds, 'No, that's not a dog, that's a horse.' Whereas before the concept 'dog' covered the whole class of furred animals, it has now become more restricted; it does not now apply to 'horse'. By a constant process of reduction and negation children learn the concepts which apply in the social and physical world around them. Occasionally a concept is introduced in a non-negative fashion: 'Look, Sally, a truck!', or, 'Wave bye-bye to Auntie!' — with the child's arm being shaken vigorously up and down.

It is important to recognize what is involved here. The child is performing an action arising out of a motivation which is unknown to the adult. The adult interrupts the child's action with a prohibition that arises out of a set of rules known to the adult, rules which are derived from the society in which the adult lives. The child's individual action is prohibited, and the adult society's rule imposed on the child. To the child the adult's intervention must appear at least as arbitrary as the child's action appeared to the adult. The child will (either immediately or eventually) acquiesce in the adult's behaviour, for the adult's prohibition is supported by superior power. The question about the child's motivations rarely arises in a serious fashion; to the adult the child was merely doing 'something silly', something potentially danger-ous', 'the wrong thing', or perhaps the child was 'being a nuisance'. The only way in which the question of the child's motivation arises is in the form 'isn't he being a nosey little thing, always into my cupboards'. That is, it is assumed that the child is naturally inquisitive.

In such interaction two things therefore remain unexamined for the adult: firstly, the grounds of his or her intervention in the child's actions and any question about the adult's 'rightness' in doing so; and secondly, the possibility that the child may be acting with motives which are perfectly consistent with and appropriate to the child's wishes and needs. The social bases of the adult's actions and their challengeability remain invisible to the adult, who presents his own actions to himself as 'only natural': 'it's only natural to . . .'

Learning language is no exception though, in so far as no physical harm can come to the child or to the adults as a result of the child's verbal actions, correction is not so obviously insistent. Language is somewhat less visible as activity, and to the extent that humans are constantly immersed in it language is perhaps less noticed than physical activity. Nevertheless, those who are constantly with children - parents, relatives, teachers, childminders - spend a vast amount of time on corrections: these normally take the form of repeating the child's utterance in the 'correct' form. When the child reaches school, language learning is fully formalized, and noticeable to the child as a school activity like other school activities. In school, language occurs not only in a formal setting, for formal purposes, embedded in ritual, it also occurs in a new mode, in writing. Most children come to school unable to read or write, and hence school is the place which conveys mastery over the language which the children already know, but in a mode which they do not know. As a result, the children's language knowledge is set aside, and only the knowledge which the school can give is relevant. The child is back in a situation very much like that described above: treated as being without knowledge, without motives or, at any rate, without rational, legitimate and acceptable knowledge and motives. The child's linguistic behaviour is again subject to prohibitions and injunctions. From the child's point of view the adult's behaviour may well seem arbitrary and have no legitimation other than that of superior power. In school, knowledge and power are interwoven, inextricably for some children, for power is frequently the basis and legitimation of knowledge. In the case of the learning of reading and writing the child's view is closer to the reality of the matter than the adult's. The vagaries of the relationship between the sound-system of English and its representation in the written form are such as to appear anarchic to the child, and quite legitimately. A teacher's insistence that the same sound must be spelled one way here and in a different way there can only appear baffling to a child. Linguists and teachers naturally attempt to represent the relationship as a basically logical one — as many different reading-schemes and sounding/spelling rules demonstrate. But this attempt simply makes the child's position worse: a system which is largely arbitrary is presented as basically logical, the child is invited to grasp the (non-existent) logic of the system, and when he fails his inadequacies are clearly apparent and confirmed.

Adults and teachers need, of course, to hold to their view of the correctness, 'naturalness', of their own actions; if they did not, they would be seriously embarrassed in their attempts to teach children. Worse, they might be seriously embarrassed about many of their own actions. In the process children's motives are, however, overlooked. The gap between the adult's value-system — which is, ultimately, society's — and the child's, is covered over by the concept of 'error'. It enshrines a view which accepts the naturalness of sets of social value-systems (be they table-manners, duelling-codes, or spelling conventions) and thereby labels behaviour which falls outside the system as unnatural, incorrect, unacceptable, etc., without inquiring into the bases of that behaviour. More than that, by suggesting that such behaviour cannot and does not have a basis in alternative rational or logical systems, the concept of error positively inhibits serious consideration's being given to the bases of divergent behaviour.

Seen from this point of view, the category 'error' acquires great interest, as it promises to be an aid in revealing the value-system of the one who classifies the error, and of the one who has committed the error. The classification of the error, and the type of error, is a measure of the distance between the two sets of value-systems. It is important to recognize that the right to classify any kind of behaviour as being incorrect and in error derives from social power *vis-à-vis* the other person. Those who are less powerful in interactions do not classify aspects of the other person's behaviour as incorrect. Employees do not correct their boss, committee members not usually the chairperson, nor patients the doctor. Children are, in their interactions with adults always less powerful, and consequently it is their behaviour which is subject to correction, not that of adults. The equation of power and knowledge is therefore strongly reinforced for the child.

The implications of adult's corrections of children may perhaps be made more apparent by a series of oppositions which are inherent in the concept of correction. A set of opposed pairs can be constructed to describe the implicit judgments:

correct	incorrect
logical	illogical
right	wrong
true	false
FACT	ERROR

The child's behaviour falls under the labels on the right-hand side, the adult's under those on the left. When we look at this set of terms the implicit meaning of corrections becomes clearer: the child's actions are equated with the notions 'incorrect', 'illogical', 'wrong', 'false', 'ERROR'. Now it is clear that the concept 'false' cannot be applied to a child pulling books out of a bookshelf, nor can the concept of 'ERROR'. And it becomes 'wrong' only if the parent decides that it is so. And yet, while we might hesitate to apply those terms to that action, we would not feel similarly constrained in applying the terms to the child's writing (or spelling). But 'correct' spelling has no claims to either truth or fact. There are by now largely agreed spelling conventions — though in some instances the conventions are not finally settled: is it programme or program, theater or theatre, connexion or connection? The set of oppositions above should therefore be replaced by another one, namely

conventional	unconventional

If we accept this opposition it puts the discussion of error at once into quite a different domain. Out go notions of truth/falsehood, fact/ error, logicality/illogicality. Indeed, we may find that the child's action may be unconventional and yet highly logical.

ii 'Error analysis'

In what follows I wish to look at some errors, some corrections, and attempt to draw out what both child and teacher seemed to be doing. Throughout I wish to stress that what is at issue is a contest over convention, and while we may accept that the child's actions are unconventional in terms of society at large, his or her actions may have their own logic, consistency, coherence, and may indeed point towards possible alternative conventions. I wish to suggest that we ought not to pass over these unspoken, unasserted suggestions for alternative conventions too quickly and unreflectingly. Above all, we should use these as important evidence of intelligent, active, creative minds at work, rather than as evidence of insufficiency or even stupidity. The exercise of the power of correction, the imposition of the category of error, inexorably pushes the child towards and into adult convention. Even if we regard this process as ultimately necessary, we ought to pause on the way at times, and reflect on what else could be. But above all we should not allow our blindness to misconstrue the abilities and actions of children.

Text 36(a)
(the child's original)

The Drunken Dragon

(1) Once upon a time there lived a drunkin dragon. (2) He lived in the woods in a cave. (3) It was black and ~~skery~~ ~~seery~~ scarie. (4) He got a ticket for lighting a fire on a very hot day. (5) As you know dragons breathe fire and so did the officer when his pants were burnt. (6) then he had a walk and fell asleep on a log as he snored flames came through his nose he started a mighty big fire. (7) He got burnt and jumped up. (8) And then he fell of a clif and dide.

This is the text as the child (an eleven-year-old boy) wrote it and left it after he had made his own corrections. His attempts at spelling *scary* are all well motivated, both in terms of spelling conventions and of possible representations of the sounds in writing. *Sk* is a possible letter-sequence in English, and would represent the phonetic value of the spoken word, *e* is in fact a better representation than *a* in Australian English, and in particular in all but the most prestigious forms of Australian English; in other words, the child may be demonstrating great acuteness of hearing, and good judgment in his transcription. The child had at first settled for the *y* ending, and then changed it to *ie*; the latter is not a possible final letter sequence in English, but the child may, again, have opted for it as being a more accurate representation of the spoken word, especially as *y* is likely to be pronounced as in *dry*. Initially sentences 5 and 6 seem to have been one sentence. The child's alteration fits in well with the notion of topical connectedness explored in detail in Chapter 4.

Text 36(b)
(the teacher's corrections)

The Drunken Dragon

(1) Once upon a time there lived a <u>drunken</u> dragon. (2) He lived in the woods in a cave. (3) It was black and <u>scary</u>. (4) He got a ticket for lighting a fire on a very hot day. (5) As you know dragons breathe fire and so did the officer when his pants were burnt. (6) <u>Then</u> he had a walk and fell asleep on a log. (7) <u>As</u> he snored flames came through his nose <u>and</u> started a mighty big fire. (8) He got burnt and jumped up. (9) And then he fell of a <u>cliff</u> and <u>died</u>.

The teacher has corrected the spelling errors indicated. One would like to know whether he or she paused over the child's spellings and own corrections, to consider what these implied about the child's knowledge of language, perceptiveness, and care to get the transcription correct. It is of course a fact of life that the teacher will have had to mark between twenty and thirty of these pieces, and the amount of time that he or she can devote to each is strictly limited. My point is not to be critical of the teacher (who may have had to keep the class in order at the same time), but to point out that with a different conception of error the child's spelling takes on a new significance, quite unlike one which regards the misspelling as simply 'getting it wrong', a deficiency which the child must overcome. The teacher may still decide to make the same corrections but, in the light of this approach and without spending more time with the child, he or she may have a significantly different impression of the child and his abilities.

The teacher introduced a new sentence into the child's sentence 6. The change alters the textual and conceptual structure of the piece quite significantly. The child had put all events leading up to the dragon getting burned into one sentence; within that sentence the events were ordered in a temporal sequence. The teacher's change alters the conceptual order. The new sentence 6 is about 'preliminary events'; the new sentence 7 about 'consequent events'. In addition, another mode of order is introduced by the correction, namely simultaneity: one sentence, new 6, reports one set of events, the other, new 7, reports events which are at least in part simultaneous with it. This represents a different criterion for the definition of sentenceness from those employed by the child. Within the new sentence 7 the teacher introduces another change, namely deleting *he* and joining the clauses by the *and*. Two significant features are involved here. The child had simply adjoined the clause *he started a mighty big fire* to the rest of the sentence, leaving the topical connectedness to carry the work of integration and cohesion. The teacher's correction suggests that clauses within a sentence need to be syntactically as well as topically/semantically integrated. The second change may be inadvertent, but probably expresses a fundamentally different conceptual orientation. In the child's text the fire is started by the dragon (*he started a mighty big fire*); in the corrected version the flames, not the dragon directly, start the fire (. . . *flames came . . . and started a mighty big fire*). This may well represent a fundamentally different mode of seeing the world: for the child the initial cause is most prominent, he keeps his eye firmly on the dragon and responsibility lies with him. For the teacher the immediate cause is most prominent, the responsibility lies there. The contrast is paradoxical and ironic, with the child's view being the more 'truthful' or 'factual'. Of course, the teacher is unlikely to have thought of the correction in these terms. That, however, is precisely my point. For one thing, to the child the correction marks an error. For another, while the teacher may have been concerned with notions of style ('it reads better that way'), or of grammatical improvement ('that's not a proper sentence structure'), the child's intended meaning is quite overlooked. It is not a consideration. In this situation any question about the child's cognitive and perceptual models cannot really arise in a serious fashion.

It may be dangerous to speculate too far here; but one could connect this difference in view to notions of alienation, which may be more apt for the adult's world than the child's.

The teacher's correction of sentences 6 and 7 arises from the clash of two differing conceptions of what sentences are. The child's derives, as pointed out in earlier chapters, from the syntax of speech and all its contingencies; the teacher's model is that of the syntax of writing. Here the origin of the error in conventionality can be seen clearly. There is no reason other than convention why the syntax of speech should not or could not persist into writing, and with it all its attendant features. Each of the two modes of language has its own conventions, which, while they coincide in part, also differ in substantial respects. The child's own corrections of his writing clearly show that he has proceeded on the basis of a clearly understood - even if not articulated - model. For instance, the spelling correction seems to indicate that the child first aims to reproduce the phonetic quality, and *skery* is an excellent approximation within the child's dialect, Adelaide Australian. He then corrects that twice, in the direction of the convention, *sc* being more frequent as an initial consonant cluster then *sk*, and *a* being the letter that more often represents this sound in writing (e.g. daring, care, fare). The child's correction of the sentence structure, making two sentences (5 and 6) out of the previous one, is motivated by his conception of the sentence as a unit defined by topically connected material. Another example of a teacher's corrections based on a clash of models can be seen in Text 31, 'Life in the Goldfields', below. Here too one of the teacher's corrections to the story involves altering the child's sentence structure (see the alteration to the child's sentence 10).

Text 31(a)
(including the child's corrections)

Life in the Goldfields
(Items in brackets indicate the corrected item)

(1) One day (we) my mum and I went to Ballarat. (2) We went to Ballarat to dig for gold because we were poor. (3) So we started digging for gold in the goldfields in Ballarat. (4) We didn't struck gold the first, second, and third day at Ballarat. (5) But on the fourth day we struck gold. (6) We (got) struck two nuggets of gold. (7) When we made sure that it was gold we packed our bags and pulled our tent down and went back to Adelaide. (8) When we got back to Adelaide and took it home and hid it. (9) I hid it in the closet where my shirts are and I put(ted) it in one of the shirt pockets. (10) When I was putting the gold in the pocket till Monday my next door neighbour was looking through the window. (11) So when I was for (and) an hour she came in and said 'Did you get any gold' I said 'Yes'. (12) 'Where is it'. (13) 'I hid it'. (14) Then when I went to bed about 10:00 PM I checked to see if the gold was there and it was. (15) So I went to bed. (16) Then my next door neighbour came in the house and

took the gold. (17) Then when I got up in the morning I went
to see (the) if the gold was (still) not there. (18) So I called
my mum.

The writer (a twelve-year-old boy) has made a number of corrections
which show his knowledge of some of the conventions of adult writing,
as of course does most of his writing. Changing *we* to *my mum and I* in
sentence 1 shows an awareness of the absent reader, to whom the *we*
would be meaningless. That is, the act of writing is making the child
aware of the need to be explicit: whereas his first move had been to use
the implicit form, which would be appropriate to speech, on reflection
he realizes the different demands of writing. In sentence 6 the child
changes *got*, perhaps the most frequent verb in the speech of children,
to *struck*. Here the child may be making a concession to two demands:
one, a constant demand by the teacher not to use *got*, and the other,
again the demand to be as explicit as possible. Here this takes the form
of substituting a lexically explicit verb for a lexically empty verb. The
two corrections in sentence 16 may also be motivated by the child's
awareness of the need to be explicit. The child seemingly was going to
write . . . *I went to see the gold (was gone)*; that is, the child as author
knows that the neighbour has taken the gold. But he hesitates to rush
to the conclusion to which he has been building up too quickly,
probably because he feels that while as author he knows the resolution
of the story, as character in the story he does not. Similarly with *still*:
it presupposes a 'cessation of an event or state of affairs', in this case
the gold having gone. However, he needs to postpone too early a
resolution for the narrator as the hero of the story. The difficulty of
holding these two requirements apart is a little too much for him, and
the *not there* brings in the denouement too soon.

Text 31(b)
(including the teacher's corrections)

Life in the Goldfields
(Items crossed out indicate the teacher's corrections; the
underlinings are the teacher's, with 'style' written in the
margin.)

(1) One day my mum and I went to Ballarat. (2) We went
to Ballarat *there* to dig for gold because we were poor.
(3) So we started digging for gold in the goldfields in

Ballarat. (4) We didn't ~~struck~~ *strike* gold the first second
~~and~~ *or* third day at Ballarat. (5) But on the fourth day
we struck gold. (6) We ~~struck~~ *found* two nuggets of gold.
(7) When we *had* made sure that it was gold we packed
our bags and pulled our tent down and went back to
Adelaide. (8) When we got back to Adelaide and took it
home and hid it. I hid it in the closet where my shirts are
and I put it in one of the shirt pockets. (10) ~~When~~ I was putting
the gold in the pocket till Monday. (11) My next door neighbour
was looking through the window. (12) So when I was home for
an hour she came in and said 'Did you get any gold' I said
'Yes'. (13) 'Where is it'. (14) 'I hid it'. (15) Then when I went
to bed about 10:00 PM I checked to see if the gold was there
and it was. (16) So I went to bed. (17) Then my next door
neighbour came in the house and took the gold. (18) Then
when I got up in the morning I went to see if the gold was
not there. (19) So I called mum.

The teacher's corrections seem by and large to be motivated by
stylistic considerations. Under this general heading she deals with a
number of disparate features. From the teacher's circling of *got* it seems
that the assumption that the child's own correction of *got* is a response
to previous corrections by the teacher is correct. The teacher has circled
the other two occurrences of *got*; it isn't quite clear what she would
expect the child to use instead of *got up - arose*? The teacher altered
one of the child's sentences, 10; she may have wanted to encourage the
child to use a different kind of sentence construction. As it turns out,
it distorts the content of the child's sentence. The child wished to
indicate that the two events reported occurred simultaneously, so that
the neighbour was witnessing the hiding of the gold. The correction
makes the events sequential, and thus destroys a clue in this mystery-
story. Again, I do not wish to attach too much significance to this
single correction: the teacher had here come to the third sentence
starting with *when*, and her wish to make a stylistic point over-rode any
other consideration. However, if one approached the child's writing with
the firm idea that it incorporates and expresses a specific view of reality,
an alternative convention which should be considered and respected, then
such a ready intervention might be less often made. As it turns out, the
child had a specific scheme in mind. The teacher either did not recognize
it or chose to give greater importance to stylistic concerns.

Two other corrections are worth comment. Both concern alternative conceptions of time. In sentence 4 the teacher replaces the child's *and* with *or*. The two conjunctions express differing conceptions and perceptions of reality here. The *and* links the three days to form one single unit, one time-period during which no gold was found by the family. In other words, it was 'quite a long time' before gold was found. The *or* on the other hand treats the three days as three separate, discrete, alternate units, on each of which no gold was found. The difference is subtle, but important. It may well represent two fundamentally distinct modes of conceptualizing time, and events within time. Time may have quite a different quality for the child — we ourselves remember the endless-seeming *stretches* of time which separated us as children from eagerly anticipated events, a trip, a birthday, Christmas. In observing children this view of time is readily apparent. Adults' conceptions of time are more prone to be of a segmenting kind: only three more months (days, weeks) before . . . In sentence 7 the teacher's correction again concerns time, in the form of the grammatical category *tense*. In the child's version, the sequence of clauses alone is sufficient to indicate the temporal succession of the two events; the teacher's correction superimposes on this 'simple' succession another relation, an internal hierarchical ordering of two events. That is, the perfective aspect establishes a temporal dependence among events, established in relation to a given point of temporal reference. The child's version has two separate events, linked in a sequential chain which includes other events. The teacher's version presents this as a single though complex unit which consists of two separate events. These two differing versions link up with the concepts of 'stretch of time' and 'discrete units of time'. For the child the sequential chain of events is the equivalent of (or the realization of) the stretch of time; for the adult, if longer units of time have to be established from the discrete units, this is done by the creation of a complex single unit via a relation of hierarchy and dependence.

The major direction of the teacher's corrections here is in the direction of 'stylistic improvement'. If spelling and syntax are conventional, the considerations of style implied in these corrections are even more so, hence least grounded in fact, truth, or necessity. These are transgressions against style, and as such we may consider corrections of this kind as paradigm cases of the notion of error arising out of conventionality. Its function lies in coercing the one who is corrected into adherence to convention. In essence the question is one of etiquette and manners, like opening your egg on the blunt or pointed end. There is, of course, no reason why the teacher should not point out what the 'best manners' are, as parents ought not to be stopped from teaching their children to balance peas on the back of a fork. Indeed, the teacher can hardly do other than encourage mastery of conventions, given that society attaches such enormous weight to certain conventions, such as spelling. Where a young school-leaver's chances of getting or keeping a job may depend on his or her mastery of such skills, teachers must give quite inordinate attention to such otherwise trivial abilities. However, a teacher might hope to provide the child with some discrimination among conventions. Here in this text these lesser stylistic matters are treated as errors of the same kind as those of tense, of verbal morphology (strike/struck), of syntax, of lexical choice. The child is consequently not given any information about the kind of convention which is at issue, and hence no means of assessing the seriousness of the 'error' which is at issue. If the teacher were to focus on questions of convention, to make them and the degree of choice which exists in each instance a subject of discussion (none in morphology, next to none in syntax, some in tense, more in the choice of words, and much in aesthetic matters such as repetition), then the child would gain an important insight not only into the nature, function and uses of language, but also into the nature of social behaviour and its foundations in more or less rigid rules and conventions.

To include, here are three more texts. The first illustrates that children's texts are not accorded the same seriousness of reading as those of adults. The others illustrate the problems inherent in this approach: what do we do with texts which seem to have no unifying conception, coherence, schema?

Text 37(a)

My Careless Master

(1) I was born on the 11th of January. (2) I thougth life was going to be good. (3) I was worng. (4) My master was a reckless uncaring boy called Fredwick. (5) He onece got to black eyes in a month. (6) He was always making nauthey deals with people and called every girl he met a numskull. (7) Well I was broken because he made a bet with a boy that he would ride a wild horse without reins or a sadle. (8) He did for five minutes but then he

fell of. (9) I hit a stone and chiped now I look ugly and the othe big thox tooth teases me a lot.

Text 37(b)
(including the teacher's corrections)

My Careless Master

(1) I was born on the 11th of January. (2) I *thought* life was going to be good. (3) I was *wrong*. (4) My master was a reckless uncaring boy called *Fredrick*. (5) He *once* got *two* black eyes in a month. (6) He was always making *naughty* deals with people and called every girl he met a numskull. (7) Well I was broken because he made a bet with a boy that he *could* ride a wild horse without reins or a *saddle*. (8) He did it for five minutes but then he fell *off*. (9) I hit a stone and *chipped*. *(10) Now* I look ugly and the *other* big thox tooth teases me a lot.

Here the teacher's alteration of *would* to *could*, in sentence 7, quite misconstrues the child's meaning. The child sees the boy making a bet on the basis of an *intention* (irrespective of his *ability* to perform the action), which is of course completely in tune with the strong-willed and naughty character Fredrick. The teacher's correction alters the basis of the bet to one of *ability*, which is quite beside the point, for Fredrick, headstrong, wicked boy that he is, is not in the least concerned with such rational considerations.

Text 38

Little Mi

(1) Onces upon a time some one nealy strot on me. (2) Then I ran away behind a star. (3) Then we all had a test on friday I got them all writ. (4) Then I went in sib and I hib be hin a leef and I went bee hinb a leef.

The writer of this story was eight years old. I have chosen this text to pose my second question, 'What do we do with texts which seem to have no unifying conception' — not because it is a particularly bad example (anyone who has taught writing or seen the writing of children will know that this is far from being bad writing), but rather because it is so close to recognizably ordinary writing. If there is a unifying cognitive schema or conceptual model behind this text, it is far less accessible than in the other texts. Linguistically it falls short of being a well-formed text, given adult conventions, although it shows sequence and some evidence of cohesion. An initial intuitive reaction might be to say that this is not a text, and is therefore beyond interpretation.

I do not wish to enter into a psychologizing reading of the text, which would concern itself with discovering the psychological/emotional state of the writer, focusing on the emphasis of 'running away', 'being strot on', and the test. Another piece from the same class, written on the same topic, has none of those features, and shows therefore that the topic alone need not lead to such content.

Text 39

Tiny Me

Once a pond a Time I saw a fairy and my name is Paula and
they give you some money if you lose your tee and you lost
a tee and your money wou worud not get enny more.

I wish to see if an interpretation can be attached to Text 38 within the scheme that I have established in the previous chapters. I suggested in Chapter 4 that the early sentences written by children are mini-narratives, mini-texts. If that is the case, then this 'text' begins to reveal its mode of organization. We have here four mini-narratives, which centre − as the title indicates and demands − on the child, 'Little Mi'. Sentences 1 and 2 may form a larger sub-unit. In that case there are three mini-texts, each consisting of two or three clauses. These are all united in a larger unit due to the teacher's demand to write a story. As stories are about sequences of events, the child imposes sequence on these mini-narratives, and indicates this by the linguistic marker of sequence, *then*.

If such a reading is correct, then this text is not all that different from Text 9, 'The Mouse'. Like that text it is predominantly a description, here of events relating to 'Little Mi', and forced into the frame of a narrative. The teacher might now begin to work on a number of points: on the fact that the child is still at the stage of writing mini-narrative sentences; on the fact that the child is unable to find an appropriate textual model for descriptions, which leads her to use the inappropriate narrative structure; perhaps to suggest modes of expanding and structuring descriptions; to select carefully topics for descriptive writing which strongly suggest a structure. As it was, the teacher affixed a rubber stamp of a little cartoon character saying 'You can do better' at the end of the story.

iii   An alternative mode of viewing the concept 'Error'

I gave Section ii of this chapter the heading 'Error analysis' to make a direct and overt link with the mode of viewing errors in the area of foreign-language learning. There it is established practice to regard the mistakes a learner makes, the difficulties a learner has with aspects of the new language, as direct evidence of interference from the rule-system of the language of which the student is a native speaker. So if a German learner says 'de vater is cold', the teacher knows that the learner has already mastered a phonological system in which the sounds represented by *the* and *w* do not exist, which leads the learner to substitute sounds which do exist in his phonological system. If she says 'I like the Jane not', the teacher realizes that the student is using syntactic rules of German, which lead to this word order, and which permit the appearance of the definite article before a name. The point is that mistakes, errors, are seen as the result of the use of quite specific models, in this case the phonological and grammatical rules of a language. This realization has at least two consequences: it takes the learner out of the category 'fool' and shows his or her behaviour to be that of a rational human being; and it permits the teacher to make an appropriate intervention, by making the basis of the error the subject of direct discussion, by making use of the learner's established rule-system, or by establishing new rules with both the learner's and the teacher's full knowledge of what they are doing.

iv   Sources and context

There is a substantial body of work in 'error analysis' and in contrastive linguistics. The latter has as its aim to establish the grammatical system of the first language and the language to be learned, and thereby to facilitate the construction of a bridging system, which can predict where no problems will be met, and where difficulties are likely to be met. *Papers in Contrastive Linguistics*, ed. Nickel (1971) provides a survey. An article dealing with 'error analysis' is S. P. Corder's 'The significance of learners' errors' (1967).

Appendix:
List of texts

Titles marked with an asterisk are the child's own.

No. of text	Title	Sex of speaker or writer	Age of speaker or writer	Chapter
1	Spoken text	M	Adult	2
2	Written text	M	Adult	2
3	Cooking lesson (sp.)	M (+ 2 females)	3 (Adult)	3
4	Lovely Things (sp.)	Class of children (+ female teacher)	6	3
5	Zebras (sp.)	Group of children	3	3
6	Tooth-Fairies (sp.)	M F	7 4	3
7	Adventure under the Sea (sp.)	M	7	3
8	going to the Shops* (wr.)	F	6	3,4,7
9	the mouse* (wr.)	M	7	3,4,5,7
10	Scruffy (wr.)	F	7	3
11	The racehorse (wr.)	F	7	3
12	Beaked Whales (wr.)	M	12	3,4,5
13	Birds* (wr.)	F	8	3,4
14	Our trip to Ayers House* (wr.)	F	8	3,4,5,6, 7
15	The Pioneer Boy* (wr.)	F	9	3,4
16	The Wolfling (sp.)	F	9	3
17	The Cockpit (wr.)	M	12	3,4,5
18	The Empire Strikes Back (sp.)	M	12	3
19	Kingies!* (wr.)	M	14	3,5
20	The two poor people* (wr.)	M	7	4,5

No. of text	Text	Sex of speaker or writer	Age of speaker or writer	Chapter
21	The Ant* (wr.)	M	7	4
22	Father Christmas (wr.)	F	7	4,7
23	Who was Goyder* (wr.)	F	9	4
24	History of Mylor (wr.)	?	Adult	4
25	The Story of Mylor (wr.)	?	Adult	4
26	My Ambition in Life* (wr.)	F	9	4,6
27	Red Rover (wr.)	M	9	4,7
27(a)	Red Rover (wr.) (adult rewriting)	M	Adult	7
28	West Germany (wr.)	F	9	5
29	Mylor (wr.)	F	9	5
30	Mystery Story (wr.)	M	12	5
31(a), (b)	Life in the Goldfields* (wr.)	M	12	5,8
32	Confrontations (wr.)	F	14	5
33	The Fishing Trip (wr.)	M	9	7
34	The Egg Hatched By A Dog* (wr.)	M	12	7
35	The Countryside around School (wr.)	M	11	7
36(a), (b)	The Drunken Dragon (wr.)	M	11	8
37(a), (b)	My Careless Master* (wr.)	F	9	8
38	Little Mi (wr.)	F	8	8
39	Tiny Me (wr.)	F	8	8

Bibliography

Albrow, K. H. (1972) *The English Writing System: Notes Towards a Description*. London: Longman.

Basso, K. (1980) review of Jack Goody (ed.), *The Domestication of the Savage Mind* (Cambridge University Press, 1977), *Language in Society*, 9, 72–80.

Bennett, B. (1979) 'Learning to write', *English in Australia*, 50, 5–16.

Bennett, B. (1979) 'The process of writing and the development of writing abilities, 15–17: Australian research in progress'. Mimeo, English Department, University of Western Australia, Perth, Australia.

Bernstein, B. (1971) *Class, Codes and Control*, vol. 1. London: Routledge & Kegan Paul.

Bernstein, B. (1979) 'The new pedagogy: sequencing und underlying assumptions', in Maling-Keepes, J., and Keepes, B. (eds) (1979), pp. 293–302.

Bloomfield, L. (1935) *Language*. London: Allen & Unwin.

Bolinger, D. (1968) *Aspects of Language*. New York: Harcourt, Brace & World.

Brazil, D. C. (1975) *Discourse Intonation*. Discourse Analysis Monographs no. 1. Birmingham: English Language Research.

Brazil, D. C. (1978) *Discourse Intonation II*. Discourse Analysis Monographs No. 2. Birmingham: English Language Research.

Britton, J.; Burgess, T.; Martin, N.; McLeod, A.; Rosen, H. (1975) *The Development of Writing Abilities (11–18)*. London: Macmillan.

Brown, R. (1973) *A First Language*. London: Allen & Unwin.

Burgess, C., et al. (1973) *Understanding Children Writing*. Harmondsworth: Penguin.

Chomsky, C. (1969) *The Acquisition of Syntax in Children from Five to Ten*. Cambridge, Mass.: MIT Press.

Chomsky, C. (1972) 'Stages in language development and reading exposure', *Harvard Educational Review*, 42, 1–33.

Chomsky, N. A. (1975) *Syntactic Structures*. The Hague: Mouton.

Chomsky, N. A. (1965) *Aspects of the Theory of Syntax*. Cambridge, Mass.: MIT Press.

Cicourel, A. (1973) *Cognitive Sociology*. Harmondsworth: Penguin.

Comrie, B. (1976) *Aspect*. Cambridge University Press.

Corder, S. P. (1967) 'The significance of learner's errors', *IRAL*
  (*International Review of Applied Linguistics*), 5, 161–9.

Coulthard, M. (1977) *An Introduction to Discourse Analysis*. London:
  Longman.

Coulthard, M., and Brazil, D. (1979) *Exchange Structure*. Discourse
  Analysis Monographs No. 5. Birmingham: English Language Research.

Dijk, T. van (1972) *Some Aspects of Text Grammars*. The Hague: Mouton.

Dijk, T. van (1977) *Text and Context*. London: Longman.

Dijk, T. van (1979) 'From Text Grammar to Interdisciplinary Discourse
  Studies'. Paper given at the La Jolla Conference on Cognitive Science,
  University of California at San Diego, La Jolla, mimeo.

Dijk, T. van (1979) 'Discourse studies and education', *Australian
  Review of Applied Linguistics*, 5.

Dittmar, N. (1976) *Sociolinguistics*. London: Arnold.

Donaldson, M. (1978) *Children's Minds*. Glasgow: Fontana/Collins.

Doughty, R.; Pearce, J.; and Thornton, G. (1972) *Exploring Language*.
  London: Arnold.

Feldman, C. F., and Toulmin, S. (1975) 'Logic and the theory of mind',
  in W. J. Arnold (ed.), *Nebraska Symposium on Motivation 1975*.
  Lincoln, Nebr.: University of Nebraska Press, pp. 409–76.

Ferguson, C. A., and Slobin, D. I. (eds) (1973) *Studies of Child
  Language Development*. New York: Holt, Rinehart & Winston.

Ferris, D. R. (1971) 'Teaching children to write', in Lamb (ed.) (1971),
  pp. 171–208.

Foucault, M. (1974) *The Archeology of Knowledge*. London: Tavistock
  Publications.

Fowler, R.; Hodge, R.; Kress, G.; and Trew, T. (1979) *Language and
  Control*. London: Routledge & Kegan Paul.

Giglioli, P. P. (ed.) (1972) *Language and Social Context*. Harmondsworth:
  Penguin.

Gimson, A. C. (1962) *An Introduction to the Pronunciation of English*.
  London: Arnold.

Gleason, H. A. (1961) *An Introduction to Descriptive Linguistics*.
  New York: Holt, Rinehart and Winston.

Gleitman, L. (1965) 'Co-ordinating conjunction in English', *Language*,
  41, 260–93.

Goody, J. (ed.) (1968) *Literacy in Traditional Societies*. Cambridge
  University Press.

Goody, J., and Watt, I. (1972) 'The consequences of literacy', in
  Giglioli (ed.) (1972), pp. 311–57.

Gregory, M., and Carroll, S. (1978) *Language and Situation: Language
  Varieties and Their Social Contexts*. London: Routledge &
  Kegan Paul.

Halliday, M. A. K. (1967-8) 'Notes on transitivity and theme in English
  (Parts 1–3)', *Journal of Linguistics*, 3, 37–81; 3, 199–244;
  4, 179–215.

Halliday, M. A. K. (1973) *Explorations in the Functions of Language.* London: Arnold.

Halliday, M. A. K. (1975) *Learning How to Mean: Explorations in the Development of Language.* London: Arnold.

Halliday, M. A. K. (1976) *Intonation and Grammar in British English.* The Hague: Mouton.

Halliday, M. A. K. (1978) *Language as Social Semiotic.* London: Arnold.

Halliday, M. A. K. (1979) 'Linguistics in teacher education', in Maling-Keepes, J., and Keepes, B. (eds) (1979), pp. 279–86.

Halliday, M. A. K., and Hasan, Ruqaiya (1976) *Cohesion in English.* London: Longman.

Harding, D. W. (1967) 'Raids on the inarticulate', *Use of English,* 19, 99–111.

Harré, R., and Madden, E. H. (1975) *Causal Powers.* Totowa, N.J.: Rownan and Littlefield.

Hockett, C. F. (1958) *A Course in Modern Linguistics.* New York: Macmillan.

Hume, D. (1969) *A Treatise of Human Nature.* Harmondsworth: Penguin.

Hunt, K. W. (1970) *Syntactic Maturity in Schoolchildren and Adults.* Monographs of the Society for Research in Child Development, vol. 35, no. 1. University of Chicago Press.

Hymes, Dell (1972) 'On communicative competence', in Pride, J. B., and Holmes, J. (eds) (1972).

Inhelder, B., and Piaget, J. (1964) *The Early Growth of Logic in the Child: Classification and Seriation.* London: Routledge & Kegan Paul.

Jones, D. (1918) *An Outline of English Phonology.* Cambridge: Heffer.

Kilham, C. A. (1977) *Thematic Organization of Wik-Munkan Discourse.* Canberra: Pacific Linguistics, Department of Linguistics, School of Pacific Studies, The Australian National University.

Kress, G. R. (ed.) (1976) *Halliday: System and Function in Language.* London: Oxford University Press.

Kress, G. R. (1978) 'Towards an analysis of the language of European intellectuals', *Journal of European Studies,* viii, 274–91.

Kress, G. R. (1979) 'The social values of speech and writing', in Fowler et al. (1979), pp. 46–62.

Kress, G. R. (1979) 'Conjoined sentences in the writing of 7 to 9 year old children', *UEA Papers in Linguistics,* 10, 1–18.

Kress, G. R. (1980) 'The development of the concept of "sentence" in children's writing', *Australian Review of Applied Linguistics,* 3, 63–76.

Kress, G. R. (1981) 'Language, living and learning', *Australian Journal of Remedial Education,* 13, 5–10.

Kress, G. R. (1981) 'Children's speech and children's writing', in Thao Lê and Mike McCausland (eds), pp. 301–15.

Kress, G. R., and Hodge, R. I. V. (1979) *Language as Ideology.* London: Routledge & Kegan Paul.

Labov, W. (1969) 'Contraction, deletion, and inherent variability of the English copula', *Language,* 45, 715–62.

Labov, W. (1972) 'The logic of non-standard English', in Giglioli (ed.) (1972), pp. 179–215.

Lamb, P. (ed.) (1971) *Guiding Children's Language Learning*, Dubuque, Iowa: William C. Brown.

Langacker, R. W. (1968) *Language and Its Structure*. New York: Harcourt, Brace and World.

Laver, J. (1970) 'The production of speech', in Lyons (ed.) (1970), pp. 53–75.

Little, G. (1978) 'Standards', *English in Australia*, 46, 3–13.

Lyons, J. (ed.) (1970) *New Horizons in Linguistics*. Harmondsworth: Penguin.

Maling-Keepes, J., and Keepes, B. (eds) (1979) *Language in Education. The Language Development Project Phase I*. Canberra: Curriculum Development Centre, P.O. Box 52, Dickson, ACT, 2602, Australia.

Martin, J. (1977) 'Learning How to Tell: Semantic Systems and Structures in Children's Narrative.' University of Essex, PhD thesis.

Martin, J. R., and Rothery, J. (1980) *No. 1 Writing Project Report 1980*. Working Papers in Linguistics, Department of Linguistics, University of Sydney.

Mitchell, A. (1973) *Speech Communication in the Classroom*. London: Pitman.

Moffett, J. (1968) *Teaching the Universe of Discourse*. Boston: Houghton Mifflin Company.

Moffett, J., and Wagner, B. J. (1976) *Student-Centered Language Arts and Reading, K-13*. Boston: Houghton Mifflin Company.

Nickel, G. (ed.) (1971) *Papers in Contrastive Linguistics*. London: Cambridge University Press.

O'Connor, J. D., and Arnold, G. F. (1961) *Intonation of Colloquial English*. London: Longman.

Pawley, K., and Syder, A. (1979) 'Why have linguists missed the obvious over these last fifty years?' Paper delivered at the annual conference of the Australian Linguistic Society, April 1979, mimeo.

Pflaum-Connor, S. (1978) *The Development of Language and Reading in Young Children*. Columbus, Ohio: Charles E. Merrill.

Piaget, J. (1926) *The Language and Thought of the Child*. London: Routledge & Kegan Paul.

Piaget, J. (1958) *The Child's Construction of Reality*. London: Routledge & Kegan Paul.

Pike, K. L. (1943) *Phonetics*. Ann Arbor: University of Michigan Press.

Pike, K. L. (1947) *Phonemics*. Ann Arbor: University of Michigan Press.

Pride, J. B., and Holmes, J. (eds) (1972) *Sociolinguistics*. Harmondsworth: Penguin.

Slobin, D. I., and Welsh, C. A. (1973) 'Elicited imitation as a research tool in developmental psycholinguistics', in Ferguson and Slobin (eds) (1973).

Smith Churchland, P. (1980) 'Language, thought and information processing', *Noûs*, xiv, 147–70.

Southgate, V. (1970) *The Enormous Turnip*. Loughborough: Ladybird Books.

Staats, A. W. (1968) *Learning, Language and Cognition*. New York: Holt, Rinehart and Winston.

Stewig, J. W. (1974) *Exploring Language with Children*. Columbus, Ohio: Charles E. Merrill.

Sweet, H. (1892) *A Primer of Phonetics*. Oxford: Clarendon Press.

Thao Lê and Mike McCausland (eds) (1981) *Child Language Development Theory into Practice*. Launceston: Launceston Teachers Centre.

Thornton, G. (1980) *Teaching Writing*. London: Arnold.

Trubetzkoy, N. S. (1967) *Grundzüge der Phonologie*. Göttingen: Vandenhoeck and Rupprecht.

Trudgill, P. (1975) *Accent, Dialect and the School*. London: Arnold.

Vygotsky, L. S. (1962) *Thought and Language*, ed. and trans. E. Hanfmann and G. Vakar. Cambridge, Mass.: MIT Press.

Whorf, B. L. (1956) *Language, Thought and Reality: Selected Writings of Benjamin Lee Whorf*, ed. J. B. Carroll. New York: Wiley.

Index